# Contents

# ▨ Part III: Special Issues in Marriage and Family Therapy   287

# *Introduction*

*I*n the preface to *Handbook of Family Therapy*, authors Alan Gurman and David Kniskern (1981b) justified their decision not to discuss certain approaches to family therapy, including cognitive, rational emotive behavior, client-centered, Adlerian, Gestalt, and transactional analysis therapies. They acknowledged that these approaches have exerted salient influences on the practice of individual and group therapy and that aspects of these approaches have been incorporated into the work of some family clinicians. Nonetheless, Gurman and Kniskern concluded that "these therapeutic approaches have not yet exerted a significant impact on the field of family therapy" (p. xiv). Although they acknowledged Virginia Satir's tremendous impact on the family therapy field, they opted to exclude her as well because no clearly discernible school or therapeutic method has evolved from her significant contributions. In Volume II of the handbook, Gurman and Kniskern (1991) discussed recent developments of the theories covered in Volume I and introduced several new systems-based theories. They continued their exclusion of individual and group theories (except behavioral) that may be used with couples and families.

Gurman and Kniskern recognized that in the developmental stages of family therapy it was necessary to separate individual and group therapy from family therapy to ensure that family therapy would not be seen as merely another theory of treatment. However, at this stage of the development of the psychotherapy profession, we believe that much is to be gained by bridging the fields of individual and group therapy with marital and family therapy. In actual practice, much of marital and family therapy is done, and will continue to be done, by therapists who were trained primarily in individual and group therapy. We believe these therapists should be prepared as fully as possible to provide effective treatment to couples and families. Although many counseling practitioners would like to become more proficient in family therapy, they report only a minimum of family therapy training in their graduate studies (Gladding, Burggraf, & Fenell, 1987). According to a survey ("Training of Clinical Psychologists," 1981), clinical psychologists in private practice work with marital and family problems approximately 40% of the time, yet less than 5% of the therapists surveyed had any formal coursework in marriage and family therapy in their graduate programs. Conversely, many therapists trained in marriage and family programs report a minimum of individual and group therapy training in their graduate studies. In either case, the practice of psychotherapy would be improved by a more thorough training process that includes exposure to individual, group, and family therapy.

In this book we attempt to accomplish this task. We provide the reader with information about how the basic core skills that are necessary, but not sufficient, to do individual and group therapy may be used to counsel couples and families. These core skills overlap to some extent and may be translated into practice differently in individual, group, and family therapy situations. Furthermore, we identify more advanced individual and group counseling skills and techniques that are useful in counseling couples and families.

Training in marriage and family therapy has frequently been characterized by requirements or strong recommendations that trainees undergo personal therapy. We believe such recommendations are appropriate during training programs and later when needed. We believe the therapeutic abilities of trainees will be enhanced by the opportunity to examine their own family histories as well as their personal values, assumptions, and beliefs. This opportunity is an increasingly important aspect of the expanded training paradigm for therapists. Corey, Corey, and Callahan (1993, p. 38) suggested that therapy for the therapist provides an opportunity to experience being a client. More important, however, is the chance for the therapist to examine blind spots, unfinished business, and other issues that may interfere with the ability to be an effective practitioner.

Thus, we hope with this book to bridge the gaps between individual, group, and family therapies. We believe there is too much fragmentation among the helping professions today in battles for turf. Therapists from virtually all types of professional training programs will work with marital and family problems. We want each of them to be as capable as possible. We hope this book will encourage counselors and other helping professionals with individual and group training to fully recognize that they already possess skills that make them capable of providing help to couples and families. In addition, we want to encourage therapists to build on their already considerable skills in individual and group counseling through gaining specific knowledge of marital and family therapy based on general systems theory. Too often we hear of counselors discarding systems theories that may be applied to the benefit of their clients because such theories are unnecessarily clinical and do not emphasize sufficiently the importance of the therapeutic relationship between client and therapist.

We believe that therapists who are not able to integrate the key concepts of family systems therapy into their counseling practice may not be able to provide the most effective help to certain couples and families. This is not to say that systems theory is the answer to all problems. However, it offers an alternative paradigm that can be effective with many clients.

We hope this book will encourage counselors to explore and perhaps integrate systems theories and techniques into their repertoire and to use them along with the effective helping skills they have already developed.

## Terms Used in This Book

Marriage and family therapy are often referred to as simply *family therapy* in this book. The reason is that the marital couple is but one important subsystem of the larger family system. Thus, family therapy includes the marital subsystem. The terms counselor, therapist, and psychotherapist will be used interchangeably throughout this book. Additionally, the terms *marriage and family counselor* and *marriage and family therapist* will be used interchangeably. In our judgment, there is little, if any, difference between a professional counselor and a psychotherapist. Both have the task of helping individuals, couples, and families alleviate human suffering and are accorded equal status and meaning in this book.

# ▨ *Overview of the Book*

This book is organized in a way that we hope will assist counselors in developing basic skills in marriage and family therapy. In Part One we systematically introduce the reader to the field of family therapy. Specifically, we focus on the family as a system and describe the core counseling skills taught in counselor training programs and how these skills may be used in working with couples and families.

In Part Two we present both individual and systems-based theories of psychotherapy and describe how these approaches may be used in working with families. The theories are organized into four major classification categories:

1. Psychodynamic
2. Cognitive/behavioral
3. Humanistic/existential
4. Transpersonal

The first three categories are widely accepted and frequently used in counselor training programs. The fourth category, transpersonal therapy, is emerging as an important force in counselor training and may suggest a direction of future growth in the counseling profession (Weinhold & Hendricks, 1993). These organizational categories may serve as a bridge linking the individual counseling theories with the systems theories frequently employed in marriage and family therapy. The systems theories presented in this book have their basis in psychodynamic, cognitive/behavioral, and humanistic/existential theory. No systems theories have been developed that have a transpersonal basis, although transpersonal theory includes an "interactional understanding" as one of its key elements.

Thus, we hope the organization of this book will enable the reader to discover that many key principles in individually oriented psychodynamic theory may also be relevant to family systems approaches based on psychodynamic theory. Similarly, cognitive/behavioral and humanistic/existential theories used in individual therapy will have elements in common with corresponding systems-based theories. These classifications will provide familiar ground for counselors as they begin to use unfamiliar systems theories with couple and families.

We describe psychodynamic systems theories, cognitive/behavioral theories, and humanistic/existential theories in detail; we discuss their applications to family treatment and show how the individually oriented theories correspond to the systems theories. In an attempt to build bridges between individually oriented counseling theories and systems-based counseling theories, we have used a format that allows us to first describe the individually oriented theories from a particular category, then describe the systems-based theories from that same category.

The individually oriented psychodynamic theories that are presented include the classic psychoanalytic theory of Freud; Adlerian theory; and Berne's transactional analysis. The systems-based psychodynamic theories presented include Bowen's family systems theory and Framo's intergenerational systems theory.

The individually oriented cognitive/behavioral theories presented include Ellis' rational emotive behavior therapy and the behavioral theory of Jacobsen, Falloon, and others. The systems-based cognitive/behavioral theories include Minuchin's structural family therapy, functional family therapy developed by Barton, Alexander, and Parsons, and included in this second edition of the text, the brief strategic therapy of Haley and Madanes.

Individually oriented humanistic/existential theories presented include Rogers' person-centered therapy; Perls' Gestalt therapy; and Moreno's psychodrama approach to therapy. Systems-based humanistic/existential theories presented include Satir's communications theory and Whitaker's symbolic/experiential systems theory.

The transpersonal theory presented is Weinhold's transpersonal relationship therapy.

Finally, in Part Three we provide the reader with information on treating families with special needs, ethnicity and family therapy, as well as professional issues, ethics, and research in the field of marriage and family therapy.

## Purpose of the Book

The purpose of this book is to provide mental health professionals trained and experienced in psychotherapy for individuals with the basic knowledge and skills to begin counseling families with family-related problems. We present a model that describes how the core counseling skills taught in most counselor training programs may be used in therapy with couples and families. In addition, information necessary to develop skills in marital and family therapy based on systems theory is presented.

To lead the reader into each chapter, we have included a brief summary statement, a list of the key concepts covered, and a few questions for discussion to direct the reader to some of the main ideas. These items also might be good for review of the chapter after it has been read. To further assist the reader in integrating the material in the text in an experiential fashion, we have developed an optional workbook to accompany the text.

# I

# Introducing and Understanding Marriage and Family Therapy

## C H A P T E R S

# 1

## Counseling Families:

## An Introduction

*In this chapter, we will show why counselors and other mental health professionals should be trained to work with family-related problems in psychotherapy. We will discuss several specific family-related problems and suggest how counselors may help resolve these problems more effectively if the family or portions of the family are included in treatment.*

## KEY CONCEPTS

Family-related problems

Two-career families

Marital dysfunction

Single-parent families

Drug and alcohol abuse

School-related problems

Child management problems

Adolescent depression and suicide

Problems with adult children leaving home

Care of elderly parents

## QUESTIONS FOR DISCUSSION

1. Why is it important for counselors and other mental health professionals to have the knowledge and skills necessary to work with couples and families?

2. What are some specific counseling problems that may be treated with family therapy?

3. The terms counselor and psychotherapist are used interchangeably throughout this book. Do you agree with this usage? Why or why not?

*M*arriage and family therapy has become an increasingly important treatment approach in the mental health profession. The social, economic, and political demands placed on families today far exceed those experienced in previous generations and can create considerable stress for family members. Helping professionals have recognized that counseling an individual without considering, and frequently without including, other family members makes it less likely that lasting change will be possible. Because societal pressures have increased family stress and because more families are seeking help through therapy, counselors and therapists must be prepared to treat psychological problems that occur in the context of the family.

Some specific areas of concern today include the pressures of families in which both parents work, the unique stresses experienced by single-parent families, burgeoning alcohol and drug abuse, increased suicide rates in the teenage population, and increased life expectancy resulting in worries about caring for elderly parents. These are just a few of the emerging issues counselors have to be aware of and be prepared to deal with. Moreover, counselors need to understand how each of these issues affects the entire family unit.

## Family-Related Problems

A practicing counseling professional is presented with numerous problems that may be caused or supported by members of the client's family. Increasing numbers of therapists are recognizing that it is often difficult to successfully treat a client who is experiencing a psychological problem that has its roots in the family without the participation of principal family members in therapy. If the client is treated without the family, change in the client may occur as a result of treatment. However, when the client returns to the family without the support of therapy, he or she frequently reverts back to former patterns of dysfunctional behavior because, while the client has changed, the rest of the family has not.

If the behaviors of the rest of the family members remain constant, the client is likely to revert to former dysfunctional behaviors that are supported and reinforced by the family system. Therefore, it becomes extremely important that the well-trained counselor understand how to effectively treat psychological problems that are reinforced and supported by the family. This treatment often involves participation of family members in family therapy.

Certain specific family-related problems are frequently encountered by professional counselors and psychotherapists. Several of the most common family problems are briefly described here.

## Two-Career Families

Economic pressures on the family have contributed to an increase in the number of women in the workforce and the number of two-career families in the United States. Developing an effective two-career lifestyle raises many new issues and questions for the partners involved in the relationship. Frequent issues raised by dual-career couples in therapy include: (1) How will the necessary household duties be divided with both spouses working? (2) How will young children be cared for? and (3) How will finances be managed (Fenell, 1982)?

When these issues for the two-career family are not resolved, marital counseling may become necessary. If only one spouse were to come for treatment, the therapeutic alternatives would be limited because the counselor would deal with the perceptions and feelings of only one partner. However, with both spouses present in treatment, new rules can be negotiated that identify and respond to the needs and concerns of both partners. If both partners' needs are considered, there is a better chance that mutual agreements can be made and that lasting change will take place.

## Marital Dysfunction

One of the most common reasons for seeking psychotherapy is for assistance in resolving marital problems. Frequently, couples have complex and serious disagreements and do not have the communication and problem-solving skills necessary to resolve them (Sperry & Carlson, 1991). When treating one spouse alone, the therapist is limited to only one spouse's perceptions of the problem. When a spouse is treated individually for marital problems, it is more likely that deterioration in the marital relationship will occur (Gurman & Kniskern, 1978a) than if both partners are treated together. Thus, the counselor should possess the skills necessary to engage both spouses in the counseling process (Whitaker & Keith, 1981; Wilcoxon & Fenell, 1983, 1986) and should be capable of treating the couple conjointly as well as individually.

A spouse treated for marital problems in individual sessions is likely to achieve personal therapeutic growth. Because of this therapeutic growth, however, the spouse in treatment may move further away from the other partner. This development may actually complicate the marital problems and perhaps lead to divorce. If the presenting concern is a marital problem and the goal is to resolve the problem, the counselor should attempt to involve both spouses in treatment. Conjoint marital therapy is the treatment of choice for marital problems because it offers the therapist a more realistic picture of the marital problems and because the couple does not grow further apart in the marriage as a result of the treatment of only one of the partners (Gurman & Kniskern, 1978a).

## Single-Parent Families

Because of the high divorce rate in the United States, the number of single-parent families has continued to increase. There are nearly 6 million single-mother households in the United States (Goodrich, Rampage, & Ellman, 1989) and increasingly large numbers of single-father households. The parent with custody of the children frequently faces a myriad of problems that must be resolved to effectively support and nurture the family.

When single parents experience increased stress levels, they may begin to lose a sense of control of their families and perhaps of themselves. Counseling with the single parent, the children, and available support persons is frequently an effective way to help moderate the tension and stress in this most difficult situation. Moreover, problems may develop surrounding the issues of custody, child support, and visitation. Frequently, these issues cannot be successfully resolved without participation by all concerned parties in the counseling process.

## Drug and Alcohol Disorders

When a member of a family has a problem with drug and alcohol abuse, all other members of the family are affected. In addition to helping the abusing client, counselors must help other family members deal with their feelings about the abusing client. Furthermore, specific behavior patterns often develop in family members that support maintenance of the drug or alcohol abuse. Children may become over responsible and perform the duties of the parents. This behavior allows the parent or parents to continue their substance abuse and often erodes the child's self-esteem.

The spouse or children of the alcoholic often behave in a way that has been described as *co-dependent*. This term describes a spouse who has such a tremendous neurotic need to maintain the marriage relationship that he or she is unwilling to seriously challenge the drug-dependent partner's dysfunctional behavior. Thus, the co-dependent person helps perpetuate the presenting problem of drug dependency or addiction. Counseling with the family as well as with individual members of the family is a clear necessity in drug and alcohol abuse situations (George, 1990).

## School-Related Problems

Parents and teachers often suggest that children having difficulty in school receive counseling. When the difficulties are related to problems at home, counseling the child alone is rarely effective. It is important to include parents, siblings, and teachers to gain an accurate assessment of the problem. The participation of the family as well as of significant school personnel is necessary to establish effective cooperation between the school and the family and to identify ways that both systems, the school and the family, might be able to support the changes made by the identified client. The counselor must possess excellent skills to facilitate the cooperation of these two important systems to enhance the effectiveness of students experiencing school-related problems (Lambie & Daniels-Mohring, 1993).

## Child Management Problems

Family counseling is often effective when parents have difficulty managing the behavior of their children (Minuchin & Fishman, 1981). Frequently, the behavior of the child promotes disagreement between the parents on how to manage and discipline the child. When the disagreement is not resolved quickly, increased stress and instability in the marriage and the family may result and the child may become the family scapegoat (Barker, 1992). This stress, in turn, precipitates additional acting out by the child.

Family therapy is the most effective way to accurately diagnose how the roles played by each family member help to maintain the problem. Therapy can help change the dysfunctional interactional patterns of the acting-out child and the other family members and help all family members enjoy a more pleasant and functional family life.

## Adolescent Depression and Suicide

With more and more pressure being placed on adolescents to engage in behaviors they are not physically or psychologically prepared to handle, the incidence of depression and suicide among this group has increased dramatically. Parents often hold excessively high expectations for their teenagers and demand excellence in all aspects of activity, or perhaps the adolescent believes these expectations are present when the parents do not in fact hold them. In either case, when the adolescent does not live up to the real or perceived parental expectations, depression may develop.

When the depression is severe, the adolescent, out of desperation, may consider suicide. Family therapy is an excellent treatment modality for problems of adolescent depression in reaction to perceived parental pressures because it sensitizes all family members to the causes of the depression and, should suicidal potential exist, educates family members concerning warning signs and ways to deal with the problem.

## Problems with Adult Children Leaving Home

A relatively recent phenomenon in our society is the problem that many families experience in facilitating the departure of adult children from the parents' home. On the one hand, parents want their adult children to become autonomous, but on the other hand, some parents may not believe that their children will be able to succeed on their own. These parents may send subtle messages to their children suggesting that they will not be successful. Thus, the children grow into adults who doubt their own ability to succeed without parental support.

When the time comes for the adult son or daughter to leave home, all family members are in a form of crisis, and a healthy departure does not occur. This pattern can repeat itself with adult children leaving home and later returning for support during a crisis unless help is obtained to identify and break the pattern. Exploring the dynamics involved in this situation in family counseling may help the adult son or daughter leave the home and also provide assistance to the parents as they learn to use effective behaviors that support the departure.

### Care for Elderly Parents

As life expectancies increase, many couples are finding themselves responsible for the care and support of their aging parents. As interactions with parents increase in these situations, additional stresses are placed on the marriage (Montalvo & Thompson, 1988). This stress is exacerbated when the demands from aging parents coincide with problems the couple may be experiencing with their own grown children leaving home.

A spouse may feel that he or she plays "second fiddle" to the other spouse's parents. Assisting the spouses in working through the issues related to the support of elderly parents may be an effective way to resolve tensions in the marriage created by this frequently unexpected demand. It can be useful to include the elderly parents in some of the sessions to gain their perceptions of the situation and their ideas concerning what is needed from their adult children.

## The Need for Family Therapy Skills

These are a few of the classic family-related problems that clearly demonstrate that many therapeutic situations will necessitate working with the family members and the identified client. To do otherwise may not be the most effective way to treat the client with the presenting problem. Therefore, it is important for counselors and psychotherapists to have the skills necessary to respond to the myriad problems that occur in marriage and the family.

## Conclusion

Most counselors and psychotherapists receive training in basic helping skills, including empathy, respect, warmth, genuineness, concreteness, self-disclosure, and immediacy. Helping professionals are generally trained to use these skills with individual clients or in groups. Although many counselor training programs have some academic courses in marriage and family therapy, few offer practicum or internship experiences of significant duration to allow the counselor to develop effective skills with couples and families (Gladding, Burggraf, & Fenell, 1987).

Most counselor training programs have little room in their curricula for marriage and family therapy coursework and training because of the significant requirements for courses supporting individual and group psychotherapy. Only six programs have received Council on Accreditation for Counseling and Related Academic Programs (CACRAP) accreditation in marriage and family counseling/therapy (Directory, 1993). Thus, for many graduate students, formal training in marriage and family therapy may occur beyond the master's level through continuing professional education (Fenell & Hovestadt, 1986).

A further problem for students in acquiring marriage and family therapy skills is the perception that marriage and family therapy, practiced from a systems perspective, is radically different from what is taught in a master's program that focuses on individual and group therapies. Because of the mystique and different terminology surrounding marriage and family therapy, counseling professionals often believe they are not adequately prepared to work with couples and families. This book is designed to demonstrate ways counseling students can begin to apply many of the basic skills learned in individual and group work to work with couples and families. Further, we will show how these skills form bridges linking individually oriented counseling theories to systems theories, which should increase the counselor's confidence and abilities to help couples and families.

The question is not whether counselors will work with couples and families. Because of the tremendous demands for family therapy services, it is certain that the practicing professional counselor will encounter clients experiencing family-related problems. The important question is: Will counselors be adequately prepared to help clients who seek help with marriage- and family-related problems? The material in this book is designed to provide counselors with the information needed to begin to provide supervised therapy to couples, families, and others experiencing relationship difficulties.

# 2

# The Family as a System

*This chapter presents essential information concerning family therapy. To be maximally effective in working with couples and families, the counselor needs to conceptualize the family as the client and be capable of treating the family system as the client.*
*In a brief chronology of the development of family therapy, we will introduce several of the therapists who founded the family therapy movement. Following this brief introduction to the profession, we will provide information that counselors need to understand family functioning, including family health, family dysfunction, and family assessment.*

## KEY CONCEPTS

Double-bind hypothesis
Identified patient
Schizophrenic family research
Family as a living system
Subsystems
Paradigm shift
Circular causality

Family homeostasis
Subsystem boundaries
Adaptability and cohesion
Disengaged families
Enmeshed families
Family life cycle

## QUESTIONS
## FOR DISCUSSION

1. How can family systems theory be helpful to the counselor in professional practice?

2. What are the major differences between systems theory and individual theory?

3. Which terms and concepts introduced in this chapter are most useful in describing your own family?

4. How can the circumplex model be used in understanding family functioning?

5. What are key characteristics of effective communication?

6. How is the concept of family life cycle development helpful in family therapy?

$K$ey family therapy terms and concepts that will be used throughout this book are introduced in this chapter. A thorough understanding of these terms and concepts will maximize the reader's understanding of the family therapy theories presented in later sections of the book.

Most traditional theories of individual psychotherapy are based on the assumption that psychological problems reside within the individual. If the therapist can help resolve issues that are internally disturbing to the individual, then therapeutic cure has occurred. This notion that the locus of pathology resides within the individual is deeply rooted in contemporary American society, where individual achievement is highly valued and rewarded. When a person is successful, he or she is viewed as having "made it" as an individual; the individual possesses the characteristics that made the success possible.

Personal failure and psychological problems are generally viewed as deficits that also occur and are maintained within an individual. If a person is unable to succeed or experiences psychological problems, the overwhelming preponderance of social opinion suggests that the person has some character defect or flaw. Given the importance of individuality in this society, it is not difficult to understand why psychological problems are viewed primarily as residing within the individual and why treatment of psychological problems focuses on the individual.

Until the late 1940s and early 1950s, psychological theories were primarily rooted in the idea that problems reside within the individual. About this time, maverick psychiatrists and psychologists began exploring the notion that psychological problems could be caused by dysfunction occurring between persons rather than by some individual character flaw or personality defect. To better understand what conditions led these pioneers in family therapy to develop systems-based theories, we will briefly describe the early history of the family therapy movement.

# ∎ The Evolution of Marriage and Family Therapy

Freud is the acknowledged father of psychotherapy. All therapies have their origins with psychoanalytic theory. Freud was perhaps the first to recognize the importance of the family in the development of sound mental health. He believed that successful passage through a series of developmental stages between birth and late adolescence was necessary for development of a sound personality.

Difficulties could occur at any of the stages to create psychological problems in the individual. Especially critical to sound development was the resolution of the Oedipal and Electra stages of development, because it was here that healthy relationships with parents and persons of the opposite sex were established. In the widely quoted case of Little Hans, Freud (1909) actually trained a father to help treat his son to resolve the son's phobia of horses. This case was one of the earliest examples of family intervention in the psychology literature.

In the 1930s, marriage counseling emerged as a new field. Psychoanalysts had been treating individuals with problems in marriage but had rarely treated the couple together. The psychoanalysts focused on the neuroses of each individual. Early marriage counselors, in contrast, focused their treatment on what was wrong in the marriage rather than what was wrong with each individual. Pioneers in marriage counseling were Paul Popenoe, Abraham and Hannah Stone, and Emily Mudd (Broderick & Schraeder, 1991).

The next significant event in the development of marriage and family therapy was establishment of the American Association of Marriage Counselors in 1945. This organization has developed into the American Association for Marriage and Family Therapy (AAMFT), which is the primary professional organization for marriage and family therapists.

The next breakthrough in the development of the field of marriage and family therapy resulted from the work of therapists in the early 1950s studying schizophrenia. These researchers began to recognize that patients' symptoms improved when they were hospitalized but deteriorated when they were brought in contact with significant family members.

This finding encouraged researchers at the Mental Research Institute in Palo Alto, California, to study the communication patterns between schizophrenic patients and members of their families. From this research emerged the double-bind hypothesis of dysfunctional communication (Bateson, Jackson, Haley, & Weakland, 1956). According to this hypothesis, confusing and contradictory messages are sent from a parent to the schizophrenic patient. No matter how the patient responded to the message, the answer or response would always be incorrect or inappropriate. Thus, the patient was in a "no win" situation because no rational response was acceptable.

It was believed that schizophrenic patients retreated into psychosis to avoid dealing with the double-bind messages and the untenable position in which these messages placed them. The mother of the schizophrenic patient was often detected as the person communicating the double-bind messages. However, fathers also may contribute to such communication patterns. One of the reasons mothers were most frequently detected in double-bind relationships with the schizophrenic offspring was that they had intense and frequent contact with the patient more often than did the fathers.

An example of a double-bind message is when a parent tells a child to show more affection and then communicates disapproval when the child attempts to be affectionate. Repeated double-bind situations have a negative psychological impact on the child, who is placed in a situation in which no response to the situation will be satisfactory.

The double-bind research conducted by Gregory Bateson, Don Jackson, Jay Haley, and John Weakland (1956) had a tremendous impact on the mental health field. Therapists began to realize that the dysfunctional communication patterns in schizophrenic families also existed in less intense forms in other families. The member of the family who exhibited symptoms was recognized in the family therapy literature as the identified patient of a dysfunctional family. Thus, the implications of the double-bind communication theory extended beyond schizophrenic families. The researchers believed that dysfunctional communication patterns were at the root of many family problems and that therapy could focus on improving communication between members rather than on pathology within a dysfunctional family member.

When the problems in communication between members were corrected, the symptoms of identified patients were frequently found to diminish or disappear. Bodin (1981), writing about the numerous significant contributions of the Mental Research Institute to family therapy, states that the double-bind theory "stands as perhaps the most definitive landmark in the revolutionary shift from an individual to systems focus in concepts of psychopathogenesis" (p. 281). Virginia Satir (1983, 1988), another pioneer in the family therapy field, worked with Bateson and his family communications research group at the Mental Research Institute in Palo Alto, California. After several years of research with Bateson, Satir left the group and developed her own unique style of family therapy, which combined humanistic and systemic characteristics.

Two of the earliest publications on family therapy were *The Psychodynamics of Family Life* by Nathan Ackerman (1958) and John Bell's (1961) monograph, *Family Group Therapy*. These authors began to popularize family therapy and systems theory.

Another early contributor to the family therapy movement is Lyman Wynne. Wynne's early research focused on dysfunctional communication within families with schizophrenic members. Wynne coined the term *pseudomutuality* to describe families that appear to be open, caring, and clear in their relationships and communication patterns when this is not the case. These families developed elaborate patterns of relating that were often superficial and disguised underlying relationship problems.

Offspring from pseudomutual families often grew up doubting themselves and their perceptions of reality (Wynne, Ryckoff, Day, & Hirsch, 1958). Wynne's later work includes an extensive overview of family therapy research (Wynne, 1988) and expanded the definition and functions of family therapists to "family consultants" and "systems consultants." Consultants would focus more on assessing system dynamics and strengths attending to the agenda of the client (Wynne, McDaniel, & Weber, 1987).

Murray Bowen (1960, 1961, 1976, 1978), another psychiatrist and first-generation family therapist, also conducted research with schizophrenic families in the 1950s. Under Bowen's care, the mothers and fathers of patients lived in the hospital with them to facilitate family treatment. Carl Whitaker (1976; Whitaker & Keith, 1981), also a psychiatrist, began bringing spouses and eventually children into therapy as early as 1944. Both Bowen and Whitaker developed family therapy theories that will be reviewed in later chapters. Readers seeking a more detailed description of the evolution of family therapy should consult Broderick and Schraeder, (1991).

# ▨ *Developing a Family Systems Perspective*

To understand family systems and to practice counseling from a systemic approach, it is important for therapists to understand that systems exist at many levels. One of the easiest ways to understand the concept of living systems is to examine the human being. The human is a living system composed of subsystems, which in turn are composed of other subsystems.

For example, the human is composed of a nervous system, a digestive system, a circulatory system, a skeletal system, a respiratory system, and a reproductive system. Each of these systems is a subsystem of the human system. Furthermore, each of these subsystems is composed of other subsystems. The circulatory system, for example, contains the veins, arteries, and the heart. Each of these subsystems is further composed of other subsystems. The heart, for example, is composed of cells, and the cells are composed of cellular subsystems. For the body to be healthy, all subsystems must function in an effective and cooperative manner. If the heart were not functioning properly, the other subsystems (and the human being) would be radically affected.

Just as humans are living systems composed of subsystems, each individual human being is a subsystem of a larger living system, as shown in Figure 2.1. This point is critical in learning to provide therapy for families. The individual human is a subsystem of a larger living system called the family. The family is part of a living system called the extended family, which is part of a larger system called the community. The community is part of a larger system, perhaps known as the state, which is also part of a larger system, and so on.

Because of these interrelationships between systems and their subsystems, if a problem occurs in one of the subsystems of a biological organization or a social organization, that problem frequently affects other subsystems of the organization. This concept is most important when a therapist treats a family in which the problem seems to reside in only one of the members. Systems therapists recognize that although the presenting problem is exhibited by an individual it may be maintained by behaviors of other family members. Furthermore, the systems therapist recognizes that the problem behavior affects the behavior of other members of the family system.

All the theorists and researchers described in previous sections

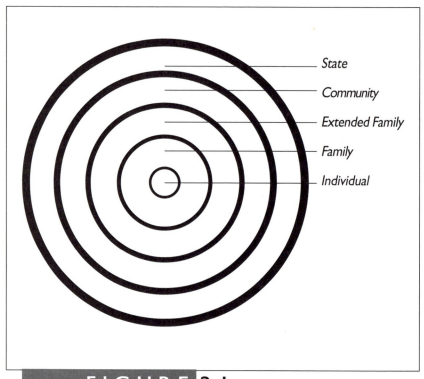

**FIGURE** 2.1

## Levels of System

of this chapter were schooled in models of psychotherapy that emphasized treatment of the individual; these models focused on problems of an intrapsychic nature that resided within the individual. Each of these theorists sought to understand the nature of problem formation in a more inclusive theoretical orientation. Rather than viewing the client's problem as being intrapsychic in nature, they came to view the psychological problem as a symptom of the dysfunctional patterns (Minuchin, 1974) in the identified patient's family system. Thus, they presented a new way of conceptualizing problem formation. With this new conceptualization of problem formation came new models and strategies for problem resolution.

The movement from an individual perspective to a systems perspective of problem formation and resolution is called a *paradigm shift* (Haley, 1971), a term frequently used in the family therapy literature. To most effectively employ systems-based counseling interventions, therapists must make this paradigm shift and learn to understand how an individual's symptoms may serve to stabilize and maintain the current family system.

A classic example of this concept is the case of a child whose symptoms divert the concern of the parents away from their marital problems and thoughts about divorce. Thus, the child has, at least temporarily, preserved the unity of the family by displaying the symptomatic behavior. The parents will rarely dwell on their marital problems when they are needed to help their child. The result of the symptomatic behavior of the child is the preservation of the larger system, the family.

## Linear and Circular Causality

Therapists who make the paradigm shift can then differentiate between linear causality and circular causality in the formation of family problems. Linear causality refers to the concept of cause and effect. One person's action causes another person's predictable reaction. An example of linear causality is:

*cause*                        *effect*

husband drinks ——————> wife nags

In this linear model, the husband's drinking causes his wife to nag. This explanation is perfectly acceptable, but it may not be a complete explanation. If we were to ask the husband to explain his drinking, he may report:

*cause*                        *effect*

wife nags ——————> husband drinks

Again we have an acceptable linear, cause-and-effect explanation for the behavior. The husband drinks because he cannot tolerate his wife's nagging, and the drinking dulls his anger toward her.

Circular causality considers both explanations and incorporates them in a more complete understanding of the problem. The wife nags to stop her husband from drinking and her husband continues to drink because it helps him tolerate his wife's nagging. This circular understanding of the problem is shown next.

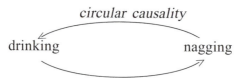

A counselor working with this couple would understand the problem more completely by conceptualizing it using the circular causality model. According to this view, the *behavior of both* persons maintains the problem behavior. The couple's problem may not necessarily be either the drinking or the nagging but, rather, their inability to resolve the power struggle concerning who will control the relationship.

## Understanding Family Health and Dysfunction

One of the most striking concepts of family systems therapy lies in how the systems therapist defines the presenting problem and conceptualizes the location of the problem. In most counseling theories, the focus of treatment is the individual because the problem is believed to reside within a single person. Family therapists base their work on the concept of systems theory as proposed by Ludwig von Bertalanffy (1968). Bertalanffy proposed that systems are composed of interrelated parts and, conversely, that the organization of the interrelated parts constitutes a higher level system.

The family, composed of the individual members of the family and their relationships, is one such higher level system. Family therapists choose to conceptualize the system as the unit to be treated in therapy rather than identifying one element or member of the system for treatment. Dysfunctional behavior exhibited by the symptomatic individual is thought to be a manifestation of problems within the family system.

For most family therapists, the whole family system, rather than a single individual in the family, is identified for treatment. The symptoms exhibited by one family member are viewed as a part of the dysfunctional interaction patterns of the family rather than a character or personality flaw residing solely within the individual. Another way of stating this is that the *identified patient,* or symptom bearer, may be signaling with his or her symptoms that a more encompassing problem exists within the family's organization.

Typically, the identified patient in a family is one of the children. When the symptoms of the child become disturbing to parents or school teachers, individual therapy for the child is usually sought. If this treatment is successful and change is maintained, the problem was with the child. However, if the treatment is not successful and the frustration of the parents or school officials continues, the parents may seek further therapy. It is at this stage that family therapy is often considered as an option. When a family seeks family therapy, it is not necessarily because they understand that the problem is systemic in nature. In fact, it is rare for a family to be aware of the interactional nature of the identified patient's symptoms prior to entering family therapy. Rather, the family is there because other forms of treatment have not been successful and they want help. Often the family comes to understand the systemic nature of the symptoms through learning that takes place in the therapy.

## Family Subsystems

Salvador Minuchin (1974) has described family systems in a helpful and understandable manner. Minuchin states that the family system is composed of smaller units called subsystems. Several family subsystems may exist, including the spouses' subsystem, the children's subsystem, the females' subsystem, the males' subsystem, and individual subsystems. In addition to these, the potential of other subsystem configurations exists, such as mother-son subsystems and father-daughter subsystems. Each family system has a set of rules that govern the behaviors of the family members, and each member has certain roles to play in the family. These rules and roles are key factors in the establishment of the family's subsystems. It is the therapist's responsibility to identify and work to change the key family subsystems involved in the maintenance of the presenting problems.

## Homeostasis

When all members abide by the family rules and act in ways consistent with their roles, family homeostasis (Minuchin, 1974), or balance, is achieved. Homeostasis is the tendency of living systems to desire to be at rest or in balance. Living systems, including families, will attempt to achieve and maintain homeostasis. When a family member or members deviate from the established family rules or roles, however, homeostasis is threatened and other members of the family system begin to engage in certain behaviors in an attempt to return the system to its former state of balance.

One classic example of homeostasis is the human body maintaining its temperature of 98.6° on a very hot day through perspiring. The perspiration evaporating on the body cools the body and maintains homeostasis. A second classic example is that of a thermostat. The thermostat senses the temperature of the air in a room and, if the temperature is too low, heat is provided. If the thermostat senses that the temperature is too hot, it shuts down heat production until it is again needed. Thus, the thermostat regulates the temperature and maintains homeostasis.

Families also exhibit homeostatic mechanisms. For example, a family rule might be that teenage children will be home by 9 o'clock on school nights. The parents allow for some fluctuations in the arrival time of the teenager. But when she regularly returns home over an hour late, the parents become upset and begin enforcing measures to bring the system back into balance. As long as the daughter maintained her behavior within an acceptable range, she experienced no problems with her parents. However, when she regularly returned home more than an hour late, the parents' tolerance level was violated and measures were taken to return the homeostasis.

As long as the daughter meets her parents' expectations, homeostasis is maintained. If she does not meet their expectations, however, additional problems such as hostility and resentment may further upset the family's homeostasis. The family might initially seek individual therapy for the daughter's "acting-out" behavior and, if this were not successful, enter family therapy.

## Boundaries

Families are composed of several levels of subsystems. The flow of information from one subsystem to another is controlled and regulated by the boundaries between the subsystems. Boundaries are created primarily by the rules the family establishes for regulating information flow between and among members. Families that are very private and do not share many thoughts and feelings have rigid boundaries. Families that share any and all information have diffuse boundaries. These families often live in homes where closed bedroom doors are not allowed and family members have detailed information about one another.

For example, a husband and wife may have a relatively impermeable boundary around their subsystem that generally does not allow the children to participate in their husband-wife interactions. However, the husband and wife also serve in the roles of mother and father to their children. When the couple is in the spousal subsystem, the participation of the children is discouraged by family rules. When the couple is in the mother-father subsystem, however, the subsystem boundaries are permeable and inclusion and appropriate participation by the children are encouraged. The family as a whole system may have a permeable boundary that readily includes members outside the family, or it may have a rigid boundary that makes inclusion of "outsiders" difficult. The character of the boundaries of the family determines the flow of information within the family and the inclusion or exclusion of participants in the family system and subsystems.

## Adaptability and Cohesion

Two characteristics of families that may be used for diagnostic purposes are those of adaptability and cohesion. Olson, Sprenkle, and Russell (1979) developed a circumplex model to assess families on these dimensions. The circumplex model, shown in Figure 2.2, has been widely used in the assessment of family health and dysfunction.

Because the constructs of adaptability and cohesion each have four levels, a possibility of sixteen types of families may be identified through the use of this model. *Adaptability* refers to the family's ability to modify its rules, roles, and structure in response to the pressures and conflicts of family life. *Chaotic* families have little structure for dealing with the problems of family life; rules are unclear and frequently unenforced. *Flexible* families are quite receptive to change and have the ability to resolve problems through appropriate changes in rules and roles. *Structured* families are less able than flexible families to modify rules and roles; however, these families are able to adapt and change when necessary. *Rigid* families are reluctant to change rules and roles and tend to maintain the status quo at all costs.

*Cohesion* refers to the degree of togetherness in the family and the amount of individual autonomy granted to family members. *Disengaged* families have low cohesion. Members are afforded maximum autonomy and may not identify significantly with their family. *Separated* families value individual autonomy; however, they have a sense of family unity and identity.

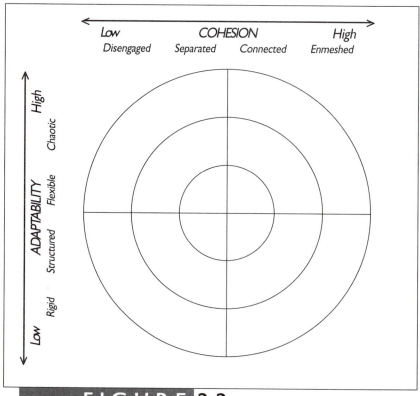

# FIGURE 2.2

## The Circumplex Model of Family Functioning

*Source:* "Circumplex Model of Marital and Family Systems: VI: Theoretical Update" by D. H. Olson, D. H. Sprenkle, and C. Russell, 1983, in *Family Process*, *22*(1), p. 71. Used by permission.

The *connected* families value closeness and may prefer it; however, connected families also recognize and support development of autonomy in their members. *Enmeshed* families value family closeness above all else. To sacrifice togetherness for independence is considered a major violation of family rules in enmeshed families. The sixteen types of families possible in the circumplex model are identified by the level of adaptability (high, midrange, or low) and the level of cohesion (high, midrange, or low) present in the family.

## Family Health and Dysfunction

Families in the midrange of the circumplex model have moderate scores on the adaptability and cohesion scales. Families with moderate scores are believed to exhibit characteristics of family health. Families at the extremes of the two dimensions are more likely to exhibit characteristics of family dysfunction. Olson and his colleagues caution, however, that all families with extreme scores are not necessarily dysfunctional and that some midrange families do experience family dysfunction. In general, however, the midrange families tend toward healthier functioning.

A summary of the characteristics of healthy and dysfunctional families is provided in Table 2.1. It is important for counselors who plan to work with families to understand family functioning and be able to classify families based on the characteristics they exhibit. The information provided in Table 2.1 should help the family counselor understand and classify family functioning.

## Family Communication

The research by Bateson et al. (1956) demonstrated that the double-bind communication style described earlier in this chapter contributed to the development of schizophrenic symptoms among family members. Similar dysfunctional communication patterns were shown to be a feature of other family systems experiencing less severe symptoms in one of their members, such as acting out or depressive reactions. Thus, the objective for many family therapists is to help their clients recognize and modify dysfunctional patterns of communication. This change in communication patterns often leads to symptom resolution. Clear, concise and open communication are hallmarks of effective family functioning.

Communication is critical to healthy family functioning because members need to be able to express their thoughts, feelings, and desires to others (Satir, 1983). When family members are unable to express their thoughts, feelings, and desires, psychological problems may develop in one or more family members. Alexander and Parsons (1982) maintain that an effective negotiation style is an important general goal for all families, because negotiation is the key to resolution of the myriad differences that will occur in families. These authors believe that effective family communication involves the following characteristics.

## TABLE 2.1
## Characteristics of Healthy and Dysfunctional Families

| Family Health | Family Dysfunction |
|---|---|
| Subsystem boundaries are clear and may be altered as family requires. | Subsystem boundaries are rigid or very diffuse and are not subject to change. |
| Family rules are clear and fairly enforced. Rules may change as family conditions change. | Rules are unchanging and rigidly enforced, or family has no rules or methods of organizing behavior. |
| Family members have a clear understanding of their roles. | Roles are rigid and may not be modified, or roles are not clearly defined and members are unsure what is required to meet expectations. |
| Individual autonomy is encouraged, and a sense of family unity is maintained. | Individual autonomy is sacrificed for family togetherness, or autonomy is required because of lack of family unity. |
| Communication is clear and direct without being coercive. | Communication is vague and indirect or coercive and authoritarian. |

**Brevity**   Communication must be short and to the point to avoid confusing the listener with too much information.

**Source Responsibility**   Wants and needs are most effectively expressed in "I statements." I statements allow the sender of the message to take responsibility for the wants, thoughts, or feelings expressed. By maintaining source responsibility, the sender avoids making accusations to the listener and keeps the communication flow on a positive level.

**Directness**   When it is necessary to identify behaviors in others that have been problematic, the communicator should identify the person and the behavior directly. Directness avoids the problem of not clearly identifying what is needed for change to occur. A nondirect statement would be, "No one in this family ever helps me in the kitchen." A more effective statement would be, "I need more help from you in the kitchen."

**Presentation of Alternatives**   Effective communicators avoid the problem of seeming to be overly demanding by presenting alternatives to solving a problem. In addition, they are open to alternative solutions suggested by the listener. For example, a husband may say to a wife, "I can't get all the rooms painted by the time your parents come. Would you like me to start on the first floor or upstairs?"

**Congruence**   Effective communicators present messages that are consistent or congruent at all levels. The verbal message is consistent with the nonverbal message, and the message is appropriate for the context of the conversation. If a husband needs more affection from his wife, he should ask for this in a pleasant manner with congruent body language rather than asking for it with a critical tone and demanding scowl on his face.

**Concreteness and Behavioral Specificity**   Effective communicators specify clearly what behavior is needed from the listener. Rather than saying, "You complain too much," the effective communicator would say, "I become angry when I hear you complain about my not helping in the kitchen." This level of specificity permits the communicators to know exactly what it is they need to work on.

**Feedback**   Effective communicators seek clarification from each other in a way that does not interrupt the purpose of the interaction or change the subject of what is being discussed. For example, when a wife tells her husband that his "long work hours are creating distance in the relationship," she would seek feedback by asking him what he understood her to say. It would be possible that the husband heard criticism from his wife when she wanted him to hear that she was lonely. An important way for couples to be sure their communication is clear is through the use of this feedback technique.

Dysfunctional communication is frequently part of the problem for families entering treatment. Family therapists can help families identify and modify their dysfunctional communication patterns by educating clients about the components of effective communication and by allowing clients to practice these skills during counseling sessions where feedback can be provided by both family members and the therapist.

# ◼ *Family Life Cycle Development*

Professional counselors and other psychotherapy practitioners must be able to design therapeutic interventions appropriate for the developmental stage of the individual receiving treatment. Therapists who treat marital and family difficulties may find the concepts of family life cycle development to be useful in their work with couples and families. Just as individuals move through predictable stages in their development, families also pass through predictable stages of development.

Carter and McGoldrick (1980) have suggested that families move through stages of development in the process of marriage, child rearing, and preparing for life as a couple with grown children. Typically, three generations of the family are involved in the life cycle process. Carter and McGoldrick suggested that specific developmental tasks must be accomplished at each of the developmental stages of the family, as described below.

1. *The unattached young adult.* During this stage, parents and children come to accept the separation that has developed between the generations. The offspring begin to develop intimate peer relationships and establish a career pattern.
2. *Marriage: The joining of two families.* During this stage, the offspring commit fully to establishment of a new family system through marriage. Critical events are the realignment of relationships with extended family and peers to meet the requirements of marriage.
3. *The family with young children.* During this stage, the couple must change the family system to make room for the child or children. The parents must increase their role responsibilities to include parenting, and they must adjust their relationships with each other and with the older generation, which assumes new roles and responsibilities as grandparents.

4. *The family with adolescents.* During this often stormy stage, parents must allow more autonomy for the adolescents. Adolescents begin to move out of the family system and begin to seriously seek autonomy. Parents deal with mid-life career and relationship issues and begin preparing to assume responsibilities of caring for the older generation.

5. *Launching children and preparing for married life without children and parents.* During this stage, the couple helps the children leave the family to establish their own lives. In addition, the spouses begin to renegotiate their relationship as a two-person system. During this stage, the couple may adopt the new roles of in-laws and grandparents. Finally, the disability and death of their own parents must be dealt with during this stage.

6. *The family in later life.* During this stage, the couple deals with passing the torch to the next generation. Specifically, the two of them must maintain their own interests in the face of declining health, support a more central role for their children (middle generation) in the family, create a place for themselves in the family system without trying to control the middle and youngest generations, and deal with the loss of spouse and preparation for one's own death.

As counselors consider this family life cycle, specific issues emerge at each of the stages. Knowledge of these stages prepares counselors to help their clients deal with these significant issues in acceptable ways. Knowledge of these stages allows counselors to reassure family members that events that seem stressful to the family are normal aspects of family development and may be handled as such. For example, parents frequently become overly critical of their teenagers when the son or daughter begins the normal process of establishing independence from the parents.

Parents often diagnose their adolescent as having emotional or psychological problems during this stage when, in fact, the teenager is only engaging in the normal life cycle process of differentiation from the family of origin. Although differentiation is often painful for both the parents and children, it is not necessarily a sign that the adolescent has psychological problems. When the counselor assures the parents and the adolescent that what is happening in the family is quite normal in family development, the stress and anxiety that had been present are often significantly reduced and healthy family functioning is enhanced.

The therapist should be careful when normalizing these family developmental issues. If this is not done effectively, family members may believe their problems are being discounted. The family therapist, while normalizing certain predictable developmental issues, may also ensure the family that there are more effective ways to deal with the issues. Family therapy may be extremely useful in this regard.

The model of family development described above is based on the rules and roles of the traditional family with three generations and two parents. Although many of the developmental tasks described are appropriate for nontraditional family systems, such as remarried families and single-parent families, frequently minority and alternative family types, such as single-parent families, have additional tasks to accomplish. Specific issues of nontraditional families will be treated in Part Three of this book.

## ▨ Summary

This chapter has provided a brief history of the family therapy movement as well as some basic information necessary to begin to understand and treat the family as a living system. Specifically, the reader has been introduced to several key figures in the development of the family therapy movement. The impact of Bateson, Haley, Weakland, Jackson, Satir, Whitaker, Bowen, Lynne, and Minuchin on the field of family therapy cannot be underestimated.

The ideas of these pioneers continue to define much of the work in family systems therapy today. The family has been described as a system and has been identified as a unit that may need to receive therapy as a coherent system. Basic concepts and terminology necessary to understand the chapters that follow were provided, as were models for understanding family health and dysfunction.

# SUGGESTED READINGS

Broderick, C. B., & Schraeder, S. S. (1991). "The History of Professional Marriage and Family Therapy." In A. S. Gurman & D. P. Kniskern, eds., *Handbook of Family Therapy*, Vol. II. New York: Brunner/Mazel.

Carter, E. A., & McGoldrick, M., eds. (1980). *The Family Life Cycle: A Framework for Family Therapy.* New York: Gardner Press.

Minuchin, S. (1974). *Families and Family Therapy.* Cambridge, MA: Harvard University Press.

# 3

# From Individual Counseling to Marriage and Family Therapy: Building Theoretical Bridges

*This chapter provides the reader with information about the similarities and differences between individual and systems theories. Too often the differences between individual and systems theories have been emphasized without sufficient consideration of their similarities. Effective therapists use both individual and systems theories appropriately in clinical practice. To understand when and how to use individual and systems theories, the therapist must be aware of the similarities and differences between the theories. This chapter also presents a five-step procedure that may be used to treat family problems by therapists with experience in individual counseling. Finally, we will describe the classification scheme used to organize the individual and systems theories presented in Part Two of the book.*

## KEY CONCEPTS

Locus of pathology

System as client

Joining

Systems therapist as expert

Expanding the definition of the problem

Paradigm shift

Brief family therapy

## QUESTIONS
## FOR DISCUSSION

1. What are the major similarities between individual and systems theory approaches to counseling?

2. What are the major differences between individual and systems theory approaches to counseling?

3. What can the counselor do to expand the definition of the presenting problem in family therapy?

4. Why is it important to join with each family member in family counseling?

5. What basic counseling techniques may be used in the joining process?

6. Why do family systems counselors consider it important to treat the whole family as the client?

7. How can family systems theory be helpful to the counselor in professional practice?

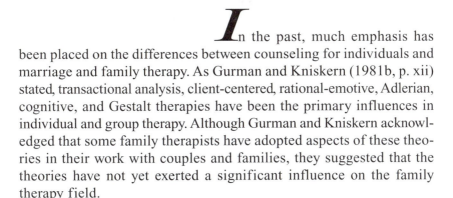

*I*n the past, much emphasis has been placed on the differences between counseling for individuals and marriage and family therapy. As Gurman and Kniskern (1981b, p. xii) stated, transactional analysis, client-centered, rational-emotive, Adlerian, cognitive, and Gestalt therapies have been the primary influences in individual and group therapy. Although Gurman and Kniskern acknowledged that some family therapists have adopted aspects of these theories in their work with couples and families, they suggested that the theories have not yet exerted a significant influence on the family therapy field.

In part, these theories about therapy for the individual have not been very influential in family therapy because of the dichotomy between the practice of individual and group therapy and family therapy. This dichotomy in essence is based on the idea that individual and group theories conceptualize problems as existing within individuals and that, for the most part, these problems are maintained by the actions of the individual or by past experiences. Family therapy, based on systems concepts, assumes that psychological problems in an individual are conspicuous elements of a more encompassing problem that involves the individual as well as those in that person's environment or interpersonal system. Most often, the interpersonal system is composed of the members of the identified patient's family.

We believe that this dichotomy between individual/group theories and systems-based theories may not be helpful for therapists with traditional individual and group therapy training, for it fails to recognize that the skills these therapists currently possess can be used effectively to help couples and families. Effective therapists will be able to conceptualize problem formation in clients from both individually oriented models and systems-based models. It is our experience that many counselors believe they are in some way being disloyal to their theoretical position if they do not adhere to the concepts in exactly the same way as the founder of the theory. This observation applies to counselors who adhere to either individual or systems-based theories. We have found that the most effective therapists are those who have identified a theoretical approach that is consistent with their own value system, and who are open to modifying their approach in response to client need, new information, and research results.

The purpose of this chapter is to clarify how counselors who have experience working from individually based theories can build bridges linking their current way of conceptualizing problem formation to a model of helping that is systems-based. To begin this process, it is important for the reader to understand the similarities and differences between individual and family systems therapies.

## ■ Similarities Between the Theories

For counselors to comfortably cross the bridge from individual to systems-based treatment, they need to reaffirm their awareness that the ultimate goal of all counseling theories, including individual and systems theories, is to help alleviate human suffering. Once the counselor recognizes that the goal of therapy is the same for all approaches, the question becomes: What is the best way to incorporate theory and technique to alleviate this human suffering? We believe that counselors who do not incorporate systems-based family therapy in their skill repertoire may not be as well-equipped to help their clients as a therapist who is able to conceptualize and treat from both individual and systems-based theoretical orientations as the client's needs dictate.

A second similarity between individual and systems-based theories is that each respects the dignity of the client. The client seeks the services of the therapist. The therapist, in turn, attempts to help the client resolve the difficulties that are negatively affecting the client's life. To be successful in helping the client, the therapist must clearly communicate that he or she respects the attempts, however ineffective, the client has made to resolve the current problems. Moreover, the therapist communicates, through respect, that the client possesses the resources necessary to make significant life changes.

If counselors accept that both individual and systems theory treatments seek to alleviate human suffering and respect the dignity of their clients, it will become easier to adopt a systems perspective in treatment. Counselors who operate from the perspective of counseling the individual need not give up their current knowledge and skills in alleviating human suffering and will not be asked to surrender their belief in the dignity of the client, as these characteristics are shared by both individual and systems theorists.

# ■ *Differences Between the Theories*

There are four specific differences between theories for treating individuals and systems theories used in family therapy. These differences highlight specific factors in the conceptualization of problem formation that should be examined and incorporated in a systems perspective. The four major differences are presented next.

## *Locus of Pathology*

Traditionally, therapists for individuals have conceptualized the locus of pathology (or the location of the problem) as being within the psyche of the individual client. According to this model, problems occur because the client has not resolved certain issues in his or her current or past experiences. The therapist helps the client examine and resolve these internal psychological issues and conflicts.

The systems therapist does not discount this model. However, the systems therapist considers an alternative hypothesis of problem formation and locus of pathology. Although the client's problem may lie within the individual's psyche, systems theorists assume that the client's problems occur as a result of dysfunctional interaction patterns between significant persons within the client's social context. This social context is frequently the client's family. Thus, for the systems theorist, the locus of pathology is within the client's social system or family. From a systems perspective, the problems experienced by one family member are believed to be conspicuous elements of a dysfunctional family. Thus, for the systems theorist, the locus of pathology is found in the client's entire social system or family.

## *Focus of Treatment Interventions*

From an individual theorist's perspective, the focus of treatment is generally on the individual client. The therapist concentrates on helping the client explore his or her past and present world and discover what could be changed to make his or her life more satisfying. In counseling the individual, the therapist gathers information based primarily on the client's perceptions of what has occurred and is occurring in his or her life. If the client is having problems dealing with a member of his or her family system, the therapist may help the client discover ways to change his or her behavior to respond more effectively to the stable conditions in the family.

The family therapist's focus of treatment is on the family system of the client. The person with the problem in the family is referred to as the *identified patient*, or *IP.* Frequently, the family therapist will treat the identified patient's entire family and will assist the family members in changing the ways they relate to each other and to the identified patient. If the therapy is successful, all family members change their patterns of interaction and the symptoms of the identified patient decrease in intensity and duration and may eventually disappear.

The therapist for an individual client usually has access only to the client's reports of the other family members' behaviors, but the family therapist can actually observe the behaviors of the identified patient and other members of the family system during the sessions. This is a major strength of family therapy. Based on observations and family interaction patterns, the systems therapist helps each member of the family adjust his or her behavior to a more satisfying state for all concerned. In family work, everyone has the opportunity to change— not just the identified client. Systems therapists believe that lasting change is more likely when all members of the system are participating in that change.

## *Unit of Treatment*

The individually oriented therapist generally treats only the individual client in therapy. Based on the theoretical assumption that the locus of pathology is within the individual, treating the individual alone makes sound theoretical sense and may be the treatment of choice.

Family therapists often seek to treat the entire family in therapy, or at least to counsel the members of the family most involved in the presenting problem. This approach, they believe, not only increases the options and alternatives for change but also resolves the presenting problems and helps the entire family more quickly and effectively than individual therapy. Because systems therapists conceptualize the locus of pathology as occurring within the family system, treating as many members of the system as possible is considered to be the treatment of choice.

## Duration of Treatment

In general, therapists for individuals attempt to help clients resolve internal conflicts that may have roots imbedded deeply in the past. Thus, treatment continues until the client has not only fully worked through problems that occurred in the past but is also functioning effectively in the present. This type of treatment may be quite lengthy, often lasting a year or more depending on the specific presenting problem and the theoretical orientation of the therapist. Such lengthy treatment also has the disadvantage of creating the possibility of client dependence on the counselor.

Family systems theorists typically attempt to provide brief treatment for the resolution of family-related problems. The systems theorist wants to help families alter their current patterns of dysfunctional behavior and then terminate the therapy in as brief a time frame as possible. Family members learn to depend on each other, rather than on the therapist, in the resolution of their difficulties. Families are encouraged to return to therapy only if further difficulties occur at a later date. Although wide variations in length of treatment can occur, family therapy tends to be briefer than most forms of treatment for individuals, often lasting six months or less. The systems therapist is not trying to help family members resolve longstanding internal conflicts. Rather, the systems therapist expects to help the family resolve only its immediate crisis through alteration of the current pattern of dysfunctional interaction among the members.

## ■ Individual Counseling Theories in Family Treatment

We have often heard counselors trained in individual and group theories report that they do not think they are adequately trained to work with families because they lack expertise in systems theory. We believe that counselors with training and experience in individual and group therapy can begin to work effectively under supervision with couples and families, using core counseling skills they have already developed (Fenell & Hovestadt, 1986). Moreover, the theories focusing on counseling individuals presented in most counselor training programs can be employed in working with couples and families, as we will demonstrate in subsequent chapters of this book. Core counseling skills may be used to accomplish a series of five steps that are important in both individual and family systems therapy. These five steps are described next.

### Establish Effective Relationships with Family Members

To help an individual or a family change through psychotherapy and to develop a productive counseling relationship, the first step for the therapist is to establish an effective relationship with each individual involved in the treatment. In our judgment, the skills counselors develop in their training programs for counseling individuals (such as empathy, respect, and genuineness) that enable the therapist to establish a therapeutic relationship with clients are the same skills the family therapist needs to develop a working relationship with a family system in family therapy. In family therapy, establishing an effective working relationship with the family members is known as *joining* (Minuchin, 1974). Joining with each family member is an important prerequisite to further work in therapy.

### Establish Self as Expert

Establishing the self as an expert who can help the family change is a step that some counselors may find inconsistent with effective therapy. Many counselors trained in therapies for individuals have been taught a person-centered theoretical orientation (Rogers, 1961). This orientation is based on the assumption that the client is the expert concerning the problem and that the client will resolve his or her own problems if the therapist can provide an effective relationship with the client. We contend, however, that even nondirective therapists establish themselves as experts in helping their clients, although they accomplish this through empathy, warmth, and genuineness rather than through more readily observable therapeutic behaviors.

Establishing yourself as an expert in helping the family change may be accomplished directly or indirectly. If a direct approach is chosen, the counselor may give specific suggestions to family members to help the family change dysfunctional patterns. The therapist may share with the family his or her perceptions of what is taking place in the family and what may need to be changed. Direct leadership may also be asserted by referring to experts in the field or citing research relevant to the presenting problem. For example, a therapist may assist a couple in marital therapy using direct leadership by citing a research study on characteristics of long-term marriages (Fenell, 1993a).

If expert leadership is established indirectly, the counselor becomes a significant source of self-esteem for the members of the family through demonstrating genuine caring, respect, and understanding of each family member. Basic relationship skills taught in most counseling programs, such as empathy, respect, warmth, and genuineness, are particularly effective in establishing expert leadership indirectly and may be effectively employed by counselors who are beginning their work with families.

## Expand the Definition of the Problem

To work most effectively with a family, the counselor must frequently define the presenting problem as one that exists and is maintained within the family system rather than one that resides entirely within the psyche of the identified patient. The definition of the problem is often expanded in this way and this redefinition enhances the effectiveness of many systems-based interventions (Haley, 1983). If the family continues to believe the problem is solely the responsibility of the identified patient, the members are less likely to make changes that could positively affect the outcome of treatment.

The counselor can help the family expand the definition of the problem by applying skills used in therapy for individuals. For example, the counselor is already trained to identify problem behaviors exhibited by the client and to communicate to the client how the behaviors maintain the undesired symptoms. In the same manner, the counselor may observe and identify behaviors in other family members that directly or indirectly affect the identified problem. By using effective communication skills learned in most counselor training programs, the counselor may help other family members discover how their behavior is part of the problem and identify what they may do to institute change.

A classic example of expanding the definition of the problem occurs when a family comes to therapy seeking help with an acting-out child. The therapist may quickly discover that the parents hold quite different opinions about how to best deal with the child's behavior. The family therapist will use this information and attempt to expand the definition of the problem to include the parents. The therapist will help the parents recognize that they send contradictory and confusing messages to the child and that the parents' behavior places the child in a bind that may have precipitated the acting-out behavior. As mentioned previously, excellent observational skills are necessary to detect important family patterns.

The therapist must accurately describe the actual behaviors of the family members in the expanded definition of the problem. By using actual family behavioral data in the expanded definition, the therapist increases the likelihood that the family will accept the expanded definition. Furthermore, if the therapist has joined with the family members and established expert leadership through the use of excellent communication skills, the chances of the family accepting the new definition of the problem is further increased.

Expanding the definition of the problem is important in family treatment. If the family's definition of the problem is maintained, the family will remain the expert on the problem. If the family is the expert, it will continue to employ different variations of the ineffective solutions it has previously attempted. If a new or expanded definition of the problem is presented and accepted by the family, the therapist becomes the expert on the problem and its resolution, and the process of change will often be expedited. When the therapist becomes the expert on the problem, the family will often defer to the therapist and more enthusiastically try new behaviors and solutions to their problem.

## Engage All Members in Solving the Problem

After the counselor has successfully expanded the definition of the problem to include other family members, it is necessary to engage the family members in solving the problem. This step can often be accomplished during a session by asking two family members to discuss how the newly defined problem can be resolved. Often, when encouraged to participate, the less verbal family members will have excellent new insights into how the family can behave in more effective ways, and the therapist should be certain all members are included in the process of problem resolution.

Remember that the family is likely to discover new and more effective ways to deal with the problem once it is redefined. Family members are not dealing with the same insoluble problem that brought them to therapy. Rather, they are dealing with a new and expanded version of the problem, which may lend itself to new and creative solutions involving all members of the family system.

## Make a Paradigm Shift

The last and possibly most difficult step in the process of working effectively with family systems is making the paradigm shift to systems thinking. Counselors are well trained to accept new ideas and to implement them when they are in the best interest of their clients. Systems therapy offers avenues for therapeutic change that cannot be easily achieved from other theoretical orientations. Thus, the well-trained counselor will want to be able to use systems therapy when it is in the best interests of the client family.

Each of the four steps listed above can be accomplished by the well-trained counselor. However, these steps will be nothing more than a set of techniques to be routinely followed if they are not supported by consistent systems-based theoretical assumptions and actions. Therefore, counselors who work with family systems need to make the paradigm shift from conceptualizing the problem as existing within the individual to conceptualizing the problem as a conspicuous aspect of a dysfunctional family system.

Too often counselors adopt a way of helping and adhere to the tenets of the theory as if it were a religion. Counseling theories are not religions; they are models developed to help clients make life changes. If one model for helping does not work, effective therapists will want to try other models. Systems theory offers a powerful alternative helping paradigm that counselors can employ with clients. However, this model cannot be effectively implemented if the counselor cannot or will not conceptualize the family as a living system and as the focus of treatment.

# Classification of Theories

The theories in this book have been organized into four categories to aid the reader in understanding the material presented. The categories are psychodynamic, cognitive/behavioral, humanistic, and transpersonal theories. The classification scheme builds on the work of Levant (1984), who developed a multilevel classification system for family therapy theories. The present classification system is unique in that it describes how theories developed to treat individual problems can be used in working with couples and families. Further, several major family therapy theories are presented that may be incorporated by counselors and psychotherapists after appropriate training and supervision.

Each of the theories will be presented in the same organizational format for the purposes of comparison and to develop the bridge between individual and systems theories. First, we will present the background for each theory and clarify why and how each theory was developed. Second, we will present the philosophical tenets of each theory and discuss the assumptions underlying each theory. It is of critical importance that counselors understand the assumptions underlying their method of providing therapeutic assistance to clients. Third, the major techniques associated with each theory will be described, including the major interventions used to bring about therapeutic change. In addition to describing these three areas for each individual and systems theory, case examples demonstrating the actual use of each theory are included. Finally, the strengths and limitations of each theory will be presented.

## ■ *Summary*

As you study each of the theories in this book, it is important to note that certain theories will make more sense to you and be more acceptable and relevant than others. This is as it should be. Each theory is based on certain assumptions and philosophical tenets. Counselors are most comfortable with theories that are based on philosophical tenets similar to their own beliefs about the development of psychological problems and the alleviation of these problems. We suggest that you initially become familiar with the theories that seem most relevant and most promising for the client and client family and use those theories in clinical practice. Then, after becoming grounded in one or more theories, carefully consider and implement theories that are less comfortable, when in the best interests of your client or family. When you are thoroughly grounded and very comfortable with a familiar theory, you will have the ability to move from that theory to study other theories carefully. A return to the familiar is always possible if the study of the new theories becomes too uncomfortable. We believe that having a strong theoretical home base permits the student to engage in a more thorough exploration of other theories.

This book describes the major individual and systems theories that can be employed in family counseling. Several of these theories may serve as a comfortable home base as the counselor studies other systems models developed for treating families.

# SUGGESTED
# READINGS

Horne, A., & Ohlsen, M., eds. (1982). *Family Counseling and Therapy*. Itasca, IL: Peacock.

Levant, R. (1984). *Family Therapy: A Comprehensive Overview*. Englewood Cliffs, NJ: Prentice Hall.

Minuchin, S., & Fishman, C. (1981). *Family Therapy Techniques*. Cambridge, MA: Harvard University Press.

# 4

# Using Core Counseling Skills in Marriage and Family Therapy

*In this chapter, twelve core counseling skills taught in most counselor education programs are described. Each of the twelve skills is identified and recommendations are made concerning how the skills may be applied in individual, group, and family therapy.*

| | |
|---|---|
| Rapport building | Reflecting feelings |
| Joining | Summarizing |
| Information gathering | Self-disclosure |
| Minimal encouragers | Confrontation |
| Genogram | Interpretation |
| Structuring | Reframing |
| Information giving | Behavior change |
| Reflecting content | Closure |

## QUESTIONS
## FOR DISCUSSION

1. Why is rapport building important in individual, group, and family counseling?

2. What steps should the family counselor take when joining with a family?

3. What is a genogram, and how is it useful in family counseling?

4. How is reflection of content different from reflection of feeling, and why are they important in counseling?

5. What is reframing, and why is it important in counseling?

6. What are the components of behavior change skills, and how are these used in individual, group, and family counseling?

*T*he five fundamental steps described in the previous chapter suggest a framework for counselors trained in individual therapy to begin working with couples and families. We assume that counselors who begin to work with couples and families are trained in the use of specific core therapeutic skills and have qualified supervision available. In this chapter we will describe twelve core counseling skills that may be used in individual, group, and marriage and family counseling. We will demonstrate how these core skills, which are already in the repertoire of most counselors, may be used as a bridge from individual and group counseling to marriage and family counseling.

## Core Skill One: Rapport Building

In counseling the individual, rapport building involves behaving in an attentive manner toward the client both verbally and nonverbally. Examples of good nonverbal attention would be sitting facing the client, maintaining good eye contact, and being relaxed. Verbal attention would include staying with the topic the client brought up and not changing the subject.

In group counseling sessions, rapport building is more difficult because of the number of people involved. The basic premise is the same, however, as with the individual. The goal in group therapy is to let the group members know you are "with them" and that you accept them rather than approve or disapprove of them. It is also useful to pay close attention to the verbs the clients use in their sentences, which will indicate their favorite way of accessing information (visual, auditory, or kinesthetic).

Research has shown that matching a client's way of accessing information is an effective way to build rapport. If a client says, "I am clear (visual) that it wasn't my fault," you might match that by saying, "You don't see why people are blaming you." Eye movements can also provide visual clues. People look up when accessing information visually, side to side when accessing in auditory ways, and down when feeling something kinesthetically. The key to letting them know you are with them is matching their verbal and nonverbal behavior (Dilts & Green, 1982).

In marriage and family therapy, rapport building with clients is called *joining* (Minuchin, 1974). Working with a couple or family requires establishing rapport with each individual in the family. The effective therapist must join with each member of the family system and the significant subsystems of the family.

## Joining with Each Family Member

Each person in a family has a story to tell. Each individual needs to tell his or her story and to know that he or she has been heard and understood by the counselor. Thus, excellent listening skills and effective verbal and nonverbal communication skills are essential in order for the counselor to let the individual know that understanding has occurred. If rapport building, or joining, is successful, the counselor will become a significant source of self-esteem for each family member (Minuchin & Fishman, 1981). When the family members look to the counselor to meet some, or most, of their self-esteem needs, the counselor's power in the family and ability to intervene effectively with the family will increase.

Unlike group counseling, in family therapy the story that each family member tells will be related to the story of every other member. The effective counselor will hear and understand each version of the story without favoring any of the versions. This skill takes practice, as the counselor's own values frequently support one family member's position over the others. If the counselor's values do become obvious, the ability to intervene in creative and powerful ways becomes limited as the counselor is "sucked" into the family system and loses therapeutic objectivity.

## Joining with the Family

In addition to successfully joining with each individual, the counselor must be able to join with the entire family and the significant subsystems within the family. The counselor must identify important patterns of behavior that the family exhibits and respect these patterns. Moreover, the counselor must be able to identify family rules early in the treatment and attempt not to violate these rules unintentionally.

Finally, there are significant subsystems in the family, such as the husband-wife, parental, and sibling subsystems. The counselor must identify and join with these subsystems. If the counselor does not join the significant (powerful) subsystems, these powerful units can hinder the therapy process. Just as individuals need to feel valued, so do family systems and subsystems. If the counselor is successful at rapport building, the prognosis for assisting the family is enhanced.

## ■ Core Skill Two: Information Gathering

In individual counseling, *open-ended questions* help the counselor gather more information than closed questions. An open-ended question allows the client to respond in several ways; a closed question lends itself to yes-no responses. An example of an open-ended question would be: "Tell me about your relationship with your husband." A closed question would be: "Do you get along with your husband?" *Minimal encouragers* also aid in information gathering. A minimal encourager prompts the client to provide additional information, as, for example, in "Tell me more" or "Give me an example of that."

In group counseling, the same techniques can be employed. The use of open-ended questions and minimal encouragement statements can have a modeling effect when used in a group. Group members may begin to use this technique with each other if it is effectively modeled by the counselor.

In marriage and family therapy, the counselor must obtain information from several persons, as in group counseling. However, the information obtained in family counseling will have a central theme and will be related to issues the family is confronting. In family counseling, the therapist needs an additional skill: *blocking information* provided by a family member who is not being addressed or who is attempting to control the flow of information in the family interview.

For example, the identified patient may be providing information to the counselor about the family situation when the mother interrupts with, "Be sure to tell him about how rude you were to your father yesterday." At this point, the counselor must block the mother's attempt to control the son's responses. The counselor can accomplish this by saying, "Thanks for your input, Mrs. Smith; however, at this point I'm interested in Tom's thoughts about the situation. If you will be patient with me for a few minutes, I will get to you and find out what you are thinking and feeling about the situation." The family counselor must begin to use blocking techniques early in the therapy to prevent more powerful family members and subsystems from controlling and limiting the flow of information provided by the family.

Another helpful information-gathering tool used primarily in family counseling is the *genogram*. The genogram is a visual depiction of the family tree that frequently covers three generations of the family. Important family information is reported on the genogram, such as names of family members, ages of family members, marital status, divorces, significant life events, and years of deaths. The genogram is a useful aid that frequently helps the counselor elicit important information concerning the family members, the problems in the family, and the emotional reactivity in the family to various members and events (McGoldrick & Gerson, 1985). An example of a three-generation genogram is shown in Figure 4.1

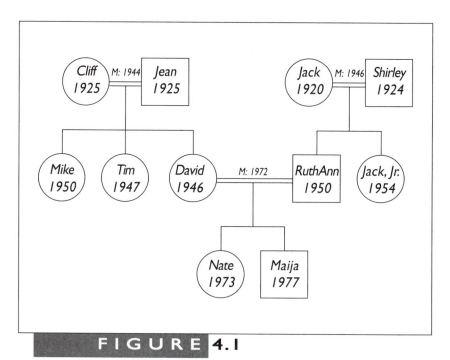

**FIGURE 4.1**

**Three-Generation Genogram**

# ■ *Core Skill Three: Structuring*

In counseling sessions for individuals, structuring the nature, limits, and goals of the session can help the client make better use of the session. It lets the client test out and clarify: (1) where he or she is, (2) who the counselor is, (3) how the counselor can or cannot help him or her, and (4) what common goals and expectations each person has for the session. Structuring also clarifies:

1. *Time limits.* Example: "We have agreed to a one-hour appointment today."
2. *Role limits.* Example: "I see my role as helping you explore your problems and concerns and helping you find solutions that are personally satisfying."
3. *Process limits.* Example: "I will help you by pointing out obstacles that I believe are getting in your way and preventing you from solving your problems."
4. *Action limits.* Example: "I will ask you to try out new ideas outside the session and report back to me."

The counselor should involve the client in the structuring process by asking open-ended questions such as, "What motivated you to come see me?" and "How may I be of most help to you?"

In group counseling, the skill is practiced in a similar way. The main difference is that in a group more time has to be devoted to structuring so all members have an equal opportunity to become involved. The time spent structuring the purpose and goals of the group is often time well spent because it helps the group members use the group time more effectively, helps encourage reluctant members to participate, and limits the participation of dominant group members.

In marriage and family therapy, structuring is of critical importance. When a couple or family enters therapy, the clients are frequently locked in a mutually reinforcing pattern of dysfunctional behavior. Despite the pain family members experience, they continue to repeat the same behaviors because those behaviors are reinforced by the complementary behaviors of other family members. A family can quickly overwhelm a therapist with dysfunctional sequences of behavior if the therapist does not take control of the session from the outset. In family therapy, this structuring begins with the initial telephone contact. Often, the person contacting the therapist will have already decided who needs treatment. The family spokesperson is already active (1) in setting up therapy, and (2) in determining who should be present in treatment. The therapist must recognize that the family member's attempts to control treatment no matter how well intentioned, may have the effect of maintaining the dysfunction. Helping the family engage in new behavior sequences can be accomplished most effectively when the therapist is able to structure the therapy without seeming authoritarian to the family members. For example: Mother may call to set up a therapy appointment and tell the therapist that everyone can attend except her husband, who is too busy with his work. The therapist must respond in a way that acknowledges the mother's concern for her husband's schedule, but that also includes him in the therapy, as his presence is important to the treatment.

# ■ Core Skill Four: Information Giving

There are times in counseling sessions for the individual when the therapist must give information to the client. At these times, called *teachable moments*, facts or data about experiences the client is having may expand the meaning or learning for the client. The three main purposes of information giving are (1) to identify alternatives, (2) to evaluate alternatives, and (3) to correct erroneous information. In giving information, it is important to be accurate and to reveal information gradually, only when the individual most needs it. In a group counseling session, this skill may be utilized in much the same way as in a session with an individual. There are many opportunities to teach group members concepts that will help them function more effectively in the group and outside the group.

In marriage and family therapy, information giving takes on an increased importance for two reasons: (1) As marriage and family therapy tends to be brief, clients need information to begin making changes relatively quickly in the therapy; and (2) to alter dysfunctional patterns, the family or couple needs to understand what these dysfunctional patterns are. The therapist identifies the dysfunctional patterns and provides the information the family needs to understand the pattern and change it. The information provided by the therapist should meet the following criteria:

1. The information is understood and accepted by the family.
2. The information does not overwhelm the family.

3. The information is accurate.
4. The information is provided at the appropriate time.

Without giving helpful information, the counselor's ability to help the family change their currently dysfunctional patterns of behavior is greatly reduced.

# ■ *Core Skill Five: Reflecting Content*

As a skill for counseling individuals, reflecting content is: (1) a way to convey to clients that you understand them, (2) a way to help clients crystallize their thoughts and feelings by having them restated in a more concise manner, and (3) a way for the counselor to check his or her perceptions to make sure they are consistent with what the client is trying to convey. Although the focus is on content, the counselor also recognizes the client's feelings. For example, if a client says, "I don't know about him—one moment he is as nice as can be and the next he is a real jerk," the counselor might say, "He seems like a pretty inconsistent guy who is hard for you to be with. His erratic behavior keeps you pretty confused."

As a group counseling skill, the reflection of content simply changes from a focus on individual content to a focus on group content. Whenever group members seem to ignore, avoid, or deny some important content, the group therapist should intervene and draw out, identify, and reflect the content. There are three specific skills involved: (1) eliciting group content, (2) identifying group content, and (3) reflecting group content. These skills are described next.

1. *Eliciting group content* usually means asking open-ended questions and making statements that draw out the content. For example, the counselor may say: "Sammy, I noticed you avoid looking at other people when you talk to them. What is going on with you? What do other members notice about this?"
2. *Identifying group content* means helping group members identify issues that they have overlooked. For example, the counselor may say: "Most of you seem to have trouble with certain subjects. I noticed that when Bill mentioned having trouble with his mother everyone got quiet, and Jim changed the subject. What have others noticed about this?"
3. *Reflecting group content* means restating or clarifying some issue in your own words. For example, the counselor may say:

"It seems to me that several of you are saying that you have problems in dealing with people in authority. Will you give me feedback on my perceptions?"

Reflecting content is an important skill for the marriage and family therapist. For the counselor to provide information to clients about their current patterns of behavior, the counselor must be able to assess current interaction patterns. When the counselor notices a certain repetitive behavior that may require modification, he or she reflects the observation of that behavior to the family. For example, the counselor may say to the family: "I notice that whenever Bill seems to have trouble gathering his thoughts, dad jumps in to help him." At this point, the counselor should check out this observation with those directly involved as well as with other family members.

In addition, this skill is critical in the joining process in the early stages of family therapy. If each member of the family feels that he or she has been heard and understood, the family is more likely to place trust in the therapist, which improves the prognosis for therapy. One of the most effective ways to ensure that family members feel heard and understood is to accurately reflect the content of each family member's communications in therapy.

# ▪ Core Skill Six: Reflecting Feelings

This skill is used in counseling individuals to help clients move toward more complete self-awareness and self-understanding. In reflection of feeling, the counselor expresses the central concern the client is feeling. There are three aspects to this skill: (1) listening for feeling, (2) timing, and (3) reflecting the feeling. In listening for feelings, listen for what is not being said. You may watch nonverbal behaviors, such as a person's breathing, a sigh, a blush, a stammer, or a swallow, as clues to feelings. Verbal clues include the use of feeling words and tone of voice. Good timing requires that the counselor wait for an appropriate moment before reflecting, being careful not to cut off an internal flow or disturb the focus of thought. It is also important not to lag behind the client. Reflecting feelings requires the use of a *feeling word* when the client may not have said one. If a client says, "I wish I could talk to my dad like this," the counselor might say, "You have been a little *afraid* to be open with your dad."

In group counseling, feelings are often overlooked or not dealt with. Most people have been conditioned not to express feelings in public. Therefore, a group counselor must help elicit, label, clarify, and reflect individual and group feelings. A group member might say: "It is hard to bring up things like that." The therapist replies: "You seem scared to talk about your problems in a group. Do any other group members share this feeling?"

According to several marriage and family therapy theories (Fisch, Weakland, & Segal, 1982; Haley, 1971; Minuchin, 1974), reflection of feeling is viewed as important in the joining process, when intense feelings about the family situation are often expressed. The counselor must accurately hear and reflect the feelings. As emotional catharsis is usually not encouraged in family therapy, feelings are not pursued unless their expression is critical to establishing more effective family patterns. However, the therapist must be careful not to discount the client's feelings even though their expression may not be contributing to specific problem resolution. In such a situation, the counselor would want to hear, understand, empathize, and reflect the feeling. When the time is appropriate, the counselor should ask if the client is ready to move to another issue. This technique contrasts with theories about counseling individuals, which teach the therapist to help the client stay with the feeling and work through it fully before moving to other issues.

The views of many family therapists toward client feelings are different from those of individual or group therapists. Family therapists recognize that family problems may evoke a great deal of affect. However, this affect is dealt with only to the extent necessary to allow the client to move on to aspects of therapy that are viewed as being more helpful in changing dysfunctional interaction patterns of all family members.

## ■ *Core Skill Seven: Summarizing Content and Feelings*

At times in individual therapy, the counselor wants to recapitulate, condense, or crystallize the essence of what the client said and felt. Although this skill resembles reflection of content and feeling, it is more comprehensive and covers more of what the client said and felt. Summarization can be used at the beginning of a session to review aspects of the previous session or at the end of a session to review what has happened. This technique can also be used when a client rambles, isn't clear, is at the end of a discussion on a particular topic, or is in conflict.

Summarization can be used in similar ways in group counseling except there is an emphasis on summarizing the collective content and feeling from the group as a whole or of several people. In a group, themes or processes should be summarized from time to time to help group members stay focused.

In marriage and family therapy, summarization pulls together critical aspects of the session for the family. Counselors will want to be certain that their summarizations include the thoughts of as many family members as possible. If the summarization of content and feeling focuses on only one member, the family (and perhaps the therapist) may have lost sight of the problem as a dysfunctional system rather than a dysfunctional individual. As noted previously, the family therapist will generally use summarization of content more frequently than summarization of feeling.

## Core Skill Eight: Self-Disclosure

Unless counselors and therapists understand themselves, they will find it difficult to understand others. In counseling individuals, there are times when counselors will want to share personal thoughts, feelings, and experiences that relate to a client's situation. At a basic level, self-disclosure involves listening to the client, reflecting content and feelings, and telling the client what you think or feel about what is being said. Carkhuff (1969a) described this skill as counselor immediacy.

In group counseling, self-disclosure can be a very useful way to give group members feedback on how their behavior affects others. For example, a group member may be critical and judgmental about his spouse. The group counselor says: "You seem so angry that I feel afraid of you when you talk that way about your wife. I get angry and want to shut you up. Can you respond to my feelings, John?" Group members may also comment on their perceptions of John's and the counselor's behaviors.

In marriage and family therapy, the use of self-disclosure is sometimes appropriate. When family members are not genuinely reacting to each other, for example, the therapist may share his or her reactions about the behavior with a member who is particularly receptive to the therapist and aware of the family's withholding information. If the counselor is on target with the self-disclosure, frequently one or more members of the family will feel more comfortable sharing the same perceptions and confronting other family members about the situation.

Family therapists must be careful not to use self-disclosure inappropriately. Frequently, counselors think self-disclosure means to share or describe a situation they experienced that was similar to what the client or family is experiencing. Because family problems are widespread and therapists are not immune to family problems of their own, it is possible that the family's behaviors or interactions will remind the therapist of a similar situation in his or her own life. The therapist should rarely discuss the similar situation with the family because it takes the focus off the family and puts it on the therapist. In general, therapists should not share this kind of personal information unless they are certain it will be therapeutic for the family by normalizing the problem or putting the family more at ease.

## ▇ *Core Skill Nine: Confrontation*

In a counseling session with an individual, a counselor may notice a discrepancy between what the client is saying and how he or she is behaving—for example, if a person is talking about a sad subject and laughs. Such discrepancies almost always have some significance for the person. They may indicate a conflict in feelings or an attempt to avoid or deny facing feelings. By confronting these discrepancies, the counselor may help the client gain insight into the problem or bring the problem out into the open so the client can deal with it. Confrontation is most effective when done from a caring position that shows respect for the client and validates him or her as a worthwhile individual. The counselor's tone of voice, posture, and gestures all contribute to the success of the confrontation.

In a group counseling situation, confrontation takes on even greater importance. Interaction within a group often reveals patterns of behavior more quickly than sessions with individuals. Within a group, members often assume roles identical to the ones they experience outside the group. Through effective confrontation, the counselor can help members understand their behaviors and change problematic behavior patterns.

Confrontation in marriage and family therapy is similar to confrontation in group counseling. However, in group counseling the client comes to recognize a pattern of behavior in the group that is similar to his or her behavior outside the group. The client must then leave the group to try new behaviors in the social setting. Furthermore, the people in the client's social setting will not be participating in the treatment and may not be prepared to reinforce the client's new behaviors. In family therapy, not only are all members experiencing their roles in the therapy but they are each in a position to change their roles with the awareness, support, and reinforcement of other family members outside the therapy session. Thus, the change is more likely to be maintained because all family members are participating in that change.

Confrontation in marriage and family therapy serves the same function as in individual and group therapies. It helps the client, group, or family recognize that what is expressed and the behavior exhibited may be incongruent. Confrontation helps the individual, group, or family clarify what it wants and encourages movement toward that goal.

## Core Skill Ten: Interpretation

Interpretation in a counseling session with an individual means the counselor presents the client with a new frame of reference through which the client can view the problems and better understand the situation. This advanced skill relies on the counselor's mastery of reflection of content and feelings. The accuracy of the interpretation determines whether the client can utilize the information. The counselor has to take the essence of what the client has said, summarize it for the client, and add new information for the client to consider. The following example illustrates this. A client with a record of absenteeism states, "I really feel bad about missing so much work." The therapist could respond with an interpretation: "You are worried about your absenteeism. You know how the company views absenteeism, and you are probably afraid you may get fired the next time it happens."

In group counseling, interpretation may include some aspect of the group process or the interaction of several group members. For example, a group member continually rescues other members whenever there is even a mild confrontation. The therapist may offer the following interpretation to the rescuer: "I have noticed that you jump in and try to protect everyone who is challenged by the group. You seem to have a real need to take care of other people. In my experience, people who have a need to protect others usually feel pretty scared and insecure themselves. Is that true for you?" In this situation, the data for the interpretation included the behavior of the client in the group context as well as the counselor's experience with other clients.

In marriage and family therapy, effective interpretation is often crucial to helping the family. When family members come into therapy, they are generally stuck in behavior patterns that seem appropriate to them given the actions of the identified patient. To help the family change, the therapist needs to understand the current behaviors of family members and recognize that these represent their *best attempt* to resolve the problems they are facing. One of the therapist's first interpretations is to acknowledge the family's genuine attempts to resolve the problem and to suggest that current methods are not resolving it. In fact, these efforts to change the identified patient may even make the problem worse.

Family members usually appreciate this interpretation because it shows them that the therapist understands that they have been trying to change and that the therapist is proficient enough to recognize that these attempts have not been effective in solving the problem. Furthermore, this interpretation *engenders hope* in the family that through therapy other ways to solve the problem may be possible.

Another interpretation critical to helping the family resolve its problems occurs when, given the information the therapist obtains from the family, the therapist presents a new understanding or interpretation of the problem. As long as the family's initial definition of the problem is used in the therapy, the family remains the expert on the problem and may disqualify many of the therapist's suggestions for alternative behavior. Typically, a family spokesperson will say, "We have tried that, and it didn't work." This type of response greatly reduces the therapist's ability to intervene effectively.

To avoid this situation, the therapist interprets the problem situation in a new way and offers the family a new understanding of the situation. This type of interpretation is called *redefining the problem* or *reframing*, and it presents the family with a new problem to solve. Because it is a new problem, the family is no longer the expert and turns to the therapist as the expert for help in resolving the problem.

A very simple example of redefining the problem can be shown by a couple beginning marital therapy. The couple is frequently in much turmoil and a great deal of anger may exist. Once the therapist determines that the couple is serious about wanting to improve the relationship, the wife's "pressuring the husband to express his feelings" may be redefined as her "need to hear that she is loved and valued by him." In the same manner, the husband's "withdrawal" may be redefined as "his feeling badly that he is unable to meet his wife's needs." Clearly, this type of interpretation must be done carefully and with appropriate timing. Attempting to redefine the problem when the partners are venting their anger toward each other or are not ready for a redefinition would almost certainly be ineffective.

# ■ *Core Skill Eleven: Behavior Change*

In counseling sessions with individuals, bringing about behavior change is an advanced skill and employs all the preceding skills. There are four stages in the process, each employing different skills.

1. *Identifying and clarifying the problem* involves use of rapport building, information gathering, structuring, reflection of content, and reflection of feeling.
2. *Establishing workable goals* requires the use of information gathering, information giving, summarization, and self-disclosure.
3. *Establishing criteria for effectiveness of the action plan* may require the use of confrontation and interpretation as well as reflection skills so both client and counselor will know when the objectives of therapy have been achieved.
4. *Implementation* involves summary skills, reflection skills, confrontation, interpretation, and closure skills. In short, the skills needed to help the client make desired changes.

In group counseling, these same skills would be useful with the additional advantage that other group members can support the changes individual members are making. Group support of its members is one of the major strengths of group therapy.

In marriage and family therapy, changing the behavior of family members is critical to system change, which is the goal of family therapy. The steps described above are appropriate for family therapy if the counselor considers the expanded uses of the core skills described for use in working with couples and families. As the family therapist identifies and clarifies the problem, she should remember that for systems therapy to be effective, the problem should be defined as an element of the functioning of the family system. Several family members should be identified as important in both the definition and the resolution of the problem.

Establishing workable goals is also important in marriage and family therapy. Determining those goals with the family based on a redefinition of the presenting problem increases the probability of successful interventions.

The marriage and family therapist, like any other therapist, must establish criteria to evaluate the effectiveness of the treatment. In family therapy, the most basic way to evaluate effectiveness is to look for change in the identified patient. Change in the identified patient, however, is not the only way to evaluate the effectiveness of the therapy.

Frequently, through change in other family members, the behaviors of the identified patient no longer have the power and influence over the family that they previously had. The behaviors of the identified patient may be relatively unchanged, but the ability of the other family members to accept or deal with the behaviors may be greatly improved. This development may be viewed by all as therapeutic success. Systems therapy offers the therapist *multiple criteria* for evaluating effectiveness. A major strength of the family systems approach to therapy is that there may be several therapeutic outcomes perceived as effective change by the family members. The therapist should be aware that system changes often occur in ways quite different from what might be expected. Such unplanned changes are every bit as effective as changes produced by well-designed treatment plans.

Behavior change in marriage and family therapy is most likely to occur when the therapist has:

- successfully joined with each family member and the family system,
- established himself or herself as an expert who is highly qualified to help the family solve the problem it confronts,
- expanded the definition of the problem to include the entire family and demonstrated how several family members are maintaining the problem through their own behaviors,

- engaged all significant family members in the solution to the problem, and
- conceptualized treatment and provided interventions from a family systems orientation.

# Core Skill Twelve: Closure

One of the most common problems in counseling individuals is termination and closure. Inexperienced counselors report that termination is a difficult time in the counseling process. Closure skills enable the counselor and the client to accomplish the following:

1. Bring a particular issue or problem to some resolution.
2. Bring a session to an end.
3. Terminate work with a client.

In the first instance, it is sometimes necessary for the therapist to ask, "Have we gone as far as we can on this problem? Is resolution complete?" If there is a specific contract with the client, it is easier to reach a mutual decision about whether resolution is complete in terms of meeting the goals of the contract. Without a contract, the counselor should summarize what has been covered, ask probing questions, and reflect content and feelings to complete the closure. Some counselors are timid and avoid closure, and others may be too aggressive and close a topic prematurely. Summarizing skills are useful in closing a session. It is usually helpful to ask the client to summarize what he or she got out of the session and to reevaluate the structure of therapy in light of the contract you have with the client.

Final termination may require several sessions to complete and usually involves self-disclosure and interpretation of the current status of the client as well as a thorough review and summary of the therapeutic contract. Some therapists write a formal evaluation of the treatment so that if the client returns to therapy or goes to another therapist a comparison can be made with the present level of functioning.

In group counseling sessions, closure of an issue being dealt with by one group member has to be complete before the emphasis can shift to another group member. Closure of a group session provides a transition for all the group members and gives them a chance to either complete unfinished business or contract to complete it outside of the group. In the final termination of a group, it is important to review the life of the group and take care of any unfinished business group members may have with each other. Some time should be spent on closure when an individual terminates from the group. Some group counselors allow graduates of a group to return for visits or remain in the group to support the work of others.

Closure in marriage and family therapy generally follows one of two patterns. In brief forms of family therapy, closure of the therapy occurs as soon as possible after the family has begun more functional behavior patterns. To keep the family in therapy after it has made basic family system changes would imply that the changes are not real or will not last. Family systems theorists believe that changes made by a family will be self-reinforcing and foster even greater change outside of therapy. Clients should be encouraged to end treatment as soon as possible and should be invited to return if and when other problems develop. The therapist needs to be able to identify when system change has occurred and should ensure that the *family feels responsible for that change* and feels capable of maintaining the change. For the family members to maintain their change, they must believe that they, not the therapist, are responsible for the good things that occurred in treatment. If the family believes the therapist is responsible for the change, it is less likely to be maintained.

In a second form of closure that occurs in family therapy after the family has made system changes, the therapist offers the family the opportunity to either terminate or remain in therapy for a time to process and learn how the changes took place as well as how to bring about similar changes when necessary in the future. This *psychoeducational approach* (Johnson, 1987) supports the idea of teaching families what it takes to bring about family system change. After this teaching stage of the therapy, termination occurs.

As you may have observed, the intense, personal relationships that are frequently established in group and individual counseling may not develop in family therapy. Therefore, many of the dependency issues that occur in the termination of individual and group treatment do not normally occur when effective family therapy ends.

## Summary

In this chapter we have shown how core counseling skills used in individual and group counseling may be effectively used in work with couples and families. Systems therapy in work with couples and families applies the basic core skills in unique ways. To most effectively help couples and families, counselors should seek additional supervision of their work to receive feedback on their counseling skills in the resolution of marital and family system problems.

In Part Two, we will discuss counseling theories that are already familiar to most counselors for individuals, show how these theories may be employed in work with couples and families, and introduce some important systems theories.

# SUGGESTED
# READINGS

Alexander, J., & Parsons, B. V. (1982). *Functional Family Therapy*. Pacific Grove, CA: Brooks/Cole.

Carkhuff, R. (1969). *Helping and Human Relations: Selection and Training*. New York: Holt, Rinehart, & Winston.

Carkhuff, R., & Anthony, W. A. (1979). *The Skills of Helping: An Introduction to Counseling*. Amherst, MA: Human Resources Development Press.

Ivey, A., & Authier, I. (1978). *Microcounseling: Innovations in Interviewing, Counseling, Psychotherapy and Psychoeducation*, 2nd ed. Springfield, IL: Charles C Thomas.

Ivey, A., & Gluckstern, N. (1984). *Basic Influencing Skills*, 2nd ed. Amherst, MA: Microtraining Associates.

Ivey, A., & Matthews, W. J. (1984). "A Meta-Model for Structuring the Clinical Interview." *Journal of Counseling and Development 65*, 237–243.

# II

# Helping Couples and Families:

# Bridging Individual and

# Systems Theories

## CHAPTERS

# 5

# *Psychodynamic Theories*

# *in Family Treatment*

*In this chapter, we will show how classical and neoclassical psychoanalytic approaches can be adapted to family therapy. The work of Harry Stack Sullivan is presented as the most family-oriented approach of this type. In addition, Adlerian approaches to family therapy are presented. Rudolf Dreikurs and Raymond Lowe are two Adlerians who have developed applications of this theory for work with families. Finally, a transactional analysis (TA) approach to family therapy is discussed. Building on the work of Eric Berne, Ruth McClendon's approach to TA-oriented family therapy is described.*

## KEY CONCEPTS

Psychosexual stages
Psychological birth
Object constancy
Symbiotic relationships
Individuation
Inferiority complex
Ego states
Strokes

Narcissistic needs
Intrapsychic conflict
Transference neurosis
Phenomenological orientation
Concept of indeterminism
Natural and logical consequences
Injunctions
Permission

## QUESTIONS
## FOR DISCUSSION

1. What are the unique aspects of psychodynamic family theories?

2. With what kinds of family problems would these approaches work best? Why?

3. With what kinds of family problems would these approaches not work? Why not?

4. Which psychodynamically oriented therapy techniques can be used most effectively in working with families?

5. As a therapist using a psychodynamic approach with a family, how would you determine the developmental issues of each of the family members?

6. How might a psychodynamically oriented family therapist handle the resistance to therapy of a family member?

7. What information would an Adlerian family therapist collect on each family member? What methods would the therapist use to collect this information?

8. How would a TA-oriented family therapist work with a family in which the father is an alcoholic?

$\mathcal{T}$he term *psychodynamic* is generally used more broadly than the term *psychoanalytic*. Psychoanalytic theories refer to Freudian principles, such as resistance, repression, narcissism, transference, libido, id, ego, and superego, as well as to Freudian techniques, such as free association and dream interpretation (Freud, 1949). Psychodynamic theorists attempt to understand the dynamic interplay of the conflicting components and experiences of the mind. They may or may not use Freudian principles or techniques. According to our definition, if a psychodynamic theory does use Freudian principles or techniques, it can be called psychoanalytic; if it does not, it is called psychodynamic. Using this definition, Sullivanians, Adlerians, Jungians, and TA theorists are classified as psychodynamic but not psychoanalytic. In this chapter, we will cover traditional psychoanalytic theory as well as two psychodynamic approaches, the Adlerian and TA theories.

## Goals of Psychodynamic Approaches

Using psychodynamic family therapy, the therapist develops insight into the family as a social unit and how family members' intrapsychic development is affected by relationships. Using such an approach, the therapist can help each family member become aware of his or her projections and take responsibility for them, which requires each family member to develop an *observing ego* to understand and integrate these awarenesses. The psychodynamic family therapist also aims to help family members set appropriate and functional ego boundaries between themselves and other family members.

One of the goals of such an approach is to strengthen and preserve the family as a social unit without interfering with the functional autonomy of each individual family member. The family and intimate family relationships are seen as excellent vehicles to help promote completion of unresolved parent-child conflicts left over from early childhood. Therapy is used to facilitate this completion process. Therapy attempts to help family members neutralize and integrate aggressive and libidinal urges so that their behavior is motivated more in the service of the ego (enlightened self-interest) and less by impulse and intrapsychic conflict.

# ▪ The Process of Psychodynamic Approaches

In general, psychodynamic family therapy involves a four-stage process.

1. *The therapy contract.* The contract includes all the administrative details of therapy, such as fees, vacations, appointment times, and so forth. The ability of clients to keep their agreements made in the therapy contract and to successfully negotiate changes as needed is seen as a clear indication of their functional level.

2. *The initial phase of treatment.* In this phase, the couple or family members gain insight into the communication patterns of the family unit. In addition, tools for effective conflict resolution are taught, and therapeutic alliances are established.

3. *The working-through stage.* The therapist actively attempts to help a couple or family members strengthen alliances with each other by helping them to reveal previously unexpressed feelings, share secrets, and develop more trust and empathy. Transference and countertransference are used to help bring out unconscious patterns of communication that are deeper than those brought out in the initial phase of treatment. These patterns often show up as resistances at this stage and should be confronted and worked through for successful therapy to take place.

4. *Termination.* When a termination date is set, conflicts and defenses often emerge. This conflict signals the need for the couple or the family to identify and work through anxiety about the impending loss. The therapist also should help clients review and identify the therapeutic gains they made during therapy.

    The goal of this phase is to help each family member reduce his or her anxiety and ambivalence about separation, to reinforce the therapeutic gains that were made, and to develop usable tools for continued growth. It is important that each person accept and understand the integrity of every other family member and be able to resolve conflicts with a minimum of psychic injury to themselves or others. Some couples or families attempt to prolong therapy rather than deal with their feelings of loss. A tapering off of sessions and periodic follow-up sessions can help a family or couple resolve this issue.

# Advantages and Disadvantages of Psychodynamic Approaches

Psychodynamic family therapy provides the therapist with a conceptual framework for understanding conscious and unconscious behavior in the context of marital and family relationships as well as a developmental framework for behavior. Freud's psychosexual stages of development, when combined with Erikson's psychosocial stages of development, provide a comprehensive model for understanding behavior at every age. The model helps to bridge the gap between inner experience and outer, social behavior.

Psychodynamic approaches offer conflicted families and couples an opportunity to achieve cognitive mastery of some causes of human suffering as well as an opportunity to learn effective interpersonal communication skills and correct misperceptions and distortions of experience that other approaches ignore. The therapeutic relationship can be used as a tool for change. Many people enter therapy because of poor relationships. This approach centers on using the therapist-client relationship as a model for teaching new relationship skills.

But psychodynamic approaches also have disadvantages. The techniques are limited in this approach, and techniques from other approaches often have to be employed. The focus on the past may lead the therapist to overlook present causes of dysfunctional family behaviors. The approach tends to overemphasize pathology rather than wellness, and there is a tendency for the therapist who is not clear on his or her own intrapsychic conflicts to create a "power-over" relationship with clients that does not get worked through.

Moreover, the transference relationship between each person and the therapist can dilute the powerful transference relationships between husband and wife or mother and child. Because the focus is often on individual behavior change rather than changes in the family structure, structural problems can be overlooked, which may cause families to maintain dysfunctional aspects despite individual changes.

# ▪ Classical and Neoclassical Psychoanalytic Approaches

Freud (1949) did not do family therapy as we now think of it. His major contributions to family therapy came from his theory on the cause of dysfunctional behavior in families. We will discuss this theory later in this chapter. Freud contributed to an understanding of the important influences of the family matrix on the development of the personality of the individual. His theory identifying the psychosexual stages of development helps us begin to chart the course of early child development and shows the importance of the early parent-child relationship for the subsequent personality development of the individual. In Freud's (1963) classical case histories, such as the case of Dora and the case of the Wolf-Man, we can see Freud's analysis of the role of family dynamics in shaping the personality and the possible psychopathology of the individual.

Colleagues of Freud also studied the influence of the family on child development (Flugel, 1921; Spitz, 1965), but psychoanalysts did not begin treating the whole family until the early 1950s, when child analysts began to treat the mother and child together (Paolino & McCrady, 1978). However, development of analytic forms of family therapy had to wait for the theoretical work of Harry Stack Sullivan (1947, 1953, 1954), Erich Fromm (1941, 1947), and Erik Erikson (1946, 1950, 1959) to provide the psychosocial focus.

Sullivan, the most family-oriented of all the American analysts, saw the growth and development of the child as a response to the social environment of the family. In addition, he was the first to demonstrate that schizophrenia could be treated by psychotherapy. He also was more interested in the clinical application of his work than in the theory itself. A number of early leaders of family therapy were heavily influenced by the work of Sullivan, including Don Jackson, Virginia Satir, and Murray Bowen.

## Philosophical Tenets

Freud was influenced by scientific realism and logical positivism, which placed emphasis on the objective knowledge of subjective experience. According to this view, the process of knowing requires an external interpreter to understand the preexisting structure of the personality. There is an essence, or preexisting human nature, that controls and governs behavior. The instinctual drives of the individual are what control human behavior.

Psychoanalytic theory assumes that much of human behavior is determined by past experience. Humans are unconscious of the process and content of their reality. They are enslaved by their past until the unconscious parts of their behavior can be brought into consciousness. In addition, the ultimate basis of morality is conscious reasoning; it is based on scientific principles that have to be understood and integrated into one's life.

## Theoretical Constructs: Theory of Cause

The works of Freud, Sullivan, and more recently, Margaret Mahler (1968; Mahler, Pine, & Bergman, 1975), showed that the human infant begins life in a symbiotic relationship with a significant mothering figure and gradually during the first two or three years of life goes through a set of developmental stages that enables the individual to achieve an independent and relatively autonomous emotional separateness from this mothering figure. The successful completion of this developmental sequence enables the person to establish a coherent sense of self, which allows the individual to develop object constancy or a constant sense of who he or she really is. Mahler calls this development the "psychological birth" of the individual.

Failure to complete this developmental process forces the individual to remain trapped in dependent relationships, never quite able to "go it alone," and to have difficulties in differentiating between himself or herself and others. These individuals remain stuck in infancy until they can learn to achieve some degree of separateness. They adopt a false sense of self that is acceptable to those they feel they are dependent on, and they gradually lose sight of their true selves. As adults, these people often have a hard time developing values or beliefs that are clearly their own. Frequently, they become excessively involved in causes, beliefs, leaders, and ideologies that they hope will provide them with the sense of stability and direction they cannot provide for themselves. If they find very few ways to establish their own identity and their lack of differentiation is severe, they may become psychotic. Neurotic behavior comes from the same source. Such people constantly need praise and cannot tolerate criticism. They look to others to build up their fragile sense of self-esteem, and they take any criticism as rejection or hostile assault.

In families where there are a number of such individuals, there is constant emotional upheaval over the competition for praise and re-assurance. Reality is distorted by these overwhelming needs. Projections abound, usually derived from repressed or split-off aspects of the individual who doesn't have enough self-esteem or ego strength to own or integrate the repressed or split-off material.

In couples, the symbiotic process is recapitulated when each partner fills in a missing part for the other to make up one complete person. This process leads to a survival orientation and a dependency relationship based on control. If either partner tries to break out of this dependency and assert his or her own needs in the face of the demands of the other or attempts to establish his or her own self-identity, he or she can expect the partner to pull out all the stops and use every form of manipulation, exploitation, pressure, rejection, and force to maintain the dependency.

In families, one member is sometimes singled out as the family scapegoat or "whipping boy" to help all the others maintain their dependent patterns. Even in a psychoanalytic approach, the interrelationship of all family members is recognized. The mobilization of one family member in the direction of autonomy and individuation will likely be seen as a threat to the security of the other family members. Therefore, some psychoanalytically oriented family therapists will insist on seeing all family members in family therapy. Others may combine individual therapy with each family member with occasional family therapy sessions.

Psychoanalytic approaches emphasize that there is a close relationship between spouse-spouse and parent-child relationships. Individuals come to the marriage relationship with unresolved narcissistic needs, and they seek to have these needs met in the marriage. When they are not met and their efforts are frustrated, the couple often has children and hopes the children will meet these needs. The child then becomes an object to fulfill the unmet needs of the parents; as such, the child cannot meet his or her own needs to develop a separate self. Thus, the cycle starts all over again with the next generation. As the child grows up in that family, this battle of wills is constantly played out until the child leaves home to start his or her own family in an effort to get the needs met that went unfulfilled while he or she was growing up.

## Main Therapeutic Interventions: Theory of Change

Psychoanalytic literature gives much more attention to a theory of cause than to a theory of cure. The recovery of the true self and the resolution of childhood intrapsychic conflicts seem to be the important goals of psychoanalytic theory. Freud (1949) defined healthy functioning as the ability to work productively and to love and be close to other people. This goal, of course, requires neutralization and integration of aggressive impulses and childhood complexes so people can behave toward themselves and others more in service of their ego and less by impulse and intrapsychic conflict.

According to psychoanalytic theory, the cure of neuroses and psychoses comes when the patient brings his or her intrapsychic and unconscious conflicts to conscious awareness and then works through the conflicts in the context of a safe therapeutic relationship. The fundamental belief in psychoanalytic theory is that the full expression of repressed or suppressed emotions and thoughts has more value than any therapeutic act on the part of the therapist. The cure for these conflicts or complexes is for the client to become aware of them and express all the formerly unconscious material in the therapy session as the therapist listens without judgment.

Psychoanalytically oriented family therapists tend to believe that insight must come first and then appropriate behavioral changes will follow. Behavioral techniques may be employed only to achieve immediate symptomatic relief, but these techniques are seen as deterrents to reaching and solving deep intrapsychic conflict. On the contrary, patients are taught that they have nothing to fear from any thought or feeling, no matter how irrational it might seem.

As the patients feel safe and secure in the therapeutic setting, the transference neurosis develops, which then provides the vehicle for patients to work through and resolve the conflicts. Transference is a regressive phenomenon by which unconscious childhood conflicts are brought to the surface. By utilizing the therapeutic alliance and by reexperiencing the conflicts within the transference situation, the patient is able to apply his or her more adult modes of thinking and reality testing to the childhood problem. Because the patients are now adults and have stronger egos, they usually have more options available to them to resolve the conflict than they did as children. The therapist has to be less intimidating or threatening than the patient's

## Psychodynamic Family Therapy

C A S E

E X A M P L E

*Mr. and Mrs. Smith had been married for three years when they first entered therapy. The reason they gave for seeking therapy was that Mrs. Smith, age 27, was interested in having children, while Mr. Smith, age 36, was not. When they got married, each had assumed that the other shared his or her values and goals about a future family.*

*In the initial phase of therapy, both shared rather openly their disappointments about the lack of common values on this issue. Mrs. Smith idolized her father and performed to meet his standards, but she felt she always fell short. She behaved toward her husband much the same way and believed she was "bad" for holding an opinion different from his. Mr. Smith, the only boy in his family, was adored and pampered by his mother and sisters. His father was cold, distant, and demanding. He expected compliance from his wife and looked to her to support the correctness of his views.*

*In the middle stage of therapy, Mrs. Smith began to understand the transference aspects of her relationship with her husband, and she developed more autonomy and self-esteem. She became more involved in her career and more sure of her wishes to have children. The therapist supported her growth. At the same time, Mr. Smith grew more fearful of parenthood. He now could separate his wife from his mother, but he wanted to express his creativity in his career and not in his family. He saw the therapist as being similar to his father and complained of the therapist's "cold, analytical style."*

*Videotape was used to help resolve the transference neurosis between Mr. Smith and the therapist. Mr. Smith began to see what was happening and gradually worked through his anger and sadness about his father. He saw that his fear of having children was related to a fear that if he became a father, he would be just like his father. He finally consented to his wife's wishes, and the couple went ahead and started a family. They continued in marital therapy during this time, and both were able to resolve their intrapsychic conflicts and become effective parents and loving partners in their relationship.*

parents were for the transference to be worked through and the childhood conflicts resolved.

In the initial stages of therapy, the therapist attempts to (1) determine the ego strengths and weaknesses of each family member, (2) determine their motivation for therapy, (3) define the goals of therapy, and (4) establish a therapeutic alliance.

Once the therapeutic alliance is established with each family member, the therapist can begin to interpret the unconscious material imbedded in the conscious statements of the clients as well as interpret the resistance and maladaptive ego defenses of the clients. Done repeatedly over time, this technique leads the client to acquire new and adaptive defense mechanisms. Through interpretation, the therapist attempts not to extinguish or encourage aggressive expression but to understand the source of the aggression and its effects on others in the family.

Videotape playback can also be used as an adjunct to therapy. Sessions are videotaped and then played back and analyzed by the therapist and the clients. This helps the client develop an observing ego and become more aware of nonverbal messages and unconscious material present in the session. Videotape is also useful when clients are denying or resisting some information or interpretation. It can also be useful in helping therapists monitor their own countertransference tendencies and make sure they do not interfere with the therapy process.

## Adlerian Approaches to Family Therapy

Adlerian family therapy has its beginnings in child guidance centers founded by Alfred Adler in Vienna during the first quarter of the twentieth century. This type of therapy focuses on relationship problems between parents and children.

Alfred Adler was a colleague of Freud but broke away from him in 1912. Adler stated that the personality was unified and not broken into id, ego, and superego, as Freud believed. Adler's social views were shaped by the writings of Charles Darwin and David Lamarck. He formulated the theory that humans have an innate social interest that enables them to contribute to the welfare of others without thought of reward (Adler, 1927).

Although Adler visited the United States frequently from 1926 to 1937, it was one of his students, Rudolf Dreikurs, who established

Adlerian family therapy in this country. Dreikurs established a family counseling center in Chicago in 1939, and Chicago remained the center of Adlerian work until 1952, when some of his students opened a center at Iowa State University. In 1959, Raymond Lowe established an Adlerian center at the University of Oregon (Lowe, 1982).

## Philosophical Tenets

Adlerian psychology was perhaps the first theory to take a phenomenological orientation toward therapy. Adlerians focus on the subjective reality of the client and how their world view or lifestyle determines how they organize their behavior. Adlerians adopt a *concept of indeterminism*, which means they believe that neither heredity nor environment determines one's behavior; rather, the individual's creative power determines what a person will or will not do.

Adlerians tend to focus more on operational reality than on ultimate reality, which they agree can never be known completely. They take the stance that what is good is determined by prevailing social values. The family is seen as a social instrument to teach sound values and help people live effectively in a democratic society. All behavior is seen as purposeful and goal-oriented (teleological versus deterministic view). The focus is more on the present and future than on the past (Corey, 1991).

## Theoretical Constructs

**Theory of Cause** Adler saw all behavior disturbances as (1) a failure to develop appropriate social interest, (2) a faulty lifestyle, and (3) a mistaken goal of success. He said that clients do not suffer from a disease but from a failure to solve life problems. Therefore, Adlerian family counseling is more of an educational model than a medical model of therapy.

Disturbances can result from either permissive or authoritarian parenting methods. In either case, children grow up with distorted views of how to get along with others. Permissive methods give the child the impression that they have no social responsibility for their behavior, and authoritarian methods teach them to fear authority and, ultimately, to rebel against it. In either case, a child can develop inferior feelings or an inferiority complex. People often compensate for these feelings of inferiority by attempting to master their environment or strive toward superiority. As such, inferiority feelings are strong motivators for purposeful, goal-oriented actions (Corey, 1991).

**Theory of Change**    The cure for disturbed behavior in Adler's framework is the use of democratic parenting methods that enable the child to establish effective limits and participate effectively in the decisions that affect him or her in the family, the school, and the larger community. To help shape the behavior along socially acceptable lines, Adlerians use the concepts of natural and logical consequences for behavior. A *natural consequence* is one that occurs naturally as a result of some action, as in sticking a finger into a light switch. Such consequences provide a natural way for humans to learn to modify their own behavior. *Logical consequences* refer to logical, agreed-upon outcomes of behavior. For example, a child who repeatedly interferes with another person by not coming to dinner on time should be told how the behavior affects the parent and that if the behavior continues he or she will not be scolded but will not be served dinner and will have to fix his or her own dinner. Depending on the age of the child, this could be a consequence or a punishment. Consequences should enable the child to assume responsibility for his or her behavior; punishment requires others to assume responsibility. Because the behavior of parents has to change before the behavior of children can change, there is inherently more responsibility placed on the parents, who are presumably more mature and able to change.

## *Main Therapeutic Interventions*

The main goal of Adlerian family counseling is to facilitate improvement of adult-child and parent-child relationships. The therapy sessions are geared toward teaching family members the skills and understanding they need to achieve and maintain effective relationships that enable everyone to grow in ways useful to themselves and to those they relate to, including the family, the neighborhood, the nation, and the world.

To accomplish this goal, the therapist attempts to help parents understand the dynamics that contribute to poor relationships and then to teach them constructive alternatives. The essential techniques therapists use include the following (Lowe, 1982):

  1. *The initial interview.* This stage is an important part of Adlerian family therapy. The structured interview form that is usually

used includes: (1) structure of the sessions, (2) information on the family constellation, (3) presenting problems, (4) working hypotheses by the therapist, (5) a description of a typical day in the family, (6) a children's interview, and (7) teacher's reports and recommendations. This information is used to diagnose children's goals, to assess the parents' discipline methods, to understand the family atmosphere, and to develop a plan of action.

2. *Role playing.* The therapist attempts to have family members act out how they perceive their situation. This technique helps the therapist teach new responses and new communication skills.

3. *Recognition reflex.* The therapist watches the response of the children to specific events. The responses are usually nonverbal, such as a slight smile or a twinkle in the eye.

4. *Disclosure and interpretation.* Adlerians use interpretation and disclosure of their own observations as a way to teach parents and children new responses.

5. *Action-oriented techniques.* Adlerians may use homework and other similar ways to promote effective practice of skills. Family councils are also recommended so that family members can practice their newly acquired skills.

6. *Information giving and teaching.* Part of the session may be devoted to teaching and giving information necessary for new learning to occur.

7. *Limit setting.* The therapist models and teaches parents how to set effective limits.

8. *Minimizing mistakes.* The therapist emphasizes what can be done rather than what was done that was wrong.

9. *Encouraging family fun.* The therapist encourages family members to plan fun activities together as a way to strengthen their work in therapy.

## Limitations of Adlerian Family Therapy

Very little research has been done to date on Adlerian family therapy. It seems to be most useful when the family pathology is not severe. It is limited in that it is very information-oriented and does not place much emphasis on the value of the therapeutic relationship. Moreover, family members can overadapt to the authority of the therapist and learn only enough to please the therapist rather than making lasting changes in the family system.

## Adlerian Family Therapy

### C A S E
### E X A M P L E

*Mr. and Mrs. Jones and their family of four children have been referred to an Adlerian family therapist because of the disturbing behavior of one of the children, Jimmy, who is 10 years old. As they discuss their typical day, the therapist finds out that Jimmy refuses to sit and eat with the family at meals. He also refuses to help out by running errands and will not cooperate with other family members. The therapist interviews the children with the parents out of the room and then brings them in and makes the following interpretation: "Jimmy is playing the role of helpless child and is the underdog in the family. Jimmy is also confused about who's boss in the family and needs to have his dad model how to be a man. Otherwise, he feels defeated and unable to do things for himself. We are going to show you, Mr. Jones, how to be a more effective role model for your son." The therapist then instructs Mr. Jones to play with his son and teaches him how to give Jimmy positive attention rather than negative attention (Lowe, 1982).*

# Transactional Analysis Approaches to Family Therapy

Building on the theoretical work of Eric Berne (1961), the founder of transactional analysis (TA), many practitioners have applied TA to family therapy. TA is an interactional therapy based on the assumption that current behavior is based on past experiences and that these past experiences cause us to make decisions about who we are, who other people are, and what the world is like. These decisions form our life script, which we can change with increased awareness and skills. Because TA was developed primarily as a group approach, it was relatively easy for practitioners to apply it to marital and family therapy. However, TA still emphasizes the dynamics of the individual, and the basic goal of TA family therapy centers on the therapy contract each person makes with the therapist. TA therapists approach work with family members cognitively, affectively, and behaviorally. Each client requires a blend of these three dimensions to make necessary changes (Corey, 1991).

## Philosophical Tenets

TA is one of the most philosophically diverse theories because its practitioners often use techniques based on many other theories, such as Gestalt, behavior therapy, and psychoanalytic therapy. As a psychodynamic theory, TA therapists still hold to the theory of an essential human nature, but there is disagreement over what the essential human nature is. Harris (1967) postulated an essential "not-OK-ness," sort of like original sin, while James and Jongeward (1971) disagreed and saw humanity as basically OK.

There is a strong phenomenological emphasis in TA as well. The meaning people give to their experiences, rather than the experiences themselves, determines how they act. The importance of the subjective reality of the client is stressed, but this reality can be understood through a set of objective laws and principles. Finally, most TA therapists regard it to be necessary for the client to gain insight about his or her behavior for change to be possible.

## Theoretical Constructs

**Theory of Cause**   According to Berne (1961), the interplay of three *ego states*, parent, adult, and child, determines an individual's personality. These ego states parallel in certain ways the structure of the personality in psychoanalytic theory. The child and id, parent and superego, and adult and ego exercise many similar functions. Thus, we have included TA among the psychodynamic theories. The pattern of *strokes* people receive determines how they view themselves and others. Strokes are verbal and nonverbal signs of acceptance and recognition, and they can be either positive or negative, conditional or unconditional.

The most damaging strokes are negative conditional or unconditional strokes, which often come from parents and other adults in the form of injunctions ("Don't be close," "Don't be you") and counterinjunctions ("Be perfect," "Try harder"). These injunctions and counterinjunctions cause people to make decisions about themselves and others such as, "I can't be who I really am" or "I am stupid." Berne (1972) saw people as victims of their injunctions and the decisions based on them.

Mary and Robert Goulding (1979) disagreed with Berne, seeing people as making conscious choices and decisions that are adaptive and changing them when they cease to be adaptive. The Gouldings insisted that many decisions children make are not the result of parental injunctions but of faulty thinking and fantasies on the part of the child. Berne (1961) discussed two types of problems that affect the structure of the personality, exclusion and contamination. *Exclusion* means that a person is stuck in stereotyped or rigid responses; the person responds from only one ego state, such as the parent ego state or the child ego state, and excludes the other two. Contamination means that material from one ego state overlaps with another, causing a double signal. A person may sound like he or she is responding from the adult ego state while using parental gestures, for example.

All of the stroking patterns, games, injunctions, and decisions make up a *life position*. There are four basic life positions that people adopt: (1) I'm OK—You're OK; (2) I'm OK—You're not OK; (3) I'm not OK—You're OK; and (4) I'm not OK—You're not OK. Generally, once a life position is chosen, it remains somewhat fixed until some intervention such as therapy occurs to help people change the stroking patterns, injunctions, and decisions. The life position was seen by Berne (1972) as representing a basic existential decision that colors all our perceptions of our transactions with the world. The life script tells us how to act out our basic life position and as such determines the patterns of our thinking, feeling, and behaving (Corey, 1991).

**Theory of Change**   To change a decision, a script, or a basic life position, TA therapists believe that people have to take responsibility for their own behavior and stop blaming their problems on other people. For most people, this is the most important and often the most difficult step in changing. Clients are seen as having the power to change their own lives. To make that shift, some clients have to reexperience aspects of their past; others can take this step in the present without much reference to the past.

Although TA is designed to help clients develop both emotional and cognitive awareness, the focus is clearly on the cognitive aspects. Understanding and insight into the functions of the ego states and the life script are usually seen as necessary for lasting behavior change to take place. Those who combine Gestalt techniques with TA theory place less emphasis on insight and cognitive understanding than on decisive action. More traditional TA approaches, however, rely on cognitive teaching methods to teach the client how to better understand his or her own behavior. In either case, the client is encouraged to develop tools to solve his or her own problems. The autonomy of the client is seen as an important part of the process of change.

## Main Therapeutic Interventions

The primary techniques used in a TA approach to family therapy vary with the stages of family therapy. McClendon (1977) proposed three main stages in a TA approach to family therapy: (1) determining the family dynamics, (2) therapy with each family member, and (3) developing a functional family.

**Stage One: Determining Family Dynamics**    The therapist looks for the patterns of communication among all family members, not just the problem member. The intention is to identify each person's role in the dynamics of the family's problem. The therapist might *interview*

Transactional
Analysis Family
Therapy

C A S E
E X A M P L E

*The White family was referred for therapy by a school counselor who had worked with Sandy. Sandy was doing poorly in school, daydreaming in class, and withdrawing from peers. The family consisted of the father, Jim, age 38; the mother, Susan, age 34; and two children, Sandy and John, ages 9 and 4. The Whites had been married for twelve years.*

*The initial session consisted of the family members introducing themselves and telling what they thought the problem was and why they had come to family therapy. Jim was on the offensive, saying that he thought the problem was his wife's inability to handle the children. He said he resented that Susan called him at work to complain about the children. Susan complained about the lack of emotional support she got from Jim, who, she said, was always working late. Sandy replied by saying she didn't know what the problem was or why they were in family therapy. John said that Sandy sometimes picked on him and teased him. Part of the session was devoted to a discussion of what the family members wanted to accomplish. Jim and Susan made a contract to spend more time together. They both agreed that the goal for the session was to help Sandy resolve her problems. The thera-*

*(continued)*

or use *open-ended questions* with each member about his or her role in the family. While doing this, the therapist watches how others behave. For example, when the father talks, the mother looks away and the oldest boy starts playing with a pencil. These observations are shared with the family to increase their awareness of family dynamics.

*Interpretation* of family dynamics may be used as well. The therapist may also use a story or *metaphor* to illustrate a point or give family members *permission* to do or say things they seem reluctant to do or say. The therapist may *confront* family members on discrepancies between their perceptions and their behavior. Therapists may also confront statements that reinforce injunctive or old script messages and give information on healthier responses, such as changing "I can't," "I won't," or "I have to" to "I choose to," "I will try," or "I will do it."

---

*(CASE EXAMPLE continued)*

*pist worked with Sandy to get her to open up about her problem. She reported that no one liked her at school and that her mother picked on her at home. She began to cry, saying, "No one likes me and I can't do anything right." It became clear that Sandy felt as if she were the victim, Susan was the persecutor, and Jim was the rescuer, although all three of them played all of these roles at different times. The therapist worked with the family, teaching ego states and identifying dysfunctional interaction patterns, making sure to include all family members in the assessment.*

*In the second phase of therapy, Susan worked on the anger she displayed with the children, especially Sandy, and her fear of expressing her needs and wants directly to Jim. Gradually in the session she began to identify what she wanted. She wanted more contact with Jim and more freedom to develop her own interests outside the home. She was encouraged to join a women's therapy group and ask for more time with Jim. As the result of script analysis, Jim learned that his life script included a pattern of working hard and keeping distant from the family. Jim saw that he was modeling his life after his father and decided to change his earlier script decision and spend more time with his family.*

*The final phase of therapy centered on couple work with Jim and Susan to restabilize the family, while Susan continued to attend her women's therapy group. Sandy's problems at school subsided, and her teachers reported that she was more attentive and had made one friend.*

**Stage Two: Therapy with Each Individual**  The focus of this stage of therapy is on individual psychodynamics and life script analysis. Clients become aware of their preferred ego states when interacting with others. The client may then choose to employ other ego states that are more functional for a given situation. This focus may require the therapist to see family members in individual therapy, work on individual issues within a family therapy framework, utilize group therapy, or work conjointly with the couple and not the family. Gestalt or psychodrama techniques may be employed to help individual family members identify and change their script decisions.

**Stage Three: Developing a Functional Family**  Reintegration aimed at developing a functional family structure is the focus of this stage. A functional family structure is one in which each person can meet his or her basic needs; the structure is designed to support the maximum development of each family member. Teaching people how to negotiate and get what they want and need is one of the techniques used during this stage. Homework assignments may be given to test the effectiveness of the family structure. In this stage, family members actively ask for what they want while also giving freely to support others.

## Limitations of TA Approaches

Little research has been done on this approach comparing it with other approaches. One limitation of TA is that it offers a cognitive approach to understanding behavior but offers very few techniques for changing behavior. Thus, it is often combined with other techniques such as Gestalt and psychodrama. Moreover, practitioners can use the structure and vocabulary of TA to avoid genuine contact with clients. Finally, clients are taught jargon that can lead them to believe they are changing when in reality they are just using new words to describe their problems. Use of jargon also can be a defense they can hide behind.

## ▨ Summary

This chapter reviewed the psychodynamic theories that have been adapted for use in marriage and family therapy. Representative psychoanalytic, Adlerian, and TA theories were described to show how these theories are being applied in working with families. These theories help to bridge individual therapy and family therapy.

In the next chapter, the major psychodynamically oriented systems theories that have been used in marriage and family therapy will be described. The skills and techniques of these systems theories will be presented, and we will show how they can be used in family therapy.

## SUGGESTED
## READINGS

Erskine, R. G. (1982). "Transactional Analysis and Family Therapy." In A. M. Horne & M. M. Ohlsen, eds., *Family Counseling and Therapy*. Itasca, IL: Peacock.

Lowe, R. N. (1982). "Adlerian/Dreikursian Family Counseling." In A. M. Horne & M. M. Ohlsen, eds., *Family Counseling and Therapy*. Itasca, IL: Peacock.

Nadelson, C. C., & Paolino, T. J. (1978). "Marital Therapy from a Psychoanalytic Perspective." In T. J. Paolino & B. S. McCrady, eds., *Marriage and Marital Therapy*. New York: Brunner/Mazel.

Sager, C. J. (1981). "Couples Therapy and Marriage Contracts." In A. S. Gurman & D. P. Kniskern, eds., *Handbook of Family Therapy*. New York: Brunner/Mazel.

# *6*

# *Psychodynamic Systems Theories*

*In this chapter we introduce the reader to two major family systems theories with psychodynamic roots. The systems theories of Murray Bowen and James Framo were selected for presentation here because each has had a major impact on the field of marriage and family therapy. Both theories have been reported widely in the literature and have a strong following. Moreover, both of these theories emphasize the impact of family-of-origin experiences on later functioning as a parent and spouse. Each theory has a systems base and underlying assumptions that are psychodynamic in nature.*

Emotional illness

Family of origin

Differentiation of self

Family projection process

Fusion

Multigenerational transmission process

Emotional cutoff

Triangulation

Family-of-origin sessions

Couples group therapy

## QUESTIONS

## FOR DISCUSSION

1. What are the major goals of Bowen's family systems therapy?

2. How may the differentiation-of-self scale be used in family therapy?

3. What are four ways fused families may dissipate the anxiety related to the fusion?

4. Why does Framo believe that sessions with one's family of origin are so effective?

5. Why does Framo use a three-phase approach to family therapy?

6. What are the specific goals of the family-of-origin session?

7. What are some of the issues in your own family of origin that have been highlighted in this chapter? Would you consider family-of-origin therapy to work on these issues? Why, or why not?

$\mathcal{T}$he two systems theories selected for discussion in this chapter are rooted in psychodynamic theory. Both have been widely used in marriage and family therapy. First we will discuss Bowen's pioneering work in family systems theory, followed by Framo's refinements in family-of-origin theory.

## Bowen's Family Systems Theory

Murray Bowen (1913–1990) was the leading proponent and developer of *family systems theory*. His shift to the family systems movement began in the early 1950s when family therapy was in its infancy. Bowen, a psychiatrist, was working at Menninger's Clinic with schizophrenic patients and their families. During this period, Bowen developed the concept of *mother-patient symbiosis*, which stated that the mother and the infant could form an intense bond that would not allow the mother to differentiate herself from the self of the child (Bowen, 1960, 1961). This intense emotional bond could make it difficult for the mother to give up the child in later years. Other psychodynamic symptoms, such as maternal deprivation, hostility, rejection, and castration anxiety were seen as secondary features of the intense attachment. Bowen believed that schizophrenia was a result of this *emotional stuck-togetherness* of the mother and child (Kerr, 1981).

Bowen modified his initial theory later to include the whole family constellation in his understanding of schizophrenia in a patient. He came to recognize that a reorientation of his psychodynamic thinking would be required to work effectively with families. He began hospitalizing entire families in his work with patients with schizophrenia and stopped all therapy with individuals to focus on family group treatment. Later, Bowen recognized that the characteristics exhibited by a schizophrenic family were similar to symptoms in many dysfunctional families and that the concepts of family systems theory could be employed with a wide range of family problems (Kerr & Bowen, 1988).

## Philosophical Tenets and Key Theoretical Constructs

Several key concepts of family systems theory are presented next. To understand these concepts fully, it is important to understand that Bowen hypothesized that individuals encounter problems in their families and in other systems when they are *emotionally impaired*. By emotionally impaired, Bowen meant that the individual was not able to "distinguish between the subjective feeling process and the intellectual thinking process" (Bowen, 1971). When this impairment occurred, the individual could not establish an "I position" to state his or her beliefs. Rather, emotionally impaired persons always work toward togetherness and agreement in their statements and discourage individuality and differentiation.

This inability to differentiate the feeling and thinking processes is called emotional illness and is much more than a disorder of the mind. Bowen believed that emotional illness is a disorder of relationships. He discontinued use of the term *mental illness* in favor of the term *emotional illness* to describe what occurs in family relationships to cause emotional impairment of one or more members.

**Emotional Triangle**   This is a three-person system considered by Bowen to be the basic molecule of any emotional system. Bowen believed that a two-person system was unstable and would always pull in a third person to create stability. These emotional triangles tend to have two stable sides and one side that is conflictual. For instance, in a mother-father-child triangle, the father and child may be stable, and the father and mother may be stable, but the mother and child may be conflictual.

**Differentiation of Self from Family of Origin**   This key concept involves an individual's ability to develop a strong sense of self and to choose behaviors that are not based on the influences of others. Bowen (1978) described the level of differentiation as the degree to which one's self fuses or merges into another self in a close emotional relationship (p. 362). Bowen developed a *conceptual scale* to describe level of differentiation, with zero indicating the least differentiation and maximum fusion and 100 representing maximum differentiation or autonomy.

The level of differentiation is believed to be established in childhood and is a reflection of how adequately the child was able to establish a sense of self separate from his or her family of origin. If a child had parents who were quite fused and undifferentiated, it would be unlikely that the child would be able to establish a high level of differentiation of self during childhood. The level of differentiation is thought to be stable throughout life unless specific actions are taken to change it. Those who are less differentiated from their family of origin have a more difficult time separating "reason from emotion" and are often controlled by their emotional system.

Fenell (1993b) described a technique that employs Bowen's differentiation-of-self scale in helping couples renegotiate the rules of their relationship and separate emotions from reason in their communication process.

Two levels of self were postulated by Bowen. The *solid self* is the part of the self that develops slowly and from within. It develops firmly held convictions that may be changed from within through rational processes but never through coercion by others. The *pseudo-self*, on the other hand, is made up of the beliefs, values, and opinions held by others. Emotional health is more likely to be found in persons whose solid self is in control of their behaviors.

Persons with very low levels of differentiation of self live in a world dominated by emotions. They are not readily able to distinguish facts from feelings. Their rational processes are frequently clouded by their emotional experiences. Much of their energy goes into seeking love and approval or punishing others for not providing that approval. Thus, there is little energy left for engaging in productive, goal-directed activities. These people have a greater incidence of emotional and physical problems.

For persons with low differentiation of self to feel satisfied, they must be receiving tremendous amounts of validation and recognition from others. Those lower on the differentiation-of-self scale may be reluctant to express their opinions if they would not meet the approval of significant others. They are quite unable to provide self-approval and are emotionally driven.

Persons with higher levels of differentiation of self are aware of the differences between thoughts and feelings. They are able to experience both without allowing their feelings to cloud the rational process. These people are able to state their positions on issues clearly and are open to modification of their positions based on new information and internal choice. The differentiation-of-self scale is shown in Figure 6.1.

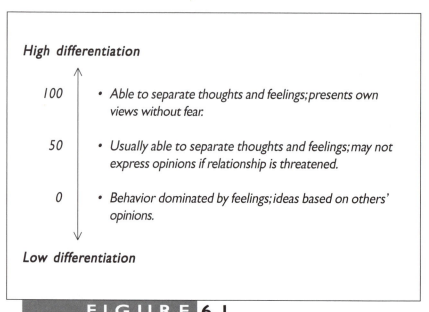

**FIGURE 6.1**

# Differentiation-of-Self Scale

**Family Projection Process**  This concept is related to the emotional triangle in that it describes how parental problems can be projected onto a child. The family projection process occurs when one parent is more emotionally focused on the child than is the other. Because of traditional gender roles, the mother is often the emotionally involved parent. The husband senses his wife's anxiety about the child and supports her in her emotional overinvolvement. The anxiety in the mother is quickly felt by the child who is most involved with the mother. The mother, with her husband's support, focuses her energy on relieving the child's anxiety rather than on dealing with her own. This activity gradually leads to increased emotional impairment for the child, and significant behavior problems often develop in adolescence. The father continues to support the behavior pattern either by backing the mother or by withdrawing from the situation when he disagrees with her. Eventually, if problems become severe, another party (frequently a counselor) will be "triangled in" to help stabilize the emotional system.

**Nuclear Family Emotional System**   This concept is a logical extension of the family projection process. The family system seeks to attain balance and stability. However, the family's attempt to balance the system may be at the expense of a vulnerable family member. All families maintain some level of fusion. *Fusion* is the act of losing one's sense of individuality in a relationship. Those who experience fusion to a greater degree are driven by their emotional processes and are less able to employ their intellectual processes. In families with high levels of fusion, there is a high level of anxiety. Families have four ways of dissipating the anxiety.

1. *Establishing emotional distance.* When persons are emotionally reactive to each other and are unsuccessful at managing that reactivity, they tend to create distance between themselves and the other (Kerr, 1981). This distancing may not be a conscious choice but a means to avoid the nuclear family emotional process. When distancing occurs, togetherness needs may be met in other relationships.
2. *Marital conflict.* Through marital conflict, spouses can meet their needs for emotional closeness and distance. However, these needs are not met through choice but through a cycle of intense anger and conflict over an issue that involves withdrawal from the partner and conflict (emotional distance) and making up and forgiveness (emotional closeness). Marital conflict in itself does not harm the children unless they are made to feel guilty or responsible for the conflict.
3. *Dysfunction of one spouse.* Another way to remove the anxiety created by the nuclear family emotional system is through the dysfunction of one spouse. In this situation, one partner becomes submissive and the other becomes dominant. In this type of marriage, each spouse believes that he or she is adapting to the other spouse. The partner who adapts the most becomes a "no-self" (Bowen, 1971) and is susceptible to physical illness, emotional illness, or social dysfunction such as alcoholism. These dysfunctions tend to become chronic and may be difficult to reverse.
4. *Projection onto children.* This occurs through the family projection process previously discussed. Children become impaired when the fusion or lack of differentiation of the parents is projected onto the child or children. Typically, because of tradi-

tional family roles, the most intense fusion may occur between the mother and an identified child. However, the fusion can be between the father and child in certain circumstances. When the child is impaired, the parents are able to focus their attentions on the child and ignore their personal anxiety concerning their lack of differentiation from their own families of origin and from each other.

**Multigenerational Transmission Process**   Bowen conceptualized the development of emotional illness as a multigenerational process in which undifferentiation or fusion is projected onto one or more of the children over a series of generations, leading to increased emotional illness with each succeeding generation. This concept, more than any other, places Bowen's systems theory among the natural systems of the universe (Friedman, 1991) and puts the focus on the historical development of symptoms over several generations. Bowen believed that people marry partners with similar levels of differentiation of self. When these couples produce children, one (or more) of the children possesses a lower level of differentiation of self than the parents. (It must be noted that one or more of the children is likely to have a higher level of differentiation than the parents.) The child with the lower level of differentiation then marries at his or her level of differentiation and produces a child who has a lower differentiation. This child marries at his or her level, and the multigenerational transmission process continues. Over the course of ten or more generations, this process may produce a severely impaired offspring. The impairment can be schizophrenia or one of many other significant problems such as serious antisocial behavior, severe chemical dependency, or severe psychosomatic physical disability (Kerr, 1981).

   The multigenerational transmission process may be slowed by favorable life circumstances that calm the anxieties of one generation. If a generation severs itself from the emotional intensity of another generation, this *emotional cutoff* may slow the multigenerational transmission process. Although emotional cutoff is commonly thought to solve the problem of emotional fusion between the generations, it actually only slows the process. It does not generally stop the dynamics that maintain the multigenerational transmission process. Frequently, couples say that their problems with the older generation were solved by moving away. Bowen would suggest that the problems may have been temporarily forestalled but would have to be dealt with through one of the four mechanisms described earlier in the Nuclear Family Emotional System section (Anonymous, 1972).

Bowen believed that the birth order of the children can serve as a predictor of adult behavior. Toman's (1961) study of birth order gives ten profiles of sibling positions. The most common are the oldest and youngest children. Typically, the oldest child will assume an overfunctioning role and believe he or she has the ability to control family events. The youngest child, who is often taken care of by older siblings, may be more reluctant to take initiative and may wait for others to be helpful. These patterns may be adaptive and functional for some. However, when there is emotional illness characterized by intense fusion and lack of differentiation of self, the birth order patterns are likely to be dysfunctional to the individual in marriage and other close relationships.

## Main Therapeutic Interventions

When families request therapy, they are asking the family systems therapist to help resolve problems in the identified patient. As Bowen suggested, the identified patient is not the source of the problem; the problem has arisen because of emotional fusion within the family. This emotional fusion leads to emotional responses and problematic situations that intensify the already charged emotional environment. Thus, the first task of the therapist is to deal with the emotionally charged situation in the family and neutralize it as much as possible.

The therapist is the key to neutralizing the emotional system in the family and must be able to remain outside the emotional forces that are in play. For the therapist to remain outside the emotional field, he must be reasonably differentiated. Bowen required therapists training with him at the Georgetown Family Institute to work on issues of differentiation of self from family of origin to prepare them to assist their client families to do the same. The method Bowen used for his own differentiation process is enlightening and is recommended reading for all family therapists (Anonymous, 1972).

The therapist neutralizes the family's emotional system by using reason to respond to each of the emotionally charged issues raised by the family members. While this process is taking place, the therapist begins to introduce the family to a systems understanding of the problem. If the emotional atmosphere has been neutralized, the family will be more readily able to rely on their intellect and conceptualize the interplay among the members that is leading to the impairment of one of the children. Bowen (1971) attempted to resolve the problems of symptomatic children through work with the family; he defined the family as the two most responsible family members. This family unit of treatment, according to Bowen, is almost always the husband and wife.

Prior to 1960, Bowen included the children in therapy. He believed his results were less than satisfactory because parents would terminate the therapy when the child's symptoms were sufficiently reduced without resolving issues of the parents' differentiation from their families of origin. After 1960, Bowen instructed the parents to enter therapy without the symptomatic child and explained to them in the initial session that problems are a result of the parents' dysfunctional relationship and that changes in the child's symptoms will occur automatically if the parents are able to redefine and modify their relationship. Bowen believed that his approach allowed the parents to focus on their relationships and the issues regarding their own differentiation of selves from their families of origin and how their lack of differentiation may be affecting the child.

Bowen (1978) believed that the therapist has four main functions in assisting the family:

1. Defining and clarifying the relationship between the spouses.
2. Keeping self detriangled from the family emotional system.
3. Teaching the functioning of emotional systems.
4. Demonstrating differentiation by taking an "I position" during the course of therapy (pp. 247–252).

Bowen suggested that spouses avoid discussing with each other subjects that create anxiety for their partners and for themselves. Thus, Bowen does not have the spouses talk to each other but to him. Bowen instructs the spouses to talk to him in the most objective and low-key manner possible. This technique prevents the spouses from engaging in emotional reactivity to each other and allows them to hear more accurately what is being said because they are not emotionally connected in the conversation. Early in the therapy process, Bowen asks the spouses to report their rational thoughts and reactions to him. Later in therapy, as the partners are better able to separate the emotions from their thoughts, he will seek the subjective opinions and feelings of the couple.

When one partner's comment created an emotional overreaction in the other and an interruption occurred in therapy, Bowen suggested that the therapist quickly turn the communication flow away from the couple and back to the therapist-client relationship by increasing questions to one partner and not attending to the interruption by the other. In this phase of therapy, the goal is to keep the couple talking about their thoughts, feelings, and reactions *to the therapist* rather than acting out these feelings and reactions with each other.

This first phase of therapy is critical. Because the spouses are talking to and through the therapist, they are able to really hear what the other is saying, perhaps for the first time in the relationship. Speaking to the therapist instead of the partner increases understanding, removes the emotional reactivity from the relationship, and allows the spouses to move on to other issues in the therapy.

The therapist must remain *detriangled* from the family's emotional system if therapy is to proceed effectively. To successfully maintain detriangulation, the therapist needs to be sufficiently differentiated from his or her own family emotional system and able to stay outside of the emotional system of the couple. The therapist needs to understand the nature of relationships and how two-person relationships always stabilize by involving a third party to form triangles. The therapist should focus on the process of what is happening in the session without becoming emotionally involved in the content.

This ability is critical to helping the family change, because one of the key assumptions of family systems theory is that "the emotional problem between two people will resolve automatically if they remain in contact with a third person who can remain free of the emotional field between them, while relating to each" (Bowen, 1971). One way a therapist can gauge if he or she is outside the emotional force of the relationship is to attempt to demonstrate to each person that there are alternative interpretations to some of their most cherished assumptions concerning the relationship. When the therapist is unable to respond with alternative conceptualizations for the situation, he or she is probably emotionally caught in the triangle.

Another technique used in family systems therapy is to teach the functioning of emotional systems to the family. This process begins by the therapist's use of "I messages," which communicate the differentiated position of the therapist and model effective behavior for the couple. Through the use of I messages, the therapist can communicate her knowledge concerning emotional systems without expecting the clients to necessarily accept the concept.

Later, the teaching is done through parables, metaphors, and descriptions of similar family situations. Much later in therapy, when the emotional reactivity and anxiety are quite low, the teaching can be didactic. When couples understand the functioning of emotional systems and are able to relate to each other, their children, and their parents in a differentiated way, therapy has been concluded successfully.

## *Strengths and Limitations of the Family Systems Approach*

Like all theories of psychotherapy, Bowen's family systems theory has strengths and limitations. The major strengths of the approach are:

1. It conceptualizes problem formation from a systems perspective. Symptoms are viewed as the result of the interactions between and among family members over several generations.
2. It does not diagnose and label an individual as having mental illness. Rather, it conceptualizes emotional illness as a systems-based phenomenon that does not label any single member of the system.
3. It conceptualizes emotional illness as resulting from a multi-generational transmission process and recognizes the importance of assisting clients in differentiation from their families of origin.
4. It recognizes the importance of neutralizing the emotional process that occurs in families to permit the couple to progress to more advanced stages of therapy.

The limitations of this approach are:

1. Because the focus of treatment is on the marital dyad, the effects of children on the system may not be fully considered.
2. Concepts such as the differentiation-of-self scale are not fully developed and have little empirical validation.
3. The approach may overemphasize past experiences at the expense of current functioning.
4. The approach may not give enough emphasis to the importance of affect in problem resolution.
5. The approach frequently requires a longer time commitment to therapy than some other systems approaches.

## Bowen's Family Systems Therapy

**CASE EXAMPLE**

*Mrs. Brown has contacted a family systems therapist because of problems she and her husband are having with their son, who has been getting into trouble at school and has not been doing his homework. The therapist suggests that the best way to approach the problem is for Mr. and Mrs. Brown to come into therapy to discover how they can best help their son.*

*Once the Browns come for therapy, the therapeutic procedures we have described are followed. The therapist helps them define and clarify the nature of their own relationship by remaining detriangled from his clients' emotional system. As their anxiety regarding their son begins to lessen, they note that considerable emotional reactivity exists between the two of them.*

*The therapist helps them move from reactions to each other based on emotions to interactions based on reason. During this portion of the therapy, the counselor describes the functioning of emotional systems to help the spouses gain insight into what happened to them in their families of origin and what has to happen in the future to establish differentiated selves in their current families.*

*Through this process of therapy, Mr. and Mrs. Brown begin to react less emotionally to their son, and gradually his problems at school begin to decrease. They start to react as differentiated selves within the family and respond to family problems through intellect rather than emotion. Specifically, the couple recognizes the following changes through therapy:*

1. *More realistic understanding of the influences of their families of origin on their concerns about their son.*
2. *An ability to recognize anxiety that is related to their previous experiences and an ability to minimize projection of that anxiety onto their son and onto each other.*
3. *An ability to remain in sustained intimate contact based on rational choice rather than neurotic dependency.*
4. *An ability to allow autonomous functioning of their children and each other without fear that this is harmful to the family.*

Bowen's family systems theory is a good example of a systems theory with psychodynamic roots. The theory relies on understanding past experiences in the development of the family emotional system. The importance placed on family-of-origin experiences and differentiation of self places Bowen's family systems theory in the category of psychodynamic family systems theories.

# ▓ Framo's Family-of-Origin Theory

James Framo, trained as a clinical psychologist, developed a family therapy theory based on the importance of dealing with the issues that emerged in a person's developing years in the family of origin. Although Framo's theory is presented in this chapter on systems theories with psychodynamic roots, it would be safe to say that Framo himself might not classify his theory in this way. Framo seems to believe that Foley's (1974) classification of his theory as that of an "integrationist" accurately describes what he has tried to accomplish. Furthermore, Framo "winces" when he finds himself categorized as a psychoanalytic family therapist (Framo, 1981). We agree that Framo is not a psychoanalytic family therapist in the classical sense, but he is indeed one of the most widely recognized systems theorists practicing today. Nonetheless, we believe that although Framo is clearly a systems thinker, many of his assumptions about therapeutic change have psychodynamic roots—thus, his inclusion in this chapter.

Framo began treating couples and families in 1958. He continually revises and modifies his therapeutic approach to meet the needs of families in distress.

## Philosophical Tenets and Key Theoretical Constructs

Framo's work is based heavily on the concepts of object relations theory as developed by Fairbairn (1954). Framo believes that families can best be treated by depth therapy and that marital and family problems result because individuals have not resolved issues that existed in their families of origin. These unresolved issues become an introjected part of the individual's personality. Thus, the individual may treat persons in close interpersonal relationships, such as spouse and children, in a manner that is based on the experiences from the family of origin rather than on actual behaviors of the family members.

Furthermore, Framo believes that when individuals deal with these issues in therapy with members of their families of origin actually present, issues that are problematic in the current marriage and with children may be resolved. Framo believes that one session with the family of origin may be more powerful in resolving current problems than several individual, marital, or family sessions (Framo, 1981). The specific tenets of Framo's (1982) theory are summarized here.

- The primary motivation in persons is to establish a successful relationship with another.
- The early relationships of children with their parents creates frustrating experiences that the child cannot change. These negative experiences are incorporated in the child's personality as introjects to surface later in life.
- The individual then forms close relationships through marrying and having children. The individual forms these relationships in a way that allows the frustrations experienced in the family of origin in childhood to be recreated with the spouse and children.
- Intrapsychic problems result because of unresolved conflicts in the family of origin.
- People select marriage partners who will precipitate reexperiencing unresolved family-of-origin conflicts.
- Unresolved issues from the family of origin are often projected onto the children. When this occurs, symptoms in the children may develop.
- Problems may be best resolved by returning to their source through sessions *with* the family of origin.
- When individuals explore the past to resolve issues with their families of origin, they are better able to perceive and relate to their own spouse and children as they actually are rather than as symbols of unresolved conflict in the family of origin.

## Main Therapeutic Interventions

Framo is most widely recognized for his work with his clients and their families of origin (Framo, 1981). It is this approach that will be addressed here. When problems arise in a family through symptoms in one of the children or through marital conflict, Framo will see the family for a few sessions to deal with the crisis that has brought the family or couple into treatment. Once the crisis is under control, Framo suggests that the marital couple may profit from continued work that will explore and perhaps correct the underlying circumstances that created the situation that brought the family to treatment.

Specifically, Framo has developed a three-phase treatment program that has provided successful therapy for his patients. The phases of the treatment program are (1) therapy with the couple, (2) couples group therapy, and (3) family-of-origin therapy.

**Therapy with the Couple**   In each stage of treatment, there are specific goals and techniques. During the first stage, the therapist works with the couple. The primary goal during this stage is to establish a solid working relationship with each spouse based on mutual trust. This goal is accomplished through the use of the relationship skills of the therapist, who (1) comes to understand the wife as an individual, (2) comes to understand the husband as an individual, and (3) comes to an accurate understanding of the relationship. Framo (1982) spends the first several sessions learning about the couple without deliberate attempts to intervene. He seeks diagnostic information by asking relevant questions in several areas, including:

- information about the referral source,
- basic demographic information about each spouse,
- brief statement of the problem from each spouse,
- length of marriage and age of children,
- previous therapy and results,
- reasons for mate selection,
- prior marriages,
- family's reaction to mate,
- fight styles,
- whether spouses love each other,
- commitment to marriage,
- characteristics of the marriage,
- quality and quantity of sexual relationship, and
- motivation of each for therapy.

Once each partner has had the opportunity to discuss these issues, the therapist has a much better sense of the quality of the relationship and the problems that are present. This initial phase of the therapy provides the therapist and the couple ample opportunity to develop a trusting relationship before beginning the intervention stage of couple therapy.

After a trusting relationship with each spouse has been established, the therapist must focus on the remaining therapeutic goals of treatment: (1) husband's goals, (2) wife's goals, and (3) therapist's goals. Framo believes it is critical for the family therapist to discover a way to conduct therapy that meets the expectations of the husband, the wife, and the therapist. If the husband and wife are not having their goals met, they are likely to drop out of treatment. If the therapist is not able to meet his goals, the chances of successful intervention are decreased. In all phases of treatment, including couple therapy, couples group therapy, and family-of-origin therapy, the therapist must be aware of the changing goals and expectations of the clients and work to meet these goals in the context of the therapist's own treatment goals.

Once the therapist's relationship with each spouse is solid, the therapist begins to defuse intense conflicts present in the marriage. This goal is accomplished through basic interventions, such as communications skills training and negotiation training, as well as by emphasizing the positive characteristics of the relationship. After any immediate crisis issues are defused, the therapist begins the process of educating the couple about object relations theory and how issues that have been long unresolved in the family of origin may be responsible for present difficulties in the marriage and family. Framo also introduces his desire to have the spouses deal directly with their families of origin in therapy at some later date. Framo recognizes that the notion of dealing directly with the family of origin causes great anxiety for many clients. He assures them that they will be adequately prepared to meet their families and will most likely benefit from the encounter.

**Couples Group Therapy**   To best prepare couples to meet with their families of origin, Framo has found that the couples group therapy format is most advantageous. There are numerous reasons why the couples group format is suggested as a step toward the family-of-origin work.

- It is reassuring to each person in therapy to know that there are other couples with similar fears and anxieties about dealing with their families of origin in therapy.
- By participating in a couples group, the individuals come to recognize the universality of problems that individuals have with their families of origin. Thus, the couple feels more normal and self-accepting.

- Couples in a successful group come to trust each other and share information that might not emerge in individual couple therapy. Furthermore, group members may be quite receptive to feedback and support from other couples.
- The genuine caring the couples feel for each other is therapeutic.
- Through feedback from group members, the couples usually come to modify their goals in productive ways.
- Through feedback and modeling by other couples, the spouses come to recognize their unrealistic expectations of their mate.
- Through effective leadership by the therapist, the group members are assisted in exploring the genesis of their unrealistic expectations of their spouses. This process returns the focus to the importance of resolving issues with the family of origin.
- Despite each person's fear of dealing with the family of origin in therapy, the members of the group are almost always supportive of other members having their family-of-origin session. This group support is often instrumental in helping members develop the courage and resolve to invite their parents to family-of-origin sessions.

The couples group is usually composed of three couples. Ideally, these couples will be at various stages of their preparation for the family-of-origin sessions. That is, the group includes one couple graduating, one couple in the middle of couples group work, and one couple joining the group after individual couple therapy sessions have just been completed. Framo always uses the couples group format unless for some reason it is impossible to place a couple in the group. He has found that the groups are most successful when the couples are similar in their family development and in other ways.

In summary, the couples group helps the spouses further understand their own relationships and improve them. It creates a sense of community in which the couples support each other in their attempts to recognize and confront unresolved issues from their families of origin that are affecting current relationships. Moreover, it provides support for the members inviting their parents to join them in therapy and provides a place to debrief after the family-of-origin sessions.

**Family-of-Origin Therapy**   As individuals become ready to meet with their families of origin, preparations are made to convene a family-of-origin session. Needless to say, the couples in a group do not always become ready for these sessions at the same time and this, of course, is not necessary. When a spouse returns to the couples group after meeting with the family of origin, the encouraging effect on the other group members may be significant.

Prior to having the family-of-origin session, the client is thoroughly prepared. Normally, Framo will meet the family of origin on a single day with four hours devoted to the session (Framo, 1981). Despite the initial reasons clients give for why the family-of-origin sessions would be impossible, the success rate of engaging the family in therapy is quite high. Framo believes that when the client recognizes the importance of the meeting, the client will communicate that importance to members of the family of origin and they will participate. This belief has been supported by experience in Framo's practice of family-of-origin therapy.

The key goal of the family-of-origin session is for the client to make contact with the family and have a "corrective experience" with the family (Framo, 1981). The family-of-origin session is held without the spouse. Framo believes that having the spouse present in these sessions can easily detract from the purpose of correcting the perceived problems between the generations and between siblings. If the spouse were present, much of the attention could be placed on the spouse and the couple's relationship, and the specific point of the family-of-origin work would be missed.

The specific goals for the family-of-origin session are as follows.

- The client makes contact with the family of origin, both parents and siblings, in a way that is based on adult (rather than child) interaction.
- The therapist may discover what from the family of origin is being projected onto the client's spouse and children.
- The client may increase differentiation (Bowen, 1971) from the family of origin, which will lead to enhanced relationships with members of the family of origin as well as with the current family.
- The meeting sets the stage for getting to know parents as real people and to share important thoughts and feelings with them.
- The meeting provides the client with an opportunity to forgive the parents for their mistakes, real and perceived, and to tell the parents that they are loved.

Framo finds that the family-of-origin sessions are generally very positive experiences for all participants. Normally, the spousal relationship is enhanced, and the relationships with parents and siblings are improved. Occasionally, however, some issues emerge that may increase tensions between the family of origin and the client. Thus, the immediate effects of the session may not be positive. Clients are prepared for this possibility and are encouraged to use the group for support if this outcome occurs.

Moreover, it is possible that when individuals complete their family-of-origin work, they may recognize that their marriage is based on projection and unfinished business with the family of origin rather than on love and respect. In these cases, the spouses may elect not to work on correcting the projections in therapy, and divorce may result. Although these negative outcomes are uncommon, clients should be made aware of the possibility that they may occur. Framo views family-of-origin work as the "major surgery" of family therapy and cautions that this therapy is not without its risks (Framo, 1981).

Framo's family-of-origin therapy is an active and directive approach to resolving issues affecting the family that have their roots in the family of origin. Framo believes that working with an opposite gender co-therapist is the most effective way to provide treatment. The opposite gender co-therapy team allows the therapists to relate to the same gender and opposite gender clients and alleviates fears that alliances by gender may be disadvantageous. Further, the co-therapy team is much better able to respond to the myriad issues that emerge in therapy. One therapist may become extremely involved in the content and affect of the situation presented, while the other may remain more detached and objective. Such co-therapy teams make it possible to effectively meet the needs of the couples. The following are other important techniques used in this approach.

- Framo does not meet with one spouse alone. He sets an appointment when both can be present. If this is not possible, he refers the couple to a colleague who treats spouses separately.
- The couple is prepared for family-of-origin sessions gradually and without coercion from the therapist. Preparation begins early in the individual couple sessions and continues more vigorously during couples group sessions.
- Spouses are specifically asked about events occurring in their families of origin. If the therapist does not seek such informa-

tion, couples normally will not view it as relevant to the current problems.

- Couples in the group who are willing to meet their families of origin help prepare couples who are reluctant.
- The group members and co-therapists encourage family-of-origin work, which causes the couple to focus on preparation for this event. Thus, the other problems in the relationship take on diminished importance and the relationship is strengthened as spouses work together for their family-of-origin sessions.
- Resistance to the family-of-origin sessions is to be expected. The combination of the therapists' interventions and group support generally leads to acceptance of the importance of the sessions. The therapist does not pressure the spouses into the sessions but allows them to become ready at their own pace. One partner may become ready for the family-of-origin session well before the other spouse. This is not a problem, however, as the spouse who has had the session can encourage the one who has not.
- The therapists help each person develop an agenda of issues to be discussed with the family of origin. This agenda assures the client that the session will have real purpose.
- Spouses are not included in the initial family-of-origin session. These sessions are between the client and his or her family.
- The spouse may be included in a later family-of-origin session if problems in the in-law relationship exist.
- The therapist and the couples group members encourage others to do family-of-origin work.
- As the family-of-origin session nears, calls from family members to the therapist are to be expected. The therapist encourages the family-of-origin members to consider any issues they may have with their son or daughter and be prepared to raise them in the session.
- To ensure a productive family-of-origin session, the therapist makes certain that caring among the family members emerges. If the session is too focused on negative content, the session may become an unproductive gripe session with potential negative outcome.

**Framo's
Family-of-Origin
Therapy**

C A S E
E X A M P L E

*Mr. and Mrs. Taylor were having difficulties with their marriage. Mrs. Taylor complained that her husband was indecisive and that she couldn't rely on him. Mr. Taylor reported that his wife was domineering and unsupportive of any attempts he made to exert leadership. Thus, he had begun to give up on the marriage.*

*The couple came to therapy for help in making the marriage better. The family-of-origin therapist, working from Framo's model, treated the couple in marital therapy to reduce the tension, the anger, and the hurt feelings through teaching communication and negotiation skills, establishing trusting relationships with both partners, and understanding each person's experience of the marital difficulties.*

*During this stage of treatment, the therapist introduced the idea of having family-of-origin sessions so that each person might come to understand how some of their present behaviors developed and seek ways to eliminate the problematic behaviors. The therapist engaged both spouses in discussions about their families of origin and the issues that existed within their families. At this point in treatment, they entered couples group therapy because they were ready to begin more advanced work on their marital problems.*

*In the group setting, Mr. and Mrs. Taylor came to feel accepted and cared for by the other two couples in the group. Each of the couples was working on relationship issues that were not unlike those the Taylors were encountering. In the couples group, the Taylors recognized that their marital issues might be the result of problems that began in their families of origin.*

*Mr. and Mrs. Edwards, another couple in the group, were each in the final stage of preparation for their family-of-origin sessions. Each was excited about the possibilities, yet fearful at the same time. The support the Edwards couple received from the therapists and the group was positive and instrumental in helping each of them have successful meetings with their families of origin. The Edwards' report to the group about their experiences encouraged the Taylors to begin serious preparation for dealing with their own families of origin. Their focus on preparing for the encounter with their*

*(continued)*

*(CASE EXAMPLE continued)*

respective families pulled the two closer together as they supported each other's attempts to prepare for the family-of-origin sessions. Thus, their original marital problems became less of a focus in therapy and at home.

Several weeks passed before Mrs. Taylor was ready for her family-of-origin session. When the day finally arrived, she was apprehensive. She went into the session armed with a list of issues to discuss with her parents and brother. Although many of the issues were not discussed because of time limitations, several of the most critical issues were covered, and Mrs. Taylor was provided with a wealth of information about herself and her family. Through the family-of-origin session, Mrs. Taylor discovered that her own father was passive and was content to let her mother deal with any problems that emerged. Mrs. Taylor discovered that she had never accepted this pattern and was angry with both parents because neither tried to change the situation. Mrs. Taylor had been certain she would not be domineering like her mother because she would marry a stronger man than her father. However, Mrs. Taylor discovered that she had recreated in her present marriage what she thought she would avoid. Thus, she was faced with the need to deal with her anger toward her parents as well as her anger toward herself for creating a similar situation. These insights provided Mrs. Taylor with plenty of information, and she was able to forgive her parents and establish more positive relationships with them. Furthermore, she discovered that her brother had similar feelings that he had not expressed before. This revelation opened the door for an improved relationship with her sibling. Finally, and perhaps most significant, she recognized that some of her husband's lack of assertiveness was indeed the result of her need to make him be the way she wanted him to be rather than accepting him as he was. This insight led to immediate marital improvements.

Mr. Taylor was ready for his family-of-origin session a few weeks later. He discovered that he had never felt adequate in relation to his father. The tasks he was asked to perform were never done quite well enough. Mr. Taylor had grown up feeling that it didn't matter how hard he tried; he would not be adequate. Thus, he married a woman who recreated that feeling.

Through the insights the Taylors achieved through family-of-origin therapy, they were able to establish a more productive marriage and more meaningful ties with their families of origin. Knowing how their behaviors were driven by unresolved family-of-origin issues helped the Taylors move forward both as individuals and as a couple.

## Strengths and Limitations of Framo's Approach

Family-of-origin therapy has several strengths. First, it is the only therapy that actually has the client deal with issues from the family of origin directly with the family in a session. Second, this theory recognizes that problems in the present marriage may be the result of unfinished business in the family of origin. Third, it recognizes the therapeutic power of the couples group and uses that power to help clients develop in their relationships. Finally, this approach offers the opportunity for individuals to create more meaningful relationships with their families of origin through direct contact about significant issues.

Framo is aware that this approach is not for everyone and acknowledges the limitations of the therapy (Framo, 1981). Specifically, family-of-origin work is not for couples with relatively minor marital difficulties that do not require intensive work. Second, some couples may not have access to their families because of death or some other circumstance. Third, this approach may highlight the need for therapy with the individual. If therapy for the individual is indicated after family-of-origin work is completed, Framo encourages referral to a therapist who specializes in such work. Fourth, this approach relies on the assumption that current problems are a result of past experiences in the family of origin. It may not be effective with clients who are unwilling to accept this assumption.

## Summary

Murray Bowen and James Framo have developed theories of family therapy that have psychodynamic roots. These theories have been included in this chapter because of the heavy emphasis that each places on the impact of early childhood and family-of-origin experiences on current family functioning. Each of these theories has been presented here with an explanation of the key theoretical tenets and techniques that counselors will want to understand as they begin to use these approaches with couples and families.

# SUGGESTED
# READINGS

Bowen, M. (1978). *Family Therapy in Clinical Practice*. New York: Jason Aronson.

Framo, J. L. (1982). *Explorations in Marital and Family Therapy*. New York: Springer.

Hovestadt, A. J., & Fine, M., eds. (1987). *Family of Origin Therapy*. Rockville, MD: Aspen.

# 7

# Cognitive/Behavioral Theories in Family Treatment

*In this chapter, we will describe the application of rational emotive behavior theory (REBT) to family therapy as a representative of the various cognitive theories. Behavioral theory is also described as it applies to family therapy as a representative of the various learning theory approaches.*

# KEY CONCEPTS

Modeling

Cognitive errors

Irrational beliefs

ABC theory

Contingency contracting

Behavioral assessment

Reinforcement

Cognitive restructuring

Behavioral rehearsal

# QUESTIONS
## FOR DISCUSSION

1. How might the REBT therapist deal with a family member who is making irrational statements to another family member?

2. Do you think the REBT therapist should teach family members a philosophy of life? Can the therapist avoid imposing his or her values?

3. How would the REBT therapist deal with a family member who starts crying and exclaiming that she feels picked on by the other family members?

4. How would a behavioral therapist handle the aggressive behavior of an older brother toward his younger sister during a family therapy session?

5. What criteria might a behavioral therapist use to determine whether the therapy has been successful?

6. How might a behavioral therapist work with a family in which the mother is an alcoholic?

*C*ognitive and behavioral approaches are often treated separately in the literature, but because they share similar philosophical underpinnings and a common focus on objective behavior, they may be considered together (Baucom & Epstein, 1990; Meichenbaum, 1977). In this chapter, we will present these theories together as the cognitive/behavioral approach.

Beck (1976) describes *cognitive therapy* as an approach that addresses the formulation of psychological problems in terms of incorrect premises and a proneness to distorted imaginal experiences. These incorrect premises and distorted internal images, also called *cognitive errors*, lead to incorrect emotional and behavioral responses to external events. Cognitive therapists attempt to change the thought patterns, beliefs, and attitudes of their clients, which they believe will lead to lasting behavior change (Ellis, 1991). Behavior therapy, on the other hand, focuses on changing specific behaviors in predetermined ways and deals only with observable events in the environment that can be objectively measured. Behavior therapy, also known as the *social learning approach*, does not require insight or a change of thinking or attitudes to be effective. This approach posits that symptoms are actual problems.

The chief contributors to cognitive therapy are Albert Ellis (1962, 1991, 1993), Aaron Beck (1976, 1991), and Donald Meichenbaum (1977). Important behavioral therapists are John Krumboltz and Carl Thoreson (1969, 1976; Thoreson, 1974), Joseph Wolpe (1958, 1969), Gerald Patterson (1971), Ian Falloon (1991), Richard Stuart (1980), Neil Jacobson (1989), and Arnold Lazarus (1971, 1981). Many behavioral therapies are based on the theoretical and research efforts of Albert Bandura (1969, 1977) and his social learning approach.

An example of a cognitive/behavioral approach can be seen in the case of a high school sophomore who is referred to the counselor's office because he is not paying attention in class, not following the teacher's instructions, and making wisecracks that disrupt the classroom. A counselor using a cognitive approach would attempt to understand the student's internal logic and help him identify the self-defeating messages with which he indoctrinates himself. For example, the student may believe it is "essential" that he be the focus of attention at all times. The counselor would help him understand that it is certainly enjoyable to be the center of attention but definitely not essential. As the student challenges this irrational idea with a more rational one, he is able to begin to change his acting-out behavior. The counselor would attempt to help the student change his self-defeating attitudes and beliefs, hoping this would improve his classroom behavior. Role playing and rehearsal techniques may be used to teach the student ways to improve his behavior.

A counselor using a behavioral approach would assume that the problem behaviors were the result of prior learning and reinforcement. The counselor would try to find reinforcement contingencies to use to help the student change the identified undesirable behavior. The counselor might also involve the teacher in the process by encouraging the teacher to reinforce the student's more acceptable behaviors with attention or grading credit and to ignore (or not reinforce) less acceptable behaviors. In this way, the counselor would assist the student in learning new and more effective behaviors.

A critical component of the behavioral approach is the counselor's development of a specific method to assess the student's behavior changes. This assessment is frequently quantified; for example, how many times did the student interrupt class discussion during the day? The behavioral counselor would expect the frequency of the undesirable behavior to decrease over time while more desirable behaviors increase.

This chapter will cover two of the main cognitive/behavioral approaches to family therapy: the rational emotive behavior therapy approach of Albert Ellis and the social learning approach of Gerald Patterson and the Oregon Social Learning Center staff. We begin the discussion with the general goals of the cognitive and behavioral approaches.

## ■ Goals of Cognitive Approaches

The two general goals of a cognitive approach are to minimize self-blame and to minimize blaming others. Specific outcomes that result from these two goals include the following:

- enlightened self-interest that respects the rights of others;
- self-direction, independence, and responsibility;
- tolerance and understanding of human fallibility;
- acceptance of the uncertainty of life;
- flexibility and openness to change;
- commitment to something outside oneself;
- risk taking and a willingness to try new things; and
- self-acceptance.

## Goals of Behavioral Approaches

The general goal of behavior therapy is development of a systematic application of experimentally established principles of learning for the purpose of changing unwanted or dysfunctional behaviors. More specific outcomes relating to the problems of the family members are also sought, including the following:

- learning to ask clearly and directly for what one wants;
- learning to give and receive both positive and negative feedback;
- being able to recognize and challenge self-destructive behaviors and thoughts;
- learning to become assertive without becoming aggressive;
- being able to say no without feeling guilty;
- developing positive methods of self-discipline, such as regular exercise, controlling eating patterns, and eliminating stress;
- learning communication and social skills; and
- learning conflict resolution strategies to cope with a variety of family situations.

## The Process of Cognitive/Behavioral Approaches

Therapy is seen as a learning process that might be viewed as follows:

1. *The courtship stage.* In this stage, the therapist assesses the problem and builds rapport. The assessment process might include standardized marital assessment devices, therapist or client ratings of the particular behaviors deemed necessary to be changed, and a clinical interview. Rapport building with each

of the family members is necessary for movement to the next stage to occur.

2. *The engagement stage.* This stage is characterized by a solidification of the therapeutic relationship. The therapist conveys commitment to the couple or family and specifies what the client is expected to contribute to the process. Goals may be determined at this stage and a plan developed to achieve these goals.

3. *The marriage stage.* This stage has two important features: (1) enhancement of communication skills between and among family members, and (2) development of a written therapy agreement to aid in the change process. The goals of the training in communication skills include teaching conflict resolution skills, teaching family members how to reduce and clarify misunderstandings, increasing positive verbal interaction, and increasing the appropriate expression of feelings. Written marital or family agreements generally involve an agreement by each family member to engage in certain specified behaviors desired by others in the family as well as an agreement on what positive or negative consequences should occur if the specified behaviors are or are not present.

4. *The disengagement stage.* In this stage, responsibility is gradually shifted from the therapist to the family members. Members are often encouraged to hold family meetings between therapy sessions and to report on the results of those meetings. In conjunction with these family meetings, family members construct and successfully carry out the agreements they make with each other. This phase provides the therapist with concrete evidence of the family's ability to solve its own problems and gets the family ready for termination.

# Advantages and Disadvantages of Cognitive/Behavioral Approaches

One of the main advantages of behavioral therapy is that it is based in research. Much research has been done to show that appropriate reinforcement contingencies can alter problem behaviors. Second, the therapist is an active participant in the therapy process and can often model effective behavior for the client. By staying with very specific observable behaviors and by using written contracts, the clients can easily understand the goals and track the progress of their own therapy. Finally, this approach allows for use of many diverse intervention methods.

Cognitive therapies have been particularly effective in the treatment of depression and in stress management (Beck et al., 1979). These approaches work well with clients who have good reasoning ability. Both cognitive and behavioral approaches tend to be brief treatment modalities.

But cognitive/behavioral therapy also has disadvantages. Critics have accused it of focusing too much on symptoms and ignoring underlying problems. In addition, the approach may be too directive and, in the hands of an unethical therapist, can be used to manipulate the client. The theory has also been criticized as having a myriad of techniques with no integrating theory to tie them together. Beck (1991) disagrees and articulates the development of cognitive theory over the past 30 years. He believes the research has supported the theoretical constructs of cognitive therapy.

## Rational Emotive Behavior Therapy

Ellis (1962) first developed rational-emotive therapy (RET) in the 1950s. Because this approach emphasizes the reciprocal interactions among cognition, emotion, and behavior, Ellis later renamed his theory "rational emotive behavior therapy (REBT)" (Corey, 1996; Ellis, 1995). He uses the ABC theory of REBT to work with individual clients as well as couples and families (Ellis, 1991, 1993):

### Problem Formation

- **A** is the *activating* event,
- **B** is the irrational *belief* about the activating event, and
- **C** is the *consequences* of the belief about the activating event.

For example, a couple complains that their son is not being as respectful as they would like. The more they insist on respect, the less they receive. The couple are becoming angry and upset, and this affects their own relationship and their relationships with their other children.

In this case the REBT therapist would help the couple identify the ABC of their presenting problem. The activating event (A) is the son's lack of respect. The consequence (C) is that the couple becomes angry and the boy is even less respectful. What this couple is not aware of is their belief (B) about the activating event. In this case, the therapist helps the couple identify their belief that "It's absolutely essential that their son show respect at all times, and if he does not, they are 'bad' parents and he is a 'bad' son." This belief would be considered an *irrational belief* because of its demanding nature and its lack of acceptance of human imperfections. The therapist helps the couple recognize that it is not their son's lack of respect that causes their anger but *their personal beliefs* about their son's behavior. Once the couple can *dispute* their irrational belief with a more rational one, such as: "It is preferable to have our son show respect, but it is not crucial. We can still admire the good in him even if he does become difficult at times. Moreover, we do not take responsibility for his actions." As the couple integrate this new, more rational belief, they stop demanding, and gradually their son's behavior toward his parents may improve.

Ellis said that irrational beliefs are effectively *disputed* (at point *D*) by challenging them logically, empirically, and rationally. This rational process causes clients to reevaluate these beliefs and actually change them to new, more effective beliefs. Ellis developed REBT as an individually oriented therapy but saw implications for its use in marital and family therapy situations. Prior to developing REBT, Ellis practiced classical psychoanalysis. He found that no matter how much insight clients gained or how well they understood how their childhood affected their present behavior they improved only slightly and often developed new symptoms. He began to realize that the clients constantly reindoctrinated themselves with irrational and childish beliefs about how they should be, how others should be, and how the world should be.

## Problem Resolution

- **A** is the *activating* event,
- **B** is irrational *belief* about activating event,
- **C** is the *consequences* of the belief about the activating event,
- **D** is rationally *disputing* the belief about the irrational activating event, and
- **E** is the *effect* of rationally disputing the irrational belief.

Ellis's thoughts differ from psychoanalysis in that he believes humans are basically irrational. He believes that this irrationality is a natural characteristic and not the result of early training. He also views humans as creatures of habit who are lazy and will take simple preferences such as a desire for love, approval, success, and pleasure and redefine them as needs or necessities. While humans are prone to irrational thought, they are capable of rational thinking that leads to a mentally healthy lifestyle. Based on these assumptions, Ellis directly attacks the self-defeating value system of clients and not clients themselves. He supports the individual but strongly attacks faulty ideas, traits, and performance (Ellis, 1974).

## Philosophical Tenets

Ellis (1962) believes in an *a priori* human nature. He thinks humans are born with strong biological predispositions to be socially involved with others. According to Ellis, humans are also naturally predisposed to disturbance and have a tendency to act against their own best interests. Their other innate values are: (1) to stay alive, (2) to enjoy themselves, (3) to live in a social group and get along with others, (4) to work productively, and (5) to seek activities that are pleasurable and satisfying.

In line with this philosophical belief, he traced the philosophical roots of his theory back to Epictetus, an early stoic philosopher who wrote that "people are disturbed not by things, but by the view which they take of them." Ellis focuses on objective thoughts, which he believes must be understood to change subjective feelings.

Ellis believes that absolute values corrupt logical and reasonable values, which are more situational. He also seems to trust the external collective values and believes the social nature of man dictates that social values are most important in guiding rational thoughts and behavior.

## Theoretical Constructs

**Theory of Cause**    Ellis stated clearly that it is not a person's behavior that has to be changed but rather a person's irrational beliefs. The cause of these beliefs, according to Ellis, is the human condition. He claimed that our basic nature is irrational, and no event or person is to blame for causing these beliefs to develop. Ellis (1993) reports that because of their nature humans are easily disturbed and that these disturbances are evident when individuals are alone, in families, or in other groups. The disturbances are the result of individuals constructing strong goals, values, and desires that initially are functional and add to their happiness. These goals, values, and desires later are elevated into grandiose demands, shoulds, oughts, and musts. When humans create these absolutes, they also create conditions that lead to their unhappiness and emotional disturbances. He identified several absolutes that lead to emotional difficulties:

- I must perform well and be approved of by the important people in my life. If I don't perform well, it is horrible or awful, and I can't stand it. I am a terrible person if I fail to perform well.
- Other people should always treat me fairly and be considerate of my needs. It is horrible if people don't treat me the way I want to be treated. They are bad individuals and cannot be trusted.
- Life must be the way I want it to be, and if it isn't, I can't stand living in such a world. It is terrible and unacceptable.

Ellis said that if family members subscribe to one or more of these core beliefs, various forms of emotional disturbances and dysfunctional behavior will result.

**Theory of Change**   For clients to change their beliefs, Ellis said that they have to learn three basic insights:

1. The causes of the emotional problems of family members are their irrational beliefs, not any external environmental condition.
2. Family members engage in self-conditioning by repeating these irrational beliefs over and over to themselves. Even if they did originally learn these beliefs from their parents, they are now responsible for the dysfunction they are causing themselves.
3. Family members will change their beliefs by being aware of them *and* by working and practicing to think, feel, and act against these irrational beliefs.

Self-acceptance is also a major factor in the theory of cure in REBT. Ellis believed that his approach taught his clients to fully accept themselves, other people, and the world, and thus live happier, more enjoyable lives. He identified several kinds of acceptances that are necessary for therapeutic change (Ellis, 1993). These are

- Accept human fallibility
- Accept the human tendency to demand
- Accept that humans may be uncaring and unloving
- Accept that humans are prone to some degree of disturbance
- Accept that we are responsible for our own disturbance by turning desires and preferences into absolute and grandiose demands
- Accept that humans choose their behaviors and that choices need not be absolute or demanded
- Accept oneself unconditionally
- Accept others unconditionally
- Accept that humans experience unchangeable frustrations
- Accept that humans may choose not to disturb themselves.

## Main Therapeutic Interventions

Three main sets of techniques are used in REBT: (1) cognitive techniques, (2) emotive techniques, and (3) behavioral techniques. Each is described briefly.

1. *Cognitive techniques.* Family members are confronted about the beliefs that cause their disturbances and are given homework assignments to keep track of their "should" and "must" beliefs. They are also given a self-help report form to fill out (Ellis, 1977). They are given other cognitive tools, such as Disputing Irrational Beliefs (DIB) (Ellis, 1974), which supply them with new and better alternatives to their present beliefs. Therapists also use imagery exercises to get them to imagine themselves making new and more effective responses. They may also be taught relaxation techniques to help them overcome anxiety and depression.

2. *Emotive techniques.* Attempts are made to get clients in touch with their worst fears and to change them to appropriate feelings. Role playing is used to help clients express and work through their feelings of unworthiness. Also, shame attacking exercises are used to elicit intense shame and self-deprecating thoughts. Humor and paradoxical intention techniques are used to attack an irrational belief or feeling. Finally, clients are given unconditional acceptance by the therapist, which shows them that they can accept themselves even when they have self-defeating behavior.

**Rational Emotive Behavior Family Therapy**

## CASE EXAMPLE

*The following case was described by Ellis (1991) and represents a good example of how rational emotive behavior family therapy works. Only brief segments of the case are presented here.*

*The family consists of a mother and father, both age 45, two sons, ages 21 and 17, and a daughter, Debbie, age 15. Debbie is the identified patient. She is very bright (140 IQ) but is getting into trouble and doing poorly in school, and this upsets her parents. The key interaction in the first session involves the therapist and Debbie.*

Therapist: *Do you want to keep getting into the kind of trouble you're in with your parents, with the school, and with your brothers?*

Debbie: *No.*

Therapist: *Why do you think you steal?*

Debbie: *'Cause I can't control myself.*

Therapist: *That's a nutty hypothesis! Horse shit! You have difficulty controlling yourself. But that doesn't mean that you can't.*

*Later in the session Debbie begins to realize how she gets herself in a self-defeating cycle.*

Debbie: *I guess I do. I keep thinking that I'm really no good. And then things get worse.*

Therapist: *Right! (therapist reinforces her awareness)*

*(continued)*

3. *Behavioral techniques.* Desensitization is a homework assignment in which the client is asked to deliberately put herself in an unpleasant marital or family situation until she no longer gets upset about it. Contracting between family members is often used to reinforce cooperative behavior. Skill training, such as assertiveness training, is used to teach new responses to family conflicts. Flooding, or asking a client to deliberately increase an unpleasant feeling, is used to deal with phobias, compulsions, and obsessions that interfere with family harmony.

*(CASE EXAMPLE continued)*

Debbie: *But how can I stop that?*

Therapist: *The best solution is to see very clearly what I said before: that some of your acts are poor or self-defeating but that you are not a worm for doing them. If we could get you to fully accept yourself, your being, your totality, even when you are screwing up and acting stupidly or badly, then we could get you to go back and work on improving your screwups. And you could change most of them.*

Debbie: *I see what you mean. But how am I going to keep seeing that and believing it?*

Therapist: *By damned hard work! By continuing to think about what you say to yourself and do. And by changing your perfectionistic, demanding thinking into preferences and desires.*

*The therapist then turned to the parents and said: "She has normal desires, but then she tells herself, I must, I must fulfill them! Now, if I can get all of you, including her, to look for the should, look for the must, which you are all bright enough to do, and if I can persuade you to tackle these absolutes and give them up, you will be able to stop upsetting yourselves, and usually solve the problem of getting along together and living happily in the world."*

*The therapist closed the session by assigning all three of them to read some REBT literature and to do some behavioral assignments, including keeping track of the times they feel upset during the week and what is happening in the family.*

## Goals of Rational Emotive Behavior Family Therapy

The goals of rational emotive behavior family therapy are as follows:

- To help family members learn not to take too seriously what other family members say or do
- To help family members surrender their absolutes (shoulds and musts) about how they would like others in the family to act
- To encourage family members to feel their feelings and use the energy generated by their feelings to help them ask for and get what they want from other family members

- To make family members aware of their irrational beliefs and teach them how to dispute and challenge their own beliefs
- To teach the clients a variety of self-therapy techniques for combating their own irrational beliefs
- To teach the clients more effective conflict resolution skills that can allow them to be happy and effective at getting what they want
- To teach the clients how to handle whatever happens in their family without getting upset or disturbed.

### Limitations of Rational Emotive Behavior Family Therapy

Rational emotive behavior therapy does have its limitations. Lyddon (1990, 1992) suggests that REBT may devalue emotion, may not be humanistic, and may not focus on deeper problems. The confrontive and directive style of the therapist may not allow the client to decide what is rational or logical thinking. New beliefs may be pushed on the client, perhaps in a way similar to how the irrational beliefs were first learned. In addition, the therapist is clearly imposing his or her value system on the client in a situation where the client may have very little power. Some critics argue that there is insufficient attention given to the desires of the client and that the therapist may "beat down" clients (Corey, 1991).

# Behavioral Family Therapy

Behavioral theory has been a major theory in psychology for about thirty years, but the application of the theory to family therapy is fairly recent (Liberman, 1970). The increased interest in family applications resulted from various research studies on social learning theory demonstrating its effectiveness with a variety of populations, including families (Falloon, 1991).

It had become apparent that the more traditional family therapies were not very effective in cases where family members displayed acting-out and aggressive behaviors. There seemed to be a need for a new theory and new approaches to deal with this kind of behavior problem. Finally, a group of psychologists at the Oregon Social Learning Center, under the direction of Gerald Patterson and John Reid, developed a behavioral treatment approach based on social learning theory. Initially, they focused on training parents and others in the acting-out child's environment to act as agents of change. Later, they broadened the approach to work with families with parent-child conflicts. They conducted extensive research, mostly on deviant behavior of children, and developed a number of effective methods for reducing and controlling deviant and disruptive behavior (Patterson, 1976; Patterson, Reid, Jones, & Conger, 1975; Reid & Patterson, 1976). Their later work focuses more on systemic family interaction patterns and avoids overfocusing on the identified patient in a family.

## Philosophical Tenets

This approach, which follows the operant conditioning model of Watson, Hull, and Skinner, stated that the most important source of knowledge (*epistemology*) is scientific knowledge discovered through rigorous, repeated laboratory research studies. Some behavioral theorists may not consider clinical judgment, subjective knowledge reported by the client, and beliefs and attitudes as valid sources of knowledge. The valid knowledge continuum would run from scientific research finds, objective findings, scientific "facts," and scientific values at the important end; mental phenomena, phenomenological methods, metaphysical inquiry, subjectivity, and interviewing variables would be at the less important end.

Behaviorists consider true reality (*ontology*) to be the external physical or sensory phenomena that can be measured and counted. This principle follows clearly the earlier philosophical tenets of Descartes, Locke, and Hume. The values (*axiology*) in behaviorism derive from certain truths that emerge as the result of logical and scientific studies. Informed reason based on the best scientific insights available is considered to be the best source of values (Corey, 1991).

As behavioral theory has evolved, it has moved from a position that views humans as the product of the environment to one that views humans as both producer and product of the environment (Bandura, 1977). Thus, we are capable of creating our destinies rather than simply being the victim of external reinforcers.

## Theoretical Constructs

**Theory of Cause**   Current behavioral theories including the social learning model, focus on the social reinforcers in a family or other social system. Social learning theorists believe, as did nonbehaviorists such as Bateson, Jackson, and Haley, that dysfunctional behavior is an understandable and logical response to the reinforcement contingencies of the family system. People and the environments in which they live are seen as reciprocal determinants of each other; thus, the concept of reciprocity or *quid pro quo* in families was developed. It was discovered that an improvement or change in one member's behavior was followed by a change in another family member's behavior (Patterson, 1971).

An interactional focus is therefore emphasized to examine the causes of dysfunctional behavior. It is impossible, however, to assign blame solely to a parent for the dysfunctional behavior of a child. The mother may present cues and reinforcers to the child that determine the behavior the child exhibits toward the mother. At the same time, the child is presenting cues and reinforcers to the mother that influence her interaction with the child. In this way, each member of a family influences the behavior and is influenced by other members of the family.

According to this view of a system, if a person or a whole family has not developed adequate positive behaviors, the cause of this problem is a lack of positive reinforcers in the individual or the family. Gottman et al. (1976) described a model of family interactions based on this premise. These authors used the metaphor that family members each have a bank account where they make deposits or investments and withdrawals analogous to their interactions with the other family members. In functional families, individuals receive a relatively high rate of exchange on their investments of time and energy with other family members because there is a long list of positive equal exchanges. In dysfunctional families, there is more time and energy spent "balancing the books" on a regular basis as each family member attempts to make sure he or she is not treated unfairly.

Patterson et al. (1975) demonstrated the limited value of coercion in creating desired change in families. An escalation of negative behaviors was more likely to occur when coercion was used to attempt to change behavior in another family member. Thus, behavioral family therapists attempt to decrease coercion while increasing reciprocity of positive behavioral exchanges (Falloon, 1991).

**Theory of Change**  The job of the therapist is to understand the social reinforcement history of an individual, a couple, or a family and begin to help them develop new positive reinforcers. The therapist has to develop a systematic process for observing the antecedents in the environment, the behaviors, and the consequences of the behaviors and then manipulate the reinforcement contingencies to provide opportunities for the clients to learn new behaviors. Any strategy designed to modify the deviant behavior of one family member must be based on changes in the behaviors of other key family members. Parents, spouses, siblings, and children are taught to eliminate their own behaviors that reinforce the deviant member's behavior and to learn and use different behaviors that are incompatible with the deviant behavior (Falloon, 1991).

In developing an understanding of the social reinforcement pattern of a family, it is important to remember a fundamental assumption of behavioral family therapy: Current behavior, no matter how dysfunctional it may seem, is the family's best attempt to deal with their current situation.

## Main Therapeutic Interventions

The main tasks of the behavioral family therapist are to analyze the problems, design appropriate interventions, and assess changes in the family. The main core skills a therapist using this approach would need are: (1) attending behavior, (2) rapport building, (3) structuring, (4) summarization, (5) interpretation, and (6) reflection of content. In addition, a social learning therapist has to be skilled in behavioral assessment. Behavioral assessment in a social learning model includes:

- Determining which environmental stimulus variables elicit the problem behaviors.
- Discovering what mediating factors exist, such as a person's thoughts and feelings about a problem behavior.
- Finding out how the individual behaves in response to his or her thoughts and feelings about the situation.
- Locating the reinforcers that affect the frequency of the problem behavior.

An important development in behavioral family therapy is the *psychoeducational approach* to family treatment. In this approach, the identified patient and family members are presented with a series of educational seminars that describe the nature of the problem and the strategies for managing the problem. This approach has been especially useful for families with a seriously impaired member (McFarlane, 1991).

## Behavioral Family Therapy

**C A S E**
**E X A M P L E**

*The following case example was taken from Horne and Ohlsen (1982, pp. 380–384). Only a portion of that case is presented here to illustrate some of the main interventions of social learning family therapists.*

*Kevin, a sixth-grade boy, along with his parents, was referred for therapy because of his difficulties in school, which included being expelled for fighting and truancy. In addition, Kevin's two younger siblings attended the sessions. Kevin was described as having a chip on his shoulder; he was often aggressive in his responses to teachers and to other students. The family's reaction was to have the therapist "fix" Kevin, and they did not see why they should be part of the therapy. As each member of the family talked, it became evident that the parents had poor parenting skills and tended to ignore the problem behaviors that resulted from their poor skills until some outside agency like the school intervened. The therapist met first with the parents, Dan and Kim.*

Therapist: *(summarizing the family situation) Kevin has had problems at school for a long time—pretty much ever since he got started—but you have figured that's the school's problem, that they should be able to handle Kevin.*

Dan: *Damned right, that's what they are there for. I was a lot like Kevin, and they certainly handled me.*

Therapist: *You pretty clearly have a kid who is more than the school can handle—he's a real expert at what he does, which is messing up.*

Kim: *We can't go to school and sit by him all the time, and we sure can't beat him all the time for coming home in trouble. That hasn't worked.*

Therapist: *I'm glad you see that.... What we do is teach parents how they can work with the school to get the changes that the school wants.... I think we can do that fairly quickly if you are interested in working with us here, but it does involve some real intensive work for awhile, and will require that you put in some time on exercises I'll assign you. It won't be easy and, in fact, will be a nuisance a lot of the time.*

*(continued)*

*(CASE EXAMPLE continued)*

Dan: *Well, maybe Kim should; she's the one that has the problem around the house, not me.*

Therapist: *That's a good point, Dan, and I'm glad you brought that up. You see, dads generally have less trouble than moms do. But, as I look at Kim, I see a tired and frustrated lady. She looks like she can use some support, some help. Since you already have pretty good control over how Kevin behaves, would you be willing to work with us to help with the program we have here in order to give Kim the backing she needs, the support she needs? … Are you willing to do that?*

Dan: *Well, I'll help out, but I don't see that I need the help.*

Therapist: *As I said, we see that all family members are involved in the welfare of the whole family.… We're asking for the family to work as a team with us. Okay?*

*The children were then brought into the session, and during the next part of the session, the parents blamed the children for misbehaving and the children blamed the parents for being too lax and ignoring conflicts. Then a co-therapist worked separately with the children while the parents completed several inventories.*

*In the interview with the children, it came out that Kevin was also having problems with his siblings around the house. The data gathered from the parents showed, among other things, that the marriage was on shaky ground. It was decided that in spite of the marriage problems, working on a behavior management contract with Kevin would help both Kevin and the marriage.*

*The family agreed to a specified number of sessions, and the members of the family were given homework assignments. Kevin's school was contacted and included in the behavior management program. After three weeks, the program progressed in the family and at school. The treatment then shifted, and conjoint therapy was done with the couple to work on the marital problems. The course of the family treatment was four months. By the end of that time, the home and school conflicts had subsided and more desirable family interactions were occurring. The family required three additional sessions six months later when the new school year began and Kevin reverted to some of his previous behavior. After the three sessions, his behavior changed back to more positive responses at school.*

The behavioral family therapist might also teach family members new communication responses using role playing or behavior rehearsal to correct any inappropriate or nonreinforcing responses. Teaching often occurs in two main areas: (1) correctional procedures, and (2) reinforcement procedures. Under the heading of *correctional procedures*, the therapist might teach family members the following skills:

- How to appropriately ignore attention-seeking problem behaviors.
- How to make effective use of natural and logical consequences.
- How to set up behavioral contingency contracts (you must do this before you get to do that).
- How to use the principle of "time out" to temporarily remove a family member from a reinforcing environment to a nonreinforcing environment.
- How to give assigned tasks to family members who don't cooperate.
- How to withhold privileges from family members when the other correctional procedures fail.

The *reinforcement procedures* often taught to family members include:

- How to properly attend to other people. This skill is the same as the nonverbal and verbal attending skills of the therapist.
- How to give social praise, including appropriate ways of demonstrating approval, appreciation, and satisfaction.
- How to give physical attention, such as hugs and touching.
- How to structure activities and spend time together.
- How to provide equal access to family activities and allow children to help plan activities that are agreeable to them and their parents.
- How to use points and other external rewards, which are effective for getting immediate involvement and behavior change but generally not useful for long-term changes.

## Limitations of Behavioral Family Therapy

The behavioral model of family therapy has a number of limitations. The method may be manipulative and used to attempt to influence and control behavior. Children, for example, who often do not have equal options or resources, must "go along" with the changes they are asked to make. In addition, this theory may reinforce the idea of the identified patient, although probably not as much as other individual theories do. However, most of the attention of behavioral family therapy is still placed on helping the parents learn to better control the behavior of their acting-out children. Furthermore, the role of the therapist is not always clear. Does the therapist consider herself a member of the family social system, or does the therapist see herself as an objective person removed from the influence of reciprocal interactions with the family?

Social learning theory may be most useful in families with acting-out or disruptive members. It is probably less useful in families where more social inhibition is present. It is also useful in marital therapy as couples work to establish mutually satisfactory *contingency contracts*. Contingency contracts help the couple establish a mutually reinforcing *quid pro quo*. When one partner does something positive, the other partner reciprocates. This is done in ways that have previously been agreed upon in therapy. It is an educational approach and as such avoids looking closely at underlying causes and deals primarily with overt symptoms. The success of this approach is often predicated on the assumption that couples or families are capable of cooperating in a reciprocal, step-by-step effort to improve their relationships. Couples or families who enter therapy, however, may not possess these capabilities.

## ▩ Summary

This chapter covered one cognitive theory (REBT) and one behavioral theory (social learning theory) that have been applied to family treatment. In the next chapter, several family systems theories with a cognitive/behavioral focus will be examined.

## SUGGESTED
## READINGS

Ellis, A. (1962). *Reason and Emotion in Psychotherapy*. Secaucus, NJ: Citadel Press.

Patterson, G. (1971). *Families: Applications of Social Learning in Family Life*. Champaign, IL: Research Press.

Patterson, G., Reid, J. B., Jonas, R. R., & Conger, R. E. (1975). *A Social Learning Approach to Family Intervention*, Vol. I. Eugene, OR: Castalia Publishing.

Ellis, A. (1995). "Rational Emotive Behavior Therapy." In R. J. Corsini & D. Wedding, eds., *Current Psychotherapies,* 5th Ed. Itasca, IL: F. E. Peacock.

Stuart, R. B. (1980). *Helping Couples Change: A Social Learning Approach to Marital Therapy*. New York: Guilford Press.

Falloon, I. R. H. (1991). "Behavioral Family Therapy." In A. S. Gurman & D. P. Kniskern, eds., *Handbook of Family Therapy*, Vol. II. New York: Brunner/Mazel.

# Cognitive/Behavioral

# Systems Theories

*In this chapter, we will examine three approaches to family systems therapy that have their roots in cognitive and behavioral theory. These approaches are quite distinct from the systems theories with psychoanalytic roots and the systems theories with humanistic/existential roots to be presented later in this book.*

*The three theories presented in this chapter are structural family therapy as developed by Salvador Minuchin, functional family therapy as developed by Cole Barton, James Alexander, and Bruce Parsons, and brief therapy as developed by the staff of the Mental Research Institute (MRI) in Palo Alto. These three theories have been selected because they are practical, concrete, relevant, and offer concepts that may be of immediate use for counselors and therapists who want to begin using systems theory in their work with couples and families.*

## KEY CONCEPTS

| | |
|---|---|
| Subsystems | Relabeling the symptom |
| Boundaries | Conceptual skills |
| Homeostasis | Technical skills |
| Joining | Interpersonal skills |
| Tracking | Paradox |
| Accommodation | Brief therapy |
| Mimesis | Therapist maneuverability |
| Enactment | 180° solution |
| Restructuring | Restraining change |
| Symptom focusing | |

## QUESTIONS
## FOR DISCUSSION

1. According to the structural family therapist, what is the relationship between family structure and family function?

2. What are the major steps the structural family therapist would use to help the family change?

3. What is meant by challenging the current family reality? Do you have any concerns about the use of this technique? Why, or why not?

4. What is the functional family therapist's conceptualization of the purpose of symptoms in the family? Do you agree with this conceptualization? Why, or why not?

5. Describe conceptual, technical, and interpersonal skills in functional family therapy. Why are each of these skill areas important?

6. How are problems identified and solved according to the brief therapy theory of the Mental Research Institute?

7. What is meant by "therapist maneuverability"? What is your reaction to this concept?

8. In the MRI approach, what is meant by "the attempted solutions are the problem?"

*S*tructural family therapy (Minuchin, 1974; Minuchin & Fishman, 1981), functional family therapy (Alexander & Parsons, 1982; Barton & Alexander, 1981), and brief therapy as practiced by the staff of the Mental Research Institute (Fisch, Weakland, & Segal, 1982; Segal, 1991; Watzlawick, Weakland, & Fisch, 1974;) have distinct characteristics that distinguish them from other systems theories presented in this book. The characteristics held in common by these theories are: (1) the focus is on discovering a practical solution to the problems presented by the family; (2) short-term tangible results are expected of therapy; (3) the goal is to take action to solve the problems rather than talking about them; (4) action is emphasized over insight; and (5) expression of feeling is viewed as a vehicle to change behavior rather than an end in itself.

Thus, the reader will learn about three of the most action-oriented systems theories in practice. Furthermore, specific techniques associated with these theories will be presented, which will offer specific suggestions for counselors beginning systems therapy with couples and families.

## Structural Family Therapy

Salvador Minuchin was born in Argentina and trained there as a physician with an interest in pediatrics. He served as a physician for the Israeli Army after Israel became a nation in 1948. He then received training in the United States as a child psychiatrist before returning to Israel to work with displaced children. Returning to the United States, Minuchin and his colleagues developed a program for working with delinquent minority children in New York City. These children frequently came from very disorganized families with few rules for conduct and little structure. Minuchin's work with these delinquent children and their families fostered many of the concepts of structural family therapy. A recounting of Minuchin and his colleagues' work with these families at the Wiltwyck School for Boys can be found in *Families of the Slums* (Minuchin, Montalvo, Guerney, Rosman, & Schumer, 1967).

From 1965 through 1975, Minuchin was the director of the Philadelphia Child Guidance Clinic. Under his leadership, it became one of the most highly acclaimed family therapy service and training institutes in the world. During the past several years, Minuchin has worked with psychosomatic families (Minuchin, Rosman, & Baker, 1978) and has written extensively about structural family therapy. He has also presented numerous training workshops and demonstrations of structural family therapy to professional audiences throughout the world.

## Philosophical Tenets and Key Theoretical Constructs

According to Minuchin (1974) the function of the family in society is to support, nurture, control, and socialize its members. "A well-functioning family is not defined by the absence of stress and conflicts, but by how effectively it handles them in the course of fulfilling its functions. This in turn depends on the *structure* and *adaptability* of the family" (Colapinto, 1991, p. 422). Structural family therapy, as its name implies, stresses the importance of the structure of the family system. In other words, how a family organizes itself is important to the well-being and effective psychological functioning of the members of the family (Minuchin, 1974).

Structural family therapists assume that there is an inherent drive toward organization within individuals and other living systems. This organization can be seen at various levels of living systems, from the cellular level all the way to the organization of a large corporation or city. These therapists assume that family *function follows structure.* Thus, structural family therapists understand behavior that occurs within a family as being a product of the *structure of the family.* When certain disturbing behaviors occur within the family, the family therapist will try to help the family reorganize its structure in a way that no longer supports or requires the disturbing behaviors. Adaptable families are those that are able to make the changes necessary to develop a new and more functional structure.

**Homeostasis and Disequilibrium**   Family systems are evolutionary. They are dynamic and changing. The system passes through periods of *homeostasis*, where change in the family occurs in rather small and acceptable ways that do not alter the current organization or structure of the family. These periods of homeostasis are interrupted by periods of *disequilibrium*, when the changes occurring in the family challenge the current family structure and require that the family structure be modified to accommodate the changes taking place. When the family system fights to retain its old organization instead of adapting to new circumstances, symptoms may develop in one or more family members. The structural family therapist will develop intervention strategies in an attempt to help the family reorganize in a more productive manner that allows for family development and change (Minuchin, 1974).

**Subsystems**   Each family is composed of subsystems that are parts of the larger family system. In an effort to help clarify the idea that a subsystem is both a whole and a part of a larger system, Minuchin used the term *holon* as a synonym for subsystem (Colapinto, 1991; Minuchin & Fishman, 1981). Each subsystem is identified by *boundaries* and *rules* that define who is in and who is out of the subsystem. For example, a subsystem of father and son may exist when the two go hunting. The rules of this subsystem may exclude mother and sister as well as friends of the father and the son. Thus, the boundaries of this subsystem are clearly defined. Four subsystems are important in a fundamental understanding of structural family therapy (Minuchin, 1974; Minuchin & Fishman, 1981).

1. *The individual subsystem.* Each member of the family is a subsystem of the family. It is important, however, not to view the family's problems as being the result of pathology within an individual. Two or more individuals form larger subsystems in the family. These larger subsystems have boundaries that describe who is a member of the subsystem. In families experiencing problems, the various subsystems are organized in a structural manner that supports the dysfunction. The therapist will seek to help the family adopt a more functional organization through treatment. In any event, all subsystems in the family are composed of individuals, and the therapist should not lose sight of this fact.

   Colapinto (1991) states that "a change in the system consists of individuals changing each other, and therefore requires the detection and mobilization of untapped individual resources"

(p. 430). While it is important to conceptualize structurally, it is individuals within the family who will behave in new ways that promote family health.

2. *The spousal subsystem.* The beginning of a new family takes place when a couple decides to unite and the partners begin to share their lives. As the two live together, they develop as a spousal subsystem. As members of the spousal subsystem, the individuals may support each other in times of crisis and indecision. Furthermore, they may work together to formulate decisions on how the family will be started, nurtured, and regulated.

One of the critical functions of the spousal subsystem is to develop boundaries that protect the couple from unwanted intrusions from either subsystems, such as parents, in-laws, or children. A strong, unified, and flexible spousal subsystem contributes much to the success of the larger family. Problems frequently occur in families in which spouses are more committed to another subsystem than to the spousal subsystem. This problem may occur when a husband is married to his work or a wife is overinvolved with her children.

When severe problems develop in the spousal subsystem and go unresolved, the effects reverberate throughout the whole family. Frequently, a child will develop psychological symptoms and may be scapegoated as a troublemaker in the family or be brought into an alliance with one of the parents against the other. An important diagnostic skill of the structural family therapist is to identify a child who is a member of a subsystem to which he or she should not be a member, such as the spousal subsystem. When a child becomes a member of the spousal subsystem, he or she often becomes allied with one parent against the other. This family structure is frequently identified in families that seek therapy.

The spousal subsystem is also known as the *executive subsystem*, as it is the subsystem primarily responsible for the regulatory functions of the family. In single-parent families, a child may be included in this subsystem to assist the parent in regulatory and support functions, and this structural form is often functional. It is important to understand that structural family therapy does not prescribe functional or dysfunctional family organizations; rather, this therapy attempts to help families develop new and more functional forms when current structures are not working.

3. *The parental subsystem.* The parental subsystem is composed of the husband and wife, or the same members as the spousal subsystem. The members of the parental subsystem have as their primary role the successful rearing of their family. Thus, the parental subsystem is specifically concerned with providing for the needs of the children in the family.

   The parental subsystem differs from the spousal subsystem in an important way. In the parental subsystem, the adults have very flexible roles and boundaries that allow for children to become temporarily parental and for parents to become temporarily childlike. This ability to spontaneously switch roles allows for the playfulness necessary for successful parenting and also allows children the opportunity to learn how to assume responsibility (parental) roles in the family.

   In contrast to the parental subsystem, the spousal or executive subsystem requires that the husband and wife work together to keep the children from intruding in their activities. When children are regularly involved in the spousal subsystem, it is not unusual to find one spouse allied with the child against the other spouse. The structural family therapist will quickly assess the functionality of both spousal and parental subsystems of the family in therapy to determine whether restructuring these subsystems may be helpful for the family.

4. *The sibling subsystem.* The fourth major subsystem is composed of the children in the family. In most functional families, communication between the members of the sibling subsystem and the parental subsystem is open and clear. As siblings recognize that they are excluded from the spousal subsystem, they form a unity, or bond, in the sibling subsystem that works cohesively to influence the adults in the parental subsystem. Although this cohesiveness in the sibling subsystem is certainly not universal and does not occur all the time, it nevertheless is often present in healthy families.

Family therapists using the structural approach will come to understand the families they work with in terms of the subsystems represented in the family. The four subsystems identified above are the most common ones noted in structural family therapy literature. It must be remembered, however, that any one of a variety of subsystems may exist within a family, and the functions of these subsystems may be either helpful or problematic for the family. The structural family therapist should be equipped to identify subsystems and their functioning before proceeding with techniques for making family system changes.

## Why Families Seek Treatment

As previously described, family systems seek organization and structure defined by the boundaries (rules) of the subsystems within the family. When the system is relatively stable, the family is in a state of homeostasis or equilibrium. When this homeostasis is altered or challenged, the family system attempts to retain its structure by not allowing change to take place. Frequently, the challenges to the family's homeostasis come from natural developmental changes in the family.

For instance, when a daughter was in her early teens, she was most compliant with her parents' rule that she be home by seven each night. However, as she became older, this rule was deemed childish by the daughter, and she rebelled and came home whenever she pleased. The parents tried everything to get their daughter to comply with their wishes. In response to their efforts to gain control, however, she only rebelled more, and the situation became worse.

This couple became angry and confused regarding their daughter's behavior and decided to seek help for her. The family came to a structural family therapist who helped the parents recognize that the current family structure or homeostasis was no longer appropriate for the developmental stage of the family. The therapist helped the family establish a new structural homeostasis with new rules and more appropriate boundaries (Minuchin & Fishman, 1981). As can be seen from this example, families come for therapy when their rules and organization are being severely challenged and all attempts to reestablish homeostasis have failed.

## Main Therapeutic Interventions

Structural family therapists assume that family dysfunction occurs because the organization of the family system has been disrupted and the family has been unsuccessful at reestablishing homeostasis or equilibrium. Thus, families come to treatment experiencing a great deal of confusion, anger, and perhaps fear. The confusion arises because they are not able to fix the problem as in the past. Anger arises because, typically, one or more family members are identified as the culprits who have caused the confusion. And fear exists because the family members who come for therapy have little idea of what to expect from the structural family therapist.

Quite naturally, effective therapy will be difficult when members are confused, angry, and afraid. The first task of the structural family therapist is to reduce these affective conditions. This is accomplished by the technique called *joining* (Minuchin, 1974).

**Joining**    For family therapy to be effective, the therapist has to establish a solid working relationship with the family members. *Joining* is the process of establishing that relationship with each family member. Joining is an especially critical technique in structural family therapy because even though the family members and the therapist share the goal of improving family functioning, the therapist and the family will often differ in their understanding of the locus of the problem, what causes the problem, and what has to be done to resolve the problem (Minuchin & Fishman, 1981).

As the therapist moves toward identifying the problem as one that is structural and involves all family members rather than as a problem with only one of its members, the rules of the family may be violated and the family may retreat in an attempt to preserve homeostasis and avoid change. Under such conditions, helping the family change becomes increasingly difficult. Thus, the family therapist joins with each member of the family, engendering trust so they will allow the therapist to use the knowledge of structural family therapy to assist them in making needed changes.

If the therapist moves too quickly in making changes before successfully joining with the family, the family may resist the therapist's attempts to help. If the therapist has successfully joined with each family member, however, they will generally be receptive to the new ideas, suggestions, and challenges the structural family therapist provides as part of treatment.

Successful joining requires that the therapist become a *significant source of self-esteem validation* for each member of the family. To be in such a position of trust, the family members must experience the therapist as *accurately understanding* the unique perspectives of each individual in the family. The therapist must be able to *communicate* to all individuals in the family that their unique perspectives are indeed understandable and make sense given the current behaviors of the other members in the family system. Thus, the therapist validates each position and, more important, each person in the family.

The specific components of joining are tracking, accommodation, and mimesis (Aponte & Van Deusen, 1981; Minuchin, 1974). *Tracking* refers to the therapist's ability to adopt the family's way of thinking about their situation. The more accurately the therapist uses the family's words, symbols, history, values, and style, the more fully understood the family will feel. The therapist uses *accommodation* in the joining process by relating to the family's current rules and roles. In this way, the therapist shows respect for family members as they are. As they understand this respect for who they are, they will be more willing to look at ways they could be even better. *Mimesis* is the joining technique that refers to the therapist becoming like a family member by adopting the family's style of communication. The therapist adopts similar body language, pace, and other communication behaviors of the family through mimesis.

Techniques for joining will be useless unless the therapist has a genuine interest in the family and is able to provide personal responsiveness. Additionally, the therapist will want to ensure that he or she does not inadvertently become organized into the family system. If the therapist is *inducted* into the family system, objectivity may be lost as the power of the family's rules organize the session. Induction is *not* joining through accommodation. In the joining process, the therapist intentionally adopts the rules of the family. Induction occurs when the therapist is inadvertently organized into the family by its rules and loses therapeutic objectivity (Colapinto, 1991).

**Activating Family Transaction Patterns and Structural Assessment**    To help families through structural family therapy, the therapist must understand and assess the current structure of the family. This process begins during the joining phase of treatment as the therapist notices rules, roles, and subsystems that govern the family's operation. The formal assessment of the family structure begins after the relationship between the therapist and the family has been solidly established. The therapist then learns how the family is structured through the technique of *enactment* (Minuchin & Fishman, 1981).

Enactment occurs when the family functions in therapy sessions as it does in the home, which allows the therapist to understand the family's current structure. Enactment may occur spontaneously in family therapy. However, when it does not, the therapist needs to facilitate the enactment. The therapist may direct certain key subsystems to discuss an acknowledged family problem or situation. As the family members behave in their accustomed ways in the session, the therapist learns how the family currently functions and how it may be able to function more effectively through structural interventions.

**Restructuring Family Transaction Patterns**  Families come to therapy to relieve stress or symptoms in one of the members. After the structural family therapist has joined with the family, created opportunities for the family to display its current patterns of functioning, and determined how the family functions and how its structure supports this functioning, it is then possible to alter the structure and the functioning of the family.

Structural family therapists have a variety of effective techniques for altering family structure and functioning. Aponte and Van Deusen (1981) have identified three major areas of restructuring: (1) system recomposition, (2) symptom focusing, and (3) structural modification. Each of these areas will be discussed briefly.

*System Recomposition*  Families seeking therapy are often organized rather rigidly into subsystems that may not adequately meet the developmental and emotional needs of the family. When the structural family therapist identifies this as a problem, recomposition of the subsystems becomes one method of treatment. Two major interventions may be used to change the composition of the family system. The first is to identify and add a new subsystem to the family. For instance, if a teenage daughter was allied with her mother against her father, the therapist may help create (or strengthen) the father-daughter subsystem by prescribing mutually enjoyable activities for them to do together. The second intervention is to eliminate subsystems that are no longer serving a productive function for the family. In the example above, the therapist may seek to eliminate the subsystem of mother and daughter allied against father and replace it with a mother-daughter-father subsystem that works jointly on tasks and issues.

*Symptom Focusing*  Frequently, families seek therapy because of some symptom being displayed by one of the family members. Quite naturally, the family members want to see the symptom eliminated. This view presents a clinical problem for the structural family therapist, who will generally see this presenting problem as a symptom of a dysfunctional family structure rather than as a problem within the identified family member. Thus, the therapist must have a variety of techniques for dealing with the symptom. The following techniques focus on the symptom either more or less intensely. Specifically, the therapist may:

- relabel the symptom,
- alter the affect of the symptom,
- expand the symptom,
- exaggerate the symptom,
- deemphasize the symptom, or
- move to a new symptom (Aponte & Van Deusen, 1981).

When a family begins therapy, it has had months or even years of practice at maintaining the symptom. When the family therapist attempts to deal with the symptom exactly as the family presents it, it may be difficult to help the family change because the family has probably tried most of the reasonable and rational approaches to changing the situation. When the therapist suggests ways to resolve the problem, it is likely that the family will have a "yes, but..." response to the therapist's suggestions for change. *Because the family is the established expert on its problem* it may disqualify the therapist's attempts to help. The therapist has to become the expert on problem resolution.

To accomplish this, the family needs to come to a new understanding of its problem as presented by the therapist. The blinders that allow the family to understand the problem in only one way have to be removed so a new understanding of the problem may occur.

Altering the nature of the symptom redefines the nature of the problem. Through this process, the dynamics of the session are altered in a way that empowers the therapist to help the family make structural changes. When the family accepts the new or revised definition of the problem, the therapist then becomes the established expert on the new problem and is in a position to assist the family in making changes. The family will then rely on the therapist's knowledge about system change and develop a curiosity about how this knowledge may be helpful in resolving the newly defined problem. The family will no longer be limited by its own extensive and unsuccessful experience with the original problem.

Six techniques for altering the symptom are described next.

1. *Relabel the symptom.* This technique is one of the most effective ways to alter tension and affect in the family if implemented correctly. It can also be quite ineffective if the therapist has not accurately assessed the family's readiness for a new understanding of the problem. Relabeling or reframing (Minuchin & Fishman, 1981) simply means that the therapist describes the symptomatic behavior in a way that makes it seem understandable and functional given the current circumstances. For instance, when a teenage girl has been consistently ignoring her schoolwork despite her parents' orders that she become more responsible, the family identifies her symptoms as rebelliousness. This definition may even be accepted by the daughter. The effective therapist may relabel the rebelliousness as "the daughter's attempts to establish herself as an autonomous young adult in the family instead of the parents' little girl." If this new label is accepted, the family has a new and potentially manageable problem that the therapist can help the family resolve.

2. *Alter the affect of the symptom.* This technique is closely related to relabeling except that it involves altering the feelings associated with the symptom rather than the definition of the symptom. In the example above, the therapist might relabel the parents' feelings about the daughter's behavior from anger at the daughter to feelings of sadness because they had not been successful in transmitting their values of the importance of education to their daughter. Once again, acceptance of this new label may open doors leading to the productive resolution of this situation.

3. *Expand the symptom.* Usually, the family will have identified one person as "the problem" and will present ample evidence of this person's guilt. In certain cases, the therapist will not be able to relabel the symptom or the affect of the symptom. In these cases, the therapist may expand the symptom by specifically identifying behaviors other family members engage in to maintain the symptom. As other members recognize their part in the problem, the identified patient will feel less pressure and may be more likely to change. Furthermore, as other family members begin to understand their roles in maintain-

ing the problem, they may make changes that support change in the identified patient.

Again, using the example above, the therapist may discover during the enactment portion of therapy that the daughter becomes most rebellious when the mother and father exhibit their disagreement about what would be the best way to get her to study. The therapist then could point out how the parents' disagreement is part of the sequence that could be defined as the symptom. This expansion of the problem takes some pressure off the daughter and encourages the parents to examine their roles in the maintenance of the problem.

4. *Exaggerate the symptom.* This *paradoxical technique* is used when other ways of altering the symptom have not been successful. In this technique, the therapist places an undue amount of emphasis on the symptom and actually suggests that the family member engage in the symptom more frequently because it is the only way the member is able to achieve the type of attention needed from the family (Minuchin & Fishman, 1981).

In the case of the teenage daughter cited above, the therapist would say that the problem was indeed a severe one. Because the daughter has no other way of obtaining her parents' attention and concern, however, she should be certain to avoid her studies even more frequently than she has been. The effects of this type of intervention are twofold. First, it normalizes and relabels the behavior as necessary to gain a positive goal (attention from parents). Second, it puts the daughter in charge of not doing homework and takes parental pressure out of the system. This exaggeration sets the stage for later changes, as the daughter could choose to be in charge of *doing* instead of *not doing* homework.

5. *Deemphasize the symptom.* This technique is designed to draw the family's energy away from the presenting symptom, as intense focus on the symptom often serves to maintain it. Deemphasizing the symptom is generally accompanied by a move to focus on a new symptom of another family member.

6. *Focus on a new symptom.* To decrease the family's intense preoccupation with the presenting symptom, the therapist will often introduce a new symptom (Minuchin, 1974). Introducing this new symptom can remove tremendous pressure from

the identified patient and place it on other less vulnerable family members. The therapist is often successful with this technique when it is introduced as follows:

> I can certainly understand your concern about your daughter's poor study habits and difficulty in school. It will be important to deal with that issue as soon as possible. First, however, it is going to be necessary for you and your husband to come to some agreement about what are acceptable study habits for your daughter. If you two are not certain what you want, we can't expect your daughter to be able to please you.

This technique allows the therapist to strengthen the spousal subsystem in the family as the couple discusses the issue, while taking pressure off and allowing change to take place in the identified patient. This technique is effective and often quite reliable in helping families change. However, the therapist must be certain that he or she has joined successfully with the family and that sufficient data has been gathered so the new symptom presented to the family will be recognized and accepted.

***Structural Modification***    When the therapist joins with the family, he or she intentionally becomes part of a system that seeks transformation. However, the family has developed certain rigid and ineffective ways to deal with change. By changing the emphasis on the symptoms, the therapist begins to assist the family in making structural changes. These structural changes are made through a variety of techniques (Minuchin & Fishman, 1981). Those most frequently employed are

- challenge the current family reality,
- create new subsystems and boundaries,
- block dysfunctional transactional patterns,
- reinforce new and adaptive family structures, and
- educate about family change.

These techniques will be described briefly next.

1. *Challenge the current family reality.* Families seeking therapy typically have certain rigid cognitive perceptions of the family and of reality in general. The structural family therapist will challenge those realities, not to convince the family that they are wrong but to show them there are other ways to be

right. For instance, a family may believe that it is critical for all family members to be home for dinner. When the wife takes a job that does not allow her to be home at dinnertime, the husband may believe she does not value her marriage and family anymore.

An alternative reality might be that the wife cares so much about her family that she is working difficult hours to help provide the necessities for comfortable living. When the family accepts a different way of thinking about the situation, structural change becomes more likely.

2. *Create new subsystems and boundaries.* This technique is a critical aspect of structural family therapy. When structure determines function and function is ineffective, then structure must be altered if family functioning is to improve. To alter family structure, the therapist can highlight relationships in the family that are appropriate for the family's developmental stage and deemphasize subsystem relationships that may be maintaining the current family problems. Typically, the therapist will make behavioral assignments that create new subsystems and provide less opportunity for dysfunctional subsystems to continue. As family members eliminate subsystems that are no longer needed and develop new, more adaptive subsystems, family functioning should be enhanced.

3. *Block dysfunctional transaction patterns.* As the therapist works with the family in the enactment stage of treatment, dysfunctional interaction patterns will be demonstrated by family members. The therapist will note and block the repetitive and ineffective communication patterns. This goal can be accomplished in several ways. The therapist may simply comment that the previous conversation did not seem to be helpful to the family and ask whether those involved could provide help in understanding what was accomplished.

Once dysfunctional subsystems and communication patterns are identified, the therapist makes assignments that direct other family members to monitor the dysfunctional subsystem and comment when problematic communications occur. This intervention not only alters the dysfunctional communication patterns identified but also alters the subsystem composition as observers become part of the subsystem.

4. *Reinforce new and adaptive family structure.* When the therapist has helped the family develop more effective subsystems and boundaries, these beneficial changes have to be maintained through reinforcement until they become self-reinforcing. To accomplish this, the therapist will enlist the assistance of other family members to report on how well the new subsystem has functioned during the week. In addition, the members of the new subsystems will be asked to evaluate their own performance. Through the positive reinforcement of the new behaviors, the changes made in the family structure can be supported and maintained.

5. *Educate about family change.* Joining, enactment, and restructuring the family may occur fairly rapidly in structural family therapy. However, after structural changes have been made, behavioral reinforcement may be accompanied by education for the family. At this stage of treatment, often only the husband and wife will continue in therapy. During the education phase of treatment, the couple will learn the basic principles of structural family therapy, including how and why some families are able to change and others have great difficulty. This education is designed to help the family develop the skills needed to manage the next opportunity for family growth through appropriate structural change. Some couples are satisfied and terminate therapy when structural changes have been made and family functioning improves. Others are curious about structural family therapy and elect to remain in therapy for the educational phase of treatment.

## Strengths and Limitations of Structural Family Therapy

Structural family therapy has a number of strengths. The theory of change is clearly explained, and the techniques closely follow the theory. The special terminology and concepts, such as subsystems and boundaries, have broad applicability to the family therapy field. The theory recognizes the identified patient's symptoms as a manifestation of structural problems in the family. Moreover, the theory focuses on active interventions with the family system to bring about change. An impressive series of studies support the efficacy of this approach (Aponte & Van Deusen, 1981; Gurman & Kniskern, 1981b; Stanton & Todd, 1979).

Structural family therapy also has limitations. The approach may overlook individual distress in searching for problems in the family structure. It minimizes the role of affect in problem resolution. In addition, therapist directiveness may take the initiative for change away from the family and foster dependence. Finally, the use of refocusing and relabeling techniques to remove the pressure from the identified patient may be considered manipulative by some therapists.

## ▨ *Functional Family Therapy*

Functional family therapy was developed by Cole Barton, James Alexander, and Bruce Parsons and has been comprehensively described in the literature (Alexander & Parsons, 1982; Barton & Alexander, 1981). These family therapists have considerable experience in using

---

### Minuchin's Structural Family Therapy

### C A S E
### E X A M P L E

*A classic example of structural family therapy is provided by reviewing the work of Braulio Montalvo with a family of four at the Philadelphia Child Guidance Clinic. In this example, the presenting problem was a young boy who feared dogs. All of the parents' efforts to help the boy had failed. When Montalvo discovered that the boy's father was a mailman who must have extensive experience dealing with dogs, he took the mother out of the primary role with the son and instructed the father to get the boy a puppy and teach him about dogs. This classic maneuver interrupted the overinvolvement of the mother-son subsystem and established a father-son subsystem, which had previously not existed. Gradually, the boy overcame his fear of dogs. At about the same time, Montalvo discovered that the parents did not have a very solid marriage. The parents were offered the opportunity to look at the marriage in therapy and to strengthen the spousal subsystem. Through the therapy, the parents were able to help their son overcome his fear of dogs and improve their own marriage. The follow-up session confirmed that the changes had been maintained.*

behavioral principles when working with families and have conducted important research and published extensively in behavioral family therapy (Alexander & Barton, 1976; Alexander, Barton, Schiavo, & Parsons, 1976; Barton & Alexander, 1977; Parsons & Alexander, 1973). As their ideas became more refined, they began writing about what they have now identified as functional family therapy (FFT).

The principles of FFT were refined for presentation to wider audiences (Barton & Alexander, 1981), and the theory was included in Gurman and Kniskern's (1981b) *Handbook of Family Therapy.* Functional family therapy was later presented in a textbook (Alexander & Parsons, 1982) for use in family therapist training. Since that time, FFT has been widely accepted as an effective approach to family therapy, largely because of its clear principles and the research that has been conducted that supports the model (Alexander, 1973; Alexander et al., 1976; Alexander & Parsons, 1973; Klein, Alexander, & Parsons, 1977; Parsons & Alexander, 1973).

## Philosophical Tenets and Key Theoretical Constructs

Functional family therapy is understood by its developers as an integration of systems theory and behaviorism. This integration is synergistic. FFT is not simply an eclectic blend of systems concepts and behavioral principles; rather, FFT is viewed as a new clinical model that emerges from systems theory and behaviorism but is distinct from each. Barton and Alexander (1981) stated that the theory was developed to have both scientific respectability and clinical usefulness. Research studies have been conducted on the effects of FFT, and a series of clinically useful techniques and instruments have been developed to assist the clinician (Alexander & Parsons, 1982).

Functional family therapy differs markedly from most behavioral models in that FFT does not simply attempt to help people change behaviors but is designed to help family members come to understand and change their *subjective conceptual and affective states* as well as their overt behaviors. Functional family therapy not only looks at actual frequencies of behaviors but also attempts to help modify the subjective attitudes family members hold about problem behaviors.

Those who would practice FFT adopt a systems perspective and seek to understand how and why the behaviors of an individual family member make sense given the actions and attitudes of the other members of the individual's family system. Rather than attempting to determine whether the behaviors are functional or dysfunctional, the therapist seeks to understand how and why the behaviors exist and how and why the behaviors are supported and maintained by the other family members. Using FFT, the therapist does not judge whether behaviors are good or bad but only understands how they *function*— thus, the name of the theory, functional family therapy.

Two key assumptions regarding FFT emerge from this perspective. The first assumption is that behavior that may be defined as "bad" is not so defined in functional family therapy. Rather, the therapist using FFT will seek to understand the behavior as serving a function for the individual and family system and may legitimize what has been defined by others as bad behavior. The second key assumption is that all behavior is adaptive. That is, behavior is not good or bad. Instead, behavior is simply a process for creating specific outcomes in interpersonal relationships. Thus, relatively novel assumptions about human behavior must be adopted to understand and treat family problems.

The functional family therapist needs to understand the behavior of individuals from a broader perspective than the therapist working only with individuals and be able to determine how that behavior makes sense given its relational context. Change occurs in FFT when family members are able to reappraise the meaning of specific behaviors in context and come to recognize the function of the behavior and that other family members are supporting the problematic behavior. Another way to understand this concept is to recognize that all family members are doing the best they can with the resources they have available to achieve their goals.

A brief example will highlight these concepts. Assume that a wife nags her husband to the point that he leaves the home. Two immediate solutions to the problem behavior would be: (1) help the wife reduce nagging, or (2) help the husband learn to deal more effectively with the wife's frustration. The functional family therapist would not necessarily move toward either solution. Rather, the therapist would seek to understand the function of the nagging and leaving behaviors. In this case, the function may be to *increase distance* between the spouses. If, in fact, the spouses need distance, are there other ways this might be accomplished? The therapist would believe that the relational outcome of distancing could be accomplished in more effective ways and would seek to help the couple learn to do so.

## Main Therapeutic Interventions

To become proficient in functional family therapy and to create conditions for effective intervention, the therapist develops three distinct sets of skills:

- Conceptual skills (how to think about families)
- Technical skills (what to do with families)
- Interpersonal skills (how to apply techniques) (Alexander & Parsons, 1982).

**Conceptual Skills**   Effective therapists need to understand the dynamics of the family's interaction to intervene successfully. To use FFT, the therapist tries to determine what will motivate the family to use identified change strategies to bring about system change. Finally, FFT is based on a distinct conceptual orientation that views the family not as harboring a patient but as a system of interacting parts behaving according to certain principles. Identifying these principles is one of the key challenges for the therapist.

**Technical Skills**   Technical skills are the basic tools of family therapy used to produce change (Alexander & Parsons, 1982). Techniques are designed to produce change in four areas of family functioning:

1. Perceptions of self and others in family.
2. Specific overt problem behaviors, such as acting-out behavior.
3. Specific psychological states, such as depression and anxiety.
4. Communication among family members that maintains the above conditions.

**Interpersonal Skills**   Research completed by Alexander et al. (1976) demonstrated that certain interpersonal skills are necessary to help families change. These skills include: (1) integrated affect and behavior, (2) nonblaming, (3) demonstrating interpersonal warmth, (4) alleviating tension with humor, and (5) appropriate self-disclosure. They also discovered that these skills have little impact in helping families change unless therapists have a solid conceptual framework and well-developed technical skills (Barton & Alexander, 1981). Thus, relationship skills taught in most counseling programs are *necessary* but not *sufficient* to bring about change in client families.

## The Process of Therapy in FFT

Before the family therapist can begin helping a family change its problematic behavior, the therapist must understand how the family functions and what has to be changed. Thus, the first stage of therapy is the *assessment* stage. In functional family therapy, the focus is on the function the behavioral sequences serve. Is the behavior creating distance? Is it creating closeness? Or is it regulating distance and closeness among family members?

To determine the function, the therapist gathers information from the family. First, the therapist discovers what the family says is occurring. At the same time, the therapist observes the interactions between and among family members to develop an understanding of how the family works and how their behaviors function to regulate intimacy in the family. When the therapist has gathered this information from the family, themes will become evident and important functions of the problematic behaviors can be determined.

Gathering data to make this assessment may present problems for the beginning family therapist if the family is not enacting its usual behaviors in the session. When the family is not providing the necessary information for an assessment, the therapist may use the following three techniques.

1. *The therapist may reflect back to the family* a behavioral sequence that was noted and ask each family member to comment on the sequence. The various perceptions of the family members regarding the sequence may open the door for further data gathering.

2. *The therapist may use the feelings or thoughts of family members* to facilitate discussion. This technique is useful when the therapist is able to pinpoint the feelings of one family member and reflect those feelings back to that member and at the same time observe and comment on the reactions of other family members.

3. *The therapist may focus on key relationships in the family* as a vehicle to gain additional information about the family. In this technique, the therapist deemphasizes the content and affect of what is said and emphasizes the recognized relationship between the parties involved. As the therapist communicates an understanding of the importance of key relationships in the

family, the family becomes more trusting and willing to provide more information for the assessment.

The second phase of therapy is designed to *institute change in the family system.* This phase of therapy is directed toward developing specific interventions to help the family change thoughts, feelings, and behaviors surrounding key family functions identified in the assessment phase of therapy. Specific techniques that may be used in this phase of therapy are

- Asking questions to clarify relationship dynamics.
- Interrelating the thoughts, feelings, and behaviors of one family member to the thoughts, feelings, and behaviors of other members.
- Offering interpretations of the function of the behaviors of family members.
- Relabeling behavior in a way that removes blame from individual family members.
- Directly discussing the impact that the removal of symptomatic behavior will have on family functioning, as the dysfunctional behavior in one member may serve to stabilize the family by directing attention away from a more critical issue.
- Shifting the focus of treatment from the identified patient to another family member (Alexander & Parsons, 1982).

Each of these specific techniques can serve to help family members think about the family differently, behave differently, and communicate more effectively.

The third phase of therapy is *maintaining change through education.* This phase of treatment begins when family hostility is reduced through the techniques presented previously. Education provides the family with the skills to resolve future issues that may arise. Specifically, during this phase of family therapy, members are taught effective communication skills, behavior management and contracting skills, and other team-building techniques. This phase is especially critical because it is here that families learn skills needed to resolve problems that will inevitably arise in the future.

## Strengths and Limitations of FFT

Functional family therapy has a solid base in research and recognizes that all behaviors serve a function. The approach identifies specific

## Functional Family Therapy

**CASE EXAMPLE**

*The Talbot family entered therapy with several concerns. Mr. and Mrs. Talbot were recently married, each for the second time. Mrs. Talbot brought her two children from the previous marriage into the home. During the courtship phase, the children seemed to like Mr. Talbot a great deal. Since the marriage, however, Scott, age 13, has been acting out and is defiant toward Mr. Talbot, who becomes angry and frustrated. When this anger and frustration is generated between Scott and Mr. Talbot, Mrs. Talbot enters the situation to defend her son, which angers Mr. Talbot further.*

*The therapist gained the family's trust by making an assessment and clearly identifying the sequence of behaviors that was disturbing the family. This accurate assessment was critical for developing a trusting atmosphere for the therapy. In the change phase of treatment, the therapist helped the family understand the functions of the behaviors of the three family members. Mr. Talbot wanted to be a good step-father, which meant providing discipline. Scott felt that Mr. Talbot's attempts to discipline him were undermining his mother, who had provided effective discipline for the past seven years since the divorce. Mrs. Talbot reacted because she was afraid Mr. Talbot no longer valued her son. Therefore, she sought to defend him. As the family came to recognize the functions the problematic behaviors were serving, tension was reduced. Finally, the family entered the education phase of treatment, and members learned effective communication skills, behavior management principles, and information about issues that typical step-families confront. The family left treatment after four months greatly improved and ready to cope more effectively with problems the family situation may present in the future.*

therapist interpersonal qualities that are necessary but not sufficient for effective therapy. Moreover, the approach focuses on specific client behaviors and understanding them from a systems perspective.

Functional family therapy is limited in that it may underestimate the intrapsychic function of affect in favor of a systemic interpretation. In addition, it may focus too specifically on overt behavior and not attend sufficiently to cognition and affect. Another danger is that the assessment phase of treatment may distance the family from the therapist. Finally, the approach does not take a stand on the moral value of negative behaviors, such as robbery, because all behavior is viewed as being functional in its context.

# The MRI Approach to Brief Therapy

In their classic text *The Tactics of Change: Doing Therapy Briefly,* Fisch, Weakland, and Segal (1982) are careful to define the brief therapy approach of the Mental Research Institute (MRI) of Palo Alto, California, as a theoretically complete model for the treatment of a wide range of human problems. They encourage their students not to confuse the MRI approach to treatment with brief crisis intervention or shortened versions of long-term approaches to therapy, made briefer by a lack of time, resources, personnel, or patient finances. MRI brief therapy is an explicit and comprehensive theory that employs innovative techniques for change and focuses treatment on the main presenting problem. Gurman and Kniskern (1991) remind us that "it is essential to keep in mind the distinction between the MRI's Brief Therapy and 'brief therapy' as a much more general reference to a style of practice that includes such diverse forms as brief psychodynamic therapy and brief cognitive therapy" (p. 173).

The history of the Mental Research Institute is closely linked with the application of *cybernetics,* the study of self-regulation to social systems. Famous names in the history of family therapy played a part in the evolution of brief therapy. Gregory Bateson, Don Jackson, Jay Haley, and John Weakland (1971) pioneered the *double-bind theory* of schizophrenia. Moreover, Haley, Jackson, Satir, Weakland, and colleagues studied the effects of *communication* and *paradox* in families (Segal, 1991). Also participating in the development of the MRI model were Milton Erickson, Richard Fisch, Paul Watzlowick, and Heinz Von Foerester. Each of these pioneers "contributed to the understanding of disturbed behavior as a function of an interpersonal system rather than an intrapsychic one, wedding cybernetic epistemology to psychiatry" (Segal, 1991, p. 173).

## Philosophical Tenets and Key Theoretical Constraints

The relationship between the theory and practice of brief therapy is critical in that embedded within the theory are the views and premises the therapist holds that govern the identification and description of psychological problems. Moreover, theory will influence what information provided by the client will become the focus of attention and what information will not be the focus. Additionally, theory will predicate what the therapist will and will not do in the treatment of the client and will determine who participates in treatment.

The brief therapist views theory as a map to help treat client problems. Theory is designed to help the therapist move from place to place; for instance, encountering a client's problem and moving to resolution of that problem. Theory should serve as a guide to treatment, as it may be useful in clarifying obstacles encountered in working with human problems. But it is important to remember that theory is only a map, and a map is not the territory. Theory, while quite important, should not be overelaborated or taken too seriously (Fisch, Weakland, & Segal, 1982).

**Defining the Problem**   Clearly, defining the problem is critical to successful implementation of brief therapy. According to Segal (1991), a problem is defined in the following ways:

- the client reports experiencing pain and distress,
- the pain/distress is attributed to the behaviors of self or others,
- the client has been trying to change this painful behavior, and
- the client has been unsuccessful at changing.

The client may be an individual or several members of a family. This approach focuses on problem solving and may involve one or several clients. The brief therapist assumes that the complaint is the problem and not the symptom of an underlying pathology. Thus, the goal of brief therapy is to identify and reduce or eliminate the client's pain. The goal may be achieved if the client's behavior changes or the behavior is no longer troubling to the client. Thus, the therapist is responsible for identifying the goals of therapy. Most frequently, the goals of therapist and client overlap, however, in this model it is the therapist who determines what will be useful for the client in bringing about change (Segal, 1991).

**How Problems Develop and Persist**   Problems result from ineffective handling of ordinary life difficulties. Brief therapy is clear on the point that problems result when behavior deviates from what is desired and that repeated attempts to return behavior to its normal state have failed. In many instances, these attempts to return behavior to its normal state actually make the problem worse. For example, a parent tells her son to go to sleep so he will be well-rested for school. The son refuses to be directed and stays awake. The more the mother attempts to solve the problem by directing him to go to sleep, the more awake the son becomes and the less sleep he gets. In this situation, trying to force the son to rest actually makes him less sleepy, and he gets even less rest. The mother's attempted solution to the problem has made the problem worse.

Segal (1991) describes four clear patterns of mishandling problems:

- forcing correction when normal life difficulties will self-correct,
- seeking a no-risk solution when normal risk is involved,
- insisting on discussion to resolve a dispute when discussion exacerbates the problem, and
- confirming the accuser's suspicion by defending oneself.

An example of forcing correction when it is inappropriate might occur when a student has a writing block over a certain assignment. The more she forces herself to write, the more overwhelming the project becomes. Forcing correction causes an ordinary difficulty to become a serious problem.

An example of seeking a no-risk solution occurs when a shy man works diligently to perfect his opening remarks to a women he wants to meet rather than allowing the conversation to develop naturally. The harder he tries to eliminate risk, the more likely he will be to become tongue-tied and interact inappropriately.

An example of insisting on discussion occurs when a husband and wife are in disagreement. It seems logical that they should talk out the disagreement, but the discussion leads to increased hostility and resentment.

An example of confirming the accuser's suspicions occurs when a teenager accuses his parents of meddling in his affairs and separates himself from the family. Without family support, he becomes depressed and withdrawn. Then the concerned parents attempt to be helpful by talking with their child, and this confirms his position that they are meddlesome.

In summary, two key assumptions underlie brief therapy. First, problems persist only if they are maintained by the actions of the client and other members of the client's family system. The problem will be resolved if those behaviors that maintain the problem are changed or eliminated.

## Main Therapeutic Interventions

Segal (1991) operationalizes brief therapy as a series of tasks to be accomplished leading to client improvement. The tasks are

- identify the family members who are motivated for treatment and arrange for them to attend the initial interview,
- collect specific data about the problem and the ways the family has tried to solve the problem,
- set a specific goal for therapy,
- develop a plan to create change in the presenting problem,
- intervene in ways that interrupt the ineffective attempted solutions,
- assess outcome of treatment, and
- terminate.

In the beginning stages of treatment the therapist will notice that the family members take *positions* on such issues as why the problem exists, which family members are helpful and which are not, why the problem is not being resolved, and often times, what the therapist must do to help. The therapist should note these positions and confirm that he or she understands them as well. However, it is critical in this approach for the therapist to maintain *therapeutic maneuverability*. The therapist needs the freedom to intervene in ways that are most helpful for the family and will resolve the presenting problem. If the therapist accepts the positions of the clients, which have not been helpful in bringing about change, the therapist is being compromised and will not have the freedom to maneuver in ways that may be helpful to the family (Fisch, Weakland, & Segal, 1982; Segal, 1991).

Therapy begins with the first phone contact. The therapist attempts to determine if the client is a *customer*, who is genuinely seeking help, or a *window shopper*, who enters therapy at someone else's direction and may not be motivated to change. The brief therapist wants to meet with the family members who are motivated to change. This may mean that the identified patient who does not want treatment will not be seen in the initial interview. Moreover, the identified patient may never enter treatment, but change may still occur as other family members identify their ineffective solutions to the problem and develop new and more effective ones.

Several specific techniques have been developed to bring about change with brief therapy. The most important technique is to understand that the problem is maintained by ineffective attempts to resolve it. The therapist's key function is to help the family implement new solutions.

A second technique is to develop with the family an achievable goal. This goal may not be total change in the problem but a step in the right direction. Segal (1991) manages this therapeutic task by structuring the goal setting in this way: "Since we only have 10 sessions, we need to define a goal of treatment that would tell us you are beginning to solve the problem. You're not completely out of the woods, so to speak, but you'll have found a trail and can find your way on your own. So, what would be the smallest, concrete, significant indicator of this?" (p. 182). Brief therapy is time limited, thus a concrete, achievable goal must be set. Once the family has achieved the goal, therapy is terminated with the expectation that they will continue to implement their new solutions to the old problem and experience relief as a result.

A third technique is for the therapist to avoid the minefield. Avoiding the minefield means that the therapist does not accept the family members' positions and is able to avoid "more of the same" solutions to the problem. If the therapist accepts family members' positions and gives directives that are similar (more of the same) to those already in place, change will not occur, and the problem may be exacerbated. For example, if a family is seeking help in having their son be more involved in family activities, a therapist would be in the minefield with any directive that attempted to command the son to be more involved.

A fourth technique is to seek a 180° shift or U-turn away from the attempted solution and implement a new solution (Fisch, Weakland, & Segal, 1982). In the example above, a 180° shift would be to direct the family to encourage the son to develop autonomy and independence. In so doing, the family could feel good about helping their son develop independence, and the son may well respond by spending more time with a supportive rather than a controlling family. Implementing this 180° shift with the family is often difficult. Such a shift often creates a solution that is counterintuitive to the family and makes no logical sense. "How can we get closer to our son by encouraging him to be distant?", they might wonder.

At this point, clients will need help in performing therapist-initiated directives that appear counterintuitive (Segal, 1991), so the therapist employs a key technique called *reframing*. Reframing is a technique defined by Watzlawick et al. (1974) that "changes the conceptual and/ or emotional setting or viewpoint in relation to which a situation is experienced and places it in another frame which fits the 'facts' of the same concrete situation equally well or even better, and thereby changes its entire meaning" (p. 95). For example, the first author of this text (Fenell) worked with a client who insisted that she was powerless to improve her marriage. She complained that no matter what she did to improve her marriage it didn't work because her husband refused to look at his dysfunctional family of origin and his previous problematic marriage.

The more she tried to get him to "do his therapy," the more he resisted. She was extremely angry and depressed. The client believed she was working to improve her marriage by insisting that her husband do family-of-origin work. The therapist reframed the situation as the client's attempt to make it difficult for her husband to demonstrate his unique attempts to improve the marriage by only recognizing one way for him to demonstrate his desire to improve the relationship. The client was surprised and shocked by this reframe and claimed she had no desire to create difficulties for her husband. Thus, she was able to accept the directive that she refrain from trying to make the marriage better for a few weeks "to see what happens." After several weeks of implementing this new solution, the client reported she was less angry and depressed and that her husband seemed to be trying new ways to respond to her needs. In this situation, the reframe worked because it used the same information the client reported and placed it in a different context (trying to improve her marriage was reframed as creating difficulties for her husband). The technique of reframing is essential to prepare the client to accept the 180° shift in the attempted solution.

Brief therapy employs a set of techniques that are considered paradoxical. The 180° solution may be considered an example of *paradox*. Change is created by directing the family to engage in solutions that seem the opposite of what should be helpful. Other examples of paradox include the directive to engage in more of the symptomatic behavior or to engage in it at a specific time. This is called *symptom prescription* and is effective for two reasons. First, if the client follows the directive and increases symptomatic behavior intentionally, he is controlling the symptom. If he can increase the frequency of the symptom, he can also use this control to decrease the frequency of the symptom. Second, if the client resists the directive, as many clients do, and does not increase symptomatic behavior, the symptoms are decreased.

Other paradoxical techniques include the directive to the client to go slowly in changing (Fisch, Weakland, & Segal, 1982). This is known as *restraining change*. This is simply another 180° shift for a client who has been desperately attempting to create change. By going slowly, the client's anxiety may be reduced, and other directives for change may be employed more carefully and with more consideration. Conversely, if the client is not progressing rapidly and is experiencing discouragement, the therapist's directive to go slowly will support the gradual change that may be about to occur or is in the process of occurring. Moreover, the therapist should be prepared to *predict relapse* so clients are prepared to deal with setbacks and do not view these setbacks as failure.

Segal (1991) warns that beginners must not erroneously assume that paradox is the essence of brief therapy. It is more important to understand the usefulness and power of the 180° shift in the attempted solution to the problem and learn to develop and implement effective reframing techniques to support this new solution.

Segal (1991) suggests that termination of therapy occurs when "(1) a small, but significant, change has been made in the problem; (2) the change appears to be durable; and (3) the patient implies or states an ability to handle things without the therapist" (p. 189). The therapist should ensure that the clients feel responsible for making the change rather than crediting the therapist with changing them. It is also important to remind the clients that relapse may occur but that they have the tools to handle future problems. If clients resist termination, the therapist may frame the termination as a temporary break from therapy while the clients consolidate their learning (Segal, 1991).

## Strengths and Limitations of Brief Therapy

The MRI approach to brief therapy has several strengths. The most notable is that problem resolution frequently occurs quite rapidly. Additionally, this approach specifically identifies and attempts to change the pattern of ineffective attempted solutions to the problem. As families learn to employ unique and sometime counterintuitive solutions to their problems, rapid change is possible. Finally, brief therapy does not look at individuals as mentally ill. The model looks at problems as the result of ineffective attempts to manage them.

There are several limitations to the approach. Brief therapy is criticized because it does not look at historical aspects of the problem and therefore only focuses on symptoms, not their cause. Others criticize the approach for its use of paradoxical techniques, which they claim are not genuine and are often manipulative.

## Summary

In this chapter, we have described three family systems approaches with their roots in cognitive/behavioral theory. Structural family therapy, functional family therapy, and brief therapy seek to help families understand their behavior and employ powerful change techniques to help families function more effectively. All three approaches are readily understood by beginning family therapists because the principles of each theory are clearly explained and the change techniques closely follow the theory. In the next two chapters, we examine individual and systems-based theories with humanistic/existential bases.

## MRI Approach to Brief Family Therapy

C A S E

E X A M P L E

*The first author of this text (Fenell) worked with a family who complained that their son was rebellious because he did not go to bed when instructed and, in fact, turned the light on in his room and read Hardy Boys mysteries into the night. All attempts to correct the behavior with verbal warnings and restrictions failed. The parents were becoming increasingly angry and coercive, to no avail. The parents framed the problem (and took the position) that they had a rebellious child who did not respect his parents. The couple was asked what small goal might indicate that things were getting back to normal. They reported that they would like to see their son getting more sleep. The presenting problem was reframed by the therapist. He described the "acting-out" son as a seemingly intelligent young man who loved to read (a positive) and was able to function well with very little sleep (another positive). The parents accepted this reframe because it was "true." It described the original situation with the same facts in a way that portrayed the son's behaviors in positive and different ways. The parents accepted the reframe and the accompanying 180° reversal solution. They were to tell their son each night that they appreciated his intelligence and interest in reading and his ability to function on so little sleep. Further, they were to tell him they trusted him to turn his light off and go to sleep when he was tired.*

*When the couple returned for the second session, they reported that they had employed the new solution each night for a week. For the first two nights, the boy read into the wee hours, but beginning with the third night, he turned his light out earlier and earlier. In fact, after one week of implementing the new solution, the parents felt the problem was solved.*

# SUGGESTED
## READINGS

Alexander, J., & Parsons, B. V. (1982). *Functional Family Therapy.* Pacific Grove, CA: Brooks/Cole.

Barton, C., & Alexander, J. F. (1981). "Functional Family Therapy." In A. S. Gurman & D. P. Kniskern, eds., *Handbook of Family Therapy.* New York: Brunner/Mazel.

Fisch, R., Weakland, J. H., & Segal, L. (1982). *The Tactics of Change: Doing Therapy Briefly.* San Francisco: Jossey-Bass.

Haley, J. (1976). *Problem Solving Therapy.* San Francisco: Jossey-Bass.

Minuchin, S. (1974). *Families and Family Therapy.* Cambridge, MA: Harvard University Press.

Minuchin, S., & Fishman, C. (1981). *Family Therapy Techniques.* Cambridge, MA: Harvard University Press.

Watzlawick, P., Weakland, J., & Fisch, R. (1974). *Change: Principles of Problem Formation and Problem Resolution.* New York: Norton.

# 9

# Humanistic/Existential Theories

# in Family Treatment

*In this chapter, we will discuss the application of several humanistic/ existential approaches to family therapy. The three approaches covered in this chapter are (1) the person-centered approach of Carl Rogers, (2) a Gestalt approach to family therapy developed by Walter Kempler, and (3) the psychodrama approach of J. L. Moreno.*

Human capacities
Self-awareness
Self-actualization
Self-determination
Relationship
Existential death
The search for meaning
Autonomy
Responsibility

Existential aloneness
Phenomenological view
Catharsis
Reflection of content/feelings
Self-disclosure
Unfinished business
Role playing
Family sculpture

## QUESTIONS
## FOR DISCUSSION

1. How would a person-centered family therapist communicate unconditional positive regard to a family?

2. What ethical issues might be raised by using a person-centered approach in family therapy?

3. How might a therapist deal with a family member who doesn't want (or is afraid) to take part in an empty chair Gestalt experiment?

4. How might a Gestalt-oriented family therapist deal with a family member who is avoiding personal responsibility?

5. How might a psychodrama-oriented therapist deal with a family member who is a drug user?

6. What are some of the possible psychological risks associated with using psychodrama techniques with a family?

*H*umanistic theory and existential theories were relegated to separate schools of thought in the past, but because of the similarities of the philosophical underpinnings and a common focus on subjective states of being, they now are often referred to together. In this chapter, we will present these theories together as the humanistic/existential approach. The leaders of this movement include Rollo May, Carl Rogers, Abraham Maslow, James Bugenthal, Viktor Frankl, and philosophers Martin Buber and Jean-Paul Sartre (Corey, 1991).

Because of their common philosophical position, humanistic/existential therapists can utilize diverse methods to work with families, including cognitive, behavioral, and action-oriented methods. The humanistic/existential theories are generally regarded as the "third force" in psychology. The approaches to therapy tend to be largely experiential and relationship-centered. Humanistic/existential theorists argue that human behavior cannot be understood by objective and cognitive methods.

For example, a therapist utilizing a humanistic/existential approach with a family that seems to be dealing with conflicts in destructive and self-defeating ways might structure the first session by saying:

> I understand that you have come to therapy because you are not able to resolve the conflicts in your family. I am pleased that you care enough about yourselves and your family to come to therapy in hope of finding some solutions to your dilemma. A place to begin the search for solutions is to first see what each of you thinks and feels about the problem. As each of you describes your view of the problem, I want the rest of the family members to listen carefully to what this person is saying rather than thinking of how you will defend or justify your position. Also, each of you might add something about how you would like your family to be different as a result of counseling.

This initial session is designed to have each family member share his or her subjective or phenomenological world. The sharing of this world with other family members and the therapist has a therapeutic effect on everybody present, particularly if everyone is really listening to each other.

In this chapter, we will cover three main humanistic/existential approaches to family therapy: (1) the person-centered approach, (2) a Gestalt-oriented approach, and (3) a psychodrama-oriented approach.

# Goals of Humanistic/Existential Approaches

The basic goal of humanistic/existential approaches is to increase the clients' awareness of their options and potentials as well as to help them make choices and decisions (Watson, 1977). Another goal is to increase autonomy and self-actualization rather than to help clients merely adjust to societal norms. Instead, clients are encouraged to discover how they want to live their lives. Helping clients to accept their own freedom to change and grow along with helping them to accept responsibility for their own existence are also important goals. But anxiety and uncertainty often accompany the acceptance of freedom and responsibility. Another goal of the approach is to help clients face and deal with these anxieties.

# The Process of Humanistic/Existential Approaches

The helping process in family therapy focuses not only on what happens within individual members but also what happens between family members. Here is a brief description of the usual process of family therapy using a humanistic/existential framework.

1. *Milling around.* At first, clients are confused and uncertain about the purpose of the therapy. They ask, "Why are we here? What is going to happen?"
2. *Resistance to therapy.* Family members are resistant to share their thoughts and feelings. They wonder if it is safe to do so.
3. *Talking about the past.* Members describe past happenings and their feelings about these events. They are focused on the "there and then."
4. *Negative feelings.* Members begin to share present negative feelings toward each other or the therapist. They may be testing the safety of the therapy situation. They ask themselves, "Is it safe to be me, even the negative me?"

5. *Expression and exploration of personally relevant issues.* At this stage, there is enough trust to permit open expression and exploration of personally relevant material. Family members begin to feel like they can help change the family to work toward what they want it to be.

6. *Full expression of feelings in the here and now.* Members express moment-to-moment feelings toward one another. Changes in the family structure begin to take place.

7. *Healing capacity of family members.* Family members begin to turn their attention to helping each other heal the pain and suffering of others in the family. A climate of trust and freedom allows for acceptance and understanding to emerge.

8. *Self-acceptance and change.* Family members begin to accept themselves as they are in the family and changes in the family take place. Members take responsibility for their actions and are in control of changing their behavior.

9. *The facades fade away.* A sense of realness develops among family members, and this becomes a norm. Those who are less real or defensive are challenged to come out with their true feelings and thoughts.

10. *Feedback is given.* Family members get and give feedback to each other. They even request feedback so they can grow more.

11. *Confrontation occurs.* Any remaining defensiveness is confronted as members drop their politeness and protectiveness. They see each other as being able to deal with confrontation.

12. *The helping family develops.* By now reports of helping interactions outside of therapy are common. Family members are being more consistent helping agents for each other.

13. *The family encounter.* The family begins to experience itself as a unit, or as a group of interdependent members. Change in one member affects all other members. A family bond develops that is felt by all members.

14. *Fuller expression of closeness.* Family members have warm and genuine feelings toward each other. They have learned to listen to and accept each other's feelings. Disputes are now resolved with less conflict and anxiety.

15. *The family is changed.* The members now experience both oneness and separateness in their interactions with each other. They have learned a process by which they can continue to explore

and clarify values, examine and make decisions, and challenge issues that come up in the family. They are able to be as open with each other on a daily basis as they once were only in therapy sessions (Thayer, 1991).

# Advantages and Disadvantages of the Humanistic/ Existential Approach

Much has been written to support this approach. It empowers people to take responsibility for their actions and provides a framework for understanding universal human concerns. In addition, it presents the positive, hopeful view that humans can continually actualize themselves and reach their potential and that families have the potential to resolve many of their own problems. This approach has contributed much to the understanding of the essential ingredients of the therapeutic relationship. Moreover, because the theory emphasizes that techniques should follow understanding, the danger of abusing the techniques is lessened.

But the humanistic/existential approach does have limitations. It uses abstract concepts and language that many clients find difficult to understand. Long-term therapy may be required to complete the process. The theory does not work as well with families that are in crisis. In addition, it may focus too much attention on individual development rather than on family dynamics. Finally, there are no set standards for training family therapists to use this approach, leading to wide variance in expertise and training.

# Person-Centered Family Therapy

Rogers (1961) discussed the implications of using person-centered therapy with families mostly by translating the principles of individual person-centered therapy to family therapy situations. The approach fits rather naturally with family therapy because of its emphasis on the process of developing effective close relationships (Rogers, 1961). Yet, to most effectively employ the person-centered approach with families, an expansion of traditional person-centered theory is required (Anderson, 1989). Rogers theorized that family members will become more trusting of each other if the therapist is able to create the right climate in the therapy sessions. The basic conditions he listed for this climate to develop are genuineness, openness, caring, acceptance, positive regard, and reflective listening.

Several of his followers (Levant, 1978; Van der Veen, 1977) have made advances in the practice of person-centered family therapy. While the *self-concept* is at the heart of person-centered therapy for individuals, the *family concept* is at the heart of person-centered family therapy (Raskin & Van der Veen, 1970). The term *family concept* describes the feelings, attitudes, and expectations a person has toward his or her family of origin and present family. This relatively stable concept organizes and influences much of a person's behavior. According to this theory, for a family to change, the members have to change their family concept.

## *Philosophical Tenets*

Rogers and other person-centered family therapists adopted a phenomenological view of human nature. According to this view, the most important source of knowledge (epistemology) is the *experience* of the individual. The view does not concentrate on the object of experience or the subject of experience but on the point of contact between being and consciousness, which includes both subject and object. The person experiences both the object and the self at the same time, although the focus is usually on one or the other (self or object). In practical terms, a phenomenological approach examines inner space and the subjective experience of the client. Understanding and empathizing with clients' views of their experiences is the therapist's best source of knowledge about a client and his or her problems.

According to this approach, the source of reality is an individual's subjective perspective of that reality. But there are differences between a purely existential view and a purely humanistic one. The existential position, as stated by Sartre, says that although we learn of our essence through our existence, that essence is largely unknowable. The humanistic view, which is more phenomenological, says that our perception of our essential nature is what we use to guide our behavior. The humanistic theorists are more concerned with discovering this perception than with finding the ultimate truth.

The source of values (axiology), according to this approach, is a set of universal principles that cannot be totally known but is reflected somewhat in the consciousness of each individual. People are seen as essentially good, and as they become more aware or conscious, they are better able to live a life based on these values. Counseling is seen as a way to increase consciousness and allow this natural outcome to occur.

## Theoretical Constructs

**Theory of Cause**   According to the person-centered approach, people develop emotional problems because they are unable to communicate what they think and feel with others, usually because of fear of punishment or rejection. This fear is a learned adaptation to the way they were treated as a child; they withdraw from people and the world. The most common family problems that person-centered family therapy is best designed to deal with are:

- Lack of realness in dealing with other family members.
- Denial or lack of expression of important feelings in the family.
- Failing to see the individuality of each family member.
- Failing to listen to others or to have much two-way communication in the family.
- The lack of a method or process through which the family can resolve conflicts as they arise. For example, most families have no way to discuss value differences.
- The lack of awareness of social and cultural effects. These effects include the demands of career, education, peers, television, wars, and world events. Does the family become a dumping ground for frustrations that arise in these other areas? (Thayer, 1991).

**Theory of Change**   The person-centered therapist sees the individual and the family, rather than the therapist, as the agent of change. The role of the therapist is to create the proper conditions for the untapped potential of the individual and the family to be explored and integrated (Gaylin, 1989). Rogers (1980) believed that individuals have within themselves vast resources for self-understanding and for altering their self-concepts, basic attitudes, and self-directed behavior; these resources can be tapped if a definable climate of facilitative psychological attitudes can be provided. The most important facilitative attitudes, according to Rogers, are genuineness, unconditional positive regard, and empathy (Rogers, 1961). The therapist teaches these qualities through modeling and helps release untapped qualities in the person.

Genuineness is a necessary prerequisite to building relationships with family members. Otherwise, they are not likely to let the therapist into their inner family system. Also, genuine responses to the pain or grief of family members can have a powerful effect on the family system. Empathy, when used in family therapy, helps the therapist understand the subtleties of meaning and feelings that family members experience in their relationships with others, rather than just understanding each individual's inner world. Giving unconditional positive regard to family members can be empowering and often helps them feel safe enough to release long-held feelings.

## Main Therapeutic Interventions

The basic attitudes mentioned above, plus the following communication skills, are seen as necessary and sufficient for a person-centered therapist. The role of the therapist is to model and thereby teach family members how to utilize these skills. *Being attentive* is a way of deepening the therapist's contact with the client (Thayer, 1991). Attending verbal and nonverbal skills are necessary if the therapist wishes to follow the process of the family dynamics. *Reflection of content* communicates respect and assures the family that the therapist is really trying to understand their perceptions of the family situation. *Reflection of feelings* is crucial in communicating empathy and requires the therapist to pay close attention to verbal and nonverbal behavior. Therapists also need to *confront* discrepancies between verbal and nonverbal messages.

*Self-disclosure* is utilized to model effective communication and is usually a response to something that happens in the moment. For example: "When you say that to John and look away, I feel sad and wonder why you don't look at him when you tell him things that are important to you." *Showing respect* is a skill that person-centered therapists use to demonstrate caring and concern for family members. Use of *intuitive hunches* is another important skill of the therapist (Thayer, 1991). The therapist needs to utilize all of his or her senses and share these "gut" reactions and hunches with family members. These intuitive feelings often can help family members reach deeper levels of awareness and growth.

O'Leary (1989) identified the complex role of the person-centered family therapist as twofold. First, the therapist needs the skill to respond to the individual meanings of each family member, and sec-

## Person-Centered Therapy

### CASE EXAMPLE

*In the following case example, Bob and Joan have been married for six years. They came to therapy because they were "not getting along with each other." Neither seem to know why, and neither seem to know what to do. The therapist, using a person-centered approach, decided to build a relationship with each of these people and in the process hoped to teach them how to get along with each other. The therapist started with Bob and began by talking to Bob about his job and his interests outside of the relationship with Joan. This formed a good foundation for the breakthrough, which began when the therapist was talking to Joan.*

Therapist: *Tell me more about your fear of Bob leaving you.*

Joan: *I'm having another feeling right now, and I think I'm going to cry.*

Therapist: *You are feeling touched because of what I asked you.*

Joan: *Yes, it suddenly dawned on me that you really care what happens to me. I don't know if it was what you said so much as it was the way you said it. There was real caring in your voice.*

Therapist: *Sounds as though you experienced a deep sense of being cared for, something you need very much, and perhaps you are realizing for the first time how much you miss that.*

*(continued)*

ond, the therapist must be able to assess and respond to the objective reality of the family's interactional patterns.

Skills generally not utilized by the person-centered therapist include *questioning*, which often implies leading and directing, and *interpretation*. The main goals are to reflect and model, leaving the interpretation to each family member.

## Limitations of Person-Centered Family Therapy

This approach may work very well in the beginning with a family that is very fearful and resistant toward therapy, but it often has to be coupled with other more action-oriented approaches for significant

---

*(CASE EXAMPLE continued)*

Joan: *I think I have wanted Bob to care about me more than he seems to. I didn't know that was behind my loneliness.*

Bob: *I can see what you mean. I, too, felt the caring in his voice. I do care for you, Joan, but I don't know how to tell you. Please help me.*

Joan: *You just did. I felt it in my body just now. Usually I'm not open to you this way. I am guarded when you talk to me, always afraid you are going to tell me I've done something wrong. (long pause)*

Therapist: *Joan, you opened yourself to me and stayed open to what Bob said to you, and our words touched a place deep within you where you have hidden this tender, somewhat fragile need of yours. I am glad that you trusted us enough to let us in. I have warm feelings toward you right now. Bob, how are you feeling toward Joan right now?*

Bob: *I am feeling lots of love and compassion. I didn't know you (Joan) felt that way. I think I sensed your fear, and not knowing what it was, I held back saying things to you.*

*As you can see, the relationship the therapist built with each of the clients helped them to lower their barriers to intimacy with each other. By helping family members experience a positive relationship with the therapist, they learn skills to build better relationships with each other.*

---

changes in the family structure to take place. The attitudes and skills required by a person-centered approach are necessary but not sufficient to produce lasting change in most family systems.

A second limitation of the approach is that it requires that the therapist be able to tolerate loose structure and ambiguity. This aspect may not only raise the anxiety of family members more than they can tolerate but may also raise the anxiety of the therapist in a similar way.

Third, being mostly reflectors or mirrors, therapists frequently remain hidden as persons. Therapists can easily become outer-directed and remain cut off from their own feelings and reactions.

Person-centered family therapists, in their efforts not to structure the family interview, often do not provide adequate screening protection or preparation for family members. Some family members may not be ready for family therapy or may need protection or preparation to make the best use of family therapy. Ethically, family therapists need to prepare people for the possible life changes that might occur and the risks involved. The therapist must also structure the therapy situation to protect weak or defenseless family members.

Finally, some practitioners object to the lack of formal certification or academic training of many person-centered family therapists. The use of minimally trained therapists is supported by research (Carkhuff, 1969b), but this lack of extensive training has led to a reluctance to accept this approach among other highly trained professionals.

# Gestalt-Oriented Family Therapy

There is nothing in Gestalt-oriented family therapy that can be considered original. It is an updated version of what has been known through human history. The story of Adam and Eve is based on the same principle of self-awareness that this approach uses. It is also seen in Socrates' admonition "Know thyself." Today, the philosophy of Gestalt-oriented family therapy is that direct knowledge of the self is the key to good mental health (Kempler, 1991).

The leaders of this approach are Fritz Perls, James Simkin, Walter Kempler, Irving and Miriam Polster, and Joseph Zinker. Kempler broke away from Perls because he objected to Perls' "one-up, hot seat" approach, in which he would frustrate, confront, and confuse clients deliberately to produce behavior change. Kempler felt that Perls kept himself "one-up" and personally removed from the therapy situation. Kempler believed that the therapist needed to be more personally involved in the therapy as a participant and needed to share personal thoughts and feelings with clients.

Perls did very little family therapy or even group therapy. Gestalt therapy is practiced as a one-to-one model of therapy. In 1961, Kempler founded the Kempler Institute for the Development of the Family, near Los Angeles, and continued to focus primarily on family therapy. There are only a handful of books in the literature on Gestalt-oriented family therapy besides Kempler's (1965, 1968, 1981, 1991) pioneering works. These include Bauer (1979), Goulding and Goulding (1979), Hatcher (1978, 1981), Kaplan and Kaplan (1978), and Rabin (1980).

The goals of Gestalt-oriented family therapy are (1) to help individuals within a family structure develop better boundaries between themselves and other family members, and (2) to help individuals become more self-aware so they can complete unfinished business and change old, familiar patterns. There is an attempt to balance individual intrapsychic problems with interpersonal problems that show up in the family interactions. Both types of problems are dealt with in Gestalt-oriented family therapy, so there often is much shifting back and forth from a focus on the individual to a focus on the family.

## Philosophical Tenets

Although Gestalt psychology is also a phenomenological approach, there are some epistemological differences between this approach and the person-centered approach. Perls, who was influenced by psychoanalytic theory, placed much more emphasis on the inner or intrapersonal sources of knowledge than the outer or interpersonal sources of knowledge emphasized by the person-centered approach. Both theories share an emphasis on the importance of the phenomenological field of perceptions.

Perls borrowed heavily from an existential framework. His emphasis on the here and now is existential in nature as is his belief that people are essentially responsible for their own conflicts and have the capacity to resolve them. Perls believed reality could be best understood by gaining more awareness of the here and now. His most significant contribution is this focus on the here and now. He showed that all unresolved conflicts from our past are with us in the here and now and therefore are resolvable in the present situation. Talking about something that happened in the past puts the person in an observer's role removed from the conflict situation; acting it out in the present brings the elements of the original conflict to life.

This approach views awareness as being good in itself. Universal human values are believed to be good, and the more aware people are of their so-called *unfinished business*, the closer they come to these universal values. Gestalt therapy clearly does not try to help people adjust to a set of social values, which are viewed as transitory ways to stay unaware. One of the universal values is becoming unified and whole as a person. The Gestalt therapist sees *awareness* as the path to this value. With awareness, people can recognize, face, and reintegrate parts of themselves they have disowned and thus become more unified and whole (Corey, 1991).

## Theoretical Constructs

**Theory of Cause**   Gestalt-oriented family therapy is based on the premise that people have the ability and desire to understand and resolve their own problems when they are aware of and take full responsibility for all aspects of their personality and behavior. When this natural desire is blocked, disturbing behavior may result. Anger and sadness are natural reactions to the blockage and are ways of expressing a desire to return to a state of awareness and cooperation as well as frustration at not being there. The causes of these blocked experiences are often forgotten but are present in the here-and-now behavior of each person. Typically, these blocked experiences occurred in a person's encounters with his or her family of origin during childhood. The therapist attempts to help the client bring these experiences back to life in the present moment so the client can begin to gain awareness and discover what was causing the problem and complete its resolution in the present.

**Theory of Change**   A model called the Gestalt experience cycle (Rabin, 1980) shows the main elements of an experience and how to complete an incomplete experience. The cycle begins with *sensations* and *perceptions* that are learned in childhood. These include messages about what we should or should not do and what we can or cannot do. Because of these experiences, we are sensitive to particular stimuli, and when we experience these stimuli, we recall some of the original stimulus events. *Awareness* results from the ability to focus on or pay attention to a sensation. If the client is confused about what really happened in his or her childhood, he or she may have trouble bringing this sensation into awareness. Enhancing awareness and helping people understand what really happened during their childhood is central to Gestalt therapy. As clients become more aware, their bodies are stimulated to action. Clients who are blocked in their awareness may experience tension or pain; others may take ineffective action. The therapist must help the client develop appropriate ways to experience and act out the conflict.

   *Contact* is the next and probably the most crucial stage of the cycle.

People who are disturbed resist making genuine contact. Their resistance takes these forms:

- *projection,* making contact with disowned parts of the self rather than with other people;
- *introjection,* incorporating aspects of the other into the self;
- *retroflection,* turning against oneself;
- *confluence,* where the boundaries between self and other are confused; and
- *deflection,* where a wall is erected to avoid contact.

In family therapy, the therapist confronts these attempts to avoid contact and helps the client learn new ways to make contact with family members.

The final stage of the cycle is *withdrawal,* which occurs after experiences have been completed. An inability to withdraw and let go of an experience usually results in unfinished business in relationships. The therapist helps the client to let go of an experience and resolve the inner conflict.

## Main Therapeutic Interventions

The goals of Gestalt-oriented family therapy are to help family members develop clear boundaries between the self and others and to increase self-awareness so they can break free from stuck patterns and experience themselves and life more completely. As Gestalt therapy is usually an individually oriented approach, it may be useful to see how it could be utilized effectively in a family therapy mode.

There are several differing views as to how to utilize Gestalt therapy with a family. Hatcher (1978) recommended a blend of both individual and family therapy. He suggested that a focus on the individual is appropriate when dealing with intrapersonal and boundary issues and that a family therapy focus is appropriate when dealing with interpersonal and transactional issues. He suggested building a contract with a family that permits the shift back and forth within the context of the family therapy session rather than scheduling separate sessions.

Bauer (1979) suggested a similar arrangement using the empty chair technique as a tool for resolving an individual's contact-boundary problems. Although he focused on the family as a whole, Bauer recommended using Gestalt experiments such as exaggeration of problem behavior, making rounds, reversal techniques, and rehearsals.

Kaplan and Kaplan (1978) focused on the process of family therapy to determine whether to intervene with the individual, with a particular subsystem, or with the family as a whole. They described three functions or skills therapists must have to promote change: observing, focusing, and facilitating. By *observing* the process carefully, the therapist can help the family become more aware of its dynamics. *Focusing* means helping the family better understand specific aspects of its process, which may include use of exaggeration techniques. *Facilitating* is defined as helping the family move toward constructive reintegration. Gestalt experiments are used in this part to help produce a new integration. The concept of *polarities* is extremely important in Gestalt therapy. For every choice of behavior a person makes, there is a polar opposite that may be a disowned aspect of the client's personality. Helping clients identify, own, and take responsibility for the polarities in their personality is a significant part of Gestalt therapy (Perls, 1969).

Gestalt-oriented family therapy can be viewed as an eclectic approach. Because it still focuses on individual change, it may be possible to utilize individually oriented techniques drawn from bioenergetics, Rolfing, TA, person-centered, and behavioral approaches.

## Limitations of Gestalt-Oriented Therapy

One limitation of Gestalt-oriented therapy is that it involves an anti-intellectual attitude that discounts the importance of cognitive understanding. Practitioners emphasize experience and feelings rather than building cognitive structures with clients. In addition, some Gestalt techniques can be abusive. There is a danger of taking a "one-up" posture with clients. The therapist often is so directive that he or she can create a dependency relationship with the client being the underdog. Gestalt therapists may utilize dramatic catharsis and then insist their clients create personal meaning from the catharsis without helping them work through and integrate the experience. Gestalt therapists can easily hide behind their techniques, and they tend to emphasize a "quick fix" instead of encouraging clients to grow and change over time. Another problem with Gestalt therapy is the jargon that the therapist and client may use to avoid deeper issues. Phrases like "stay in the here and now" or "take responsibility for yourself" can become rigid rules and not just guidelines. Finally, very little research has been done on Gestalt therapy, and virtually none has been done on Gestalt-oriented family therapy.

# ▪ *Psychodrama-Oriented Family Therapy*

Psychodrama was created in Vienna in 1921 by J. L. Moreno (1983). In that year, he opened the Theatre of Spontaneity. Those who participated in the theatre were not professional actors, nor did they use scripts. Instead, they acted out in a spontaneous manner the events reported in the daily newspaper or topics suggested by members of the audience. After an event or topic was acted out, the actors and audience were invited to comment on their experiences during the performance. Moreno found that both the actors and those in the audience experienced a catharsis or release of pent-up feelings as a result of being in the play or observing the play. As a result of this experiment, Moreno began to develop specialized therapeutic techniques that became the foundation for psychodrama.

Psychodrama is designed to help people express their feelings in a spontaneous and dramatic way through the use of role playing. Because the work involves the use of many different players, it is good to use in a group setting and lends itself to family therapy as well. Although it is interpersonally oriented, psychodrama is intended to help people explore intrapersonal aspects of their lives. Psychodrama recognizes the importance of the social environment and of action methods in the treatment of family problems (Moreno, 1983).

Psychodrama was the precursor of many other action-oriented approaches, including Gestalt, encounter groups, behavioral approaches, bioenergetics, guided fantasy, psychosynthesis, play therapy, and improvisational dramatics. Other family systems approaches, such as family sculpting and role playing, often use psychodramatic techniques originally developed by Moreno.

## Philosophical Tenets

Like Perls, Moreno based his ideas on the notion that people are the product of their experiences and are responsible for their actions. This existential position is similar to the philosophies of Camus and Sartre, both of whom emphasized that people are alone in the universe of their experience. This aloneness, however, provides a common experience for all people, a concept that forms the epistemological basis of existentialism. People share the common experience of being as well as the common fear of nonbeing. The belief that death is absolute also frees people to choose to either accept their fate and enjoy

### Gestalt Therapy

## CASE
## EXAMPLE

*This case, taken from Kempler's approach (1981, pp. 178–179), shows how a husband who feels victimized by his wife might be confronted.*

Husband: *What can I do? She stops me at every turn.*

Therapist: (sarcastically, to provoke him) *You poor thing, overpowered by that terrible lady over there.*

Husband: (ducking) *She means well.*

Therapist: *You're whimpering at me, and I can't stand to see a grown man whimpering.*

Husband: (firmer) *I tell you, I don't know what to do.*

Therapist: *Like hell you don't* (offering and at the same time pushing). *You know as well as I that if you want her off your back you just have to tell her to get the hell off your back and mean it. That's one thing you could do instead of that mealy-mouthed apology "She means well."*

Husband: (looks quizzical; obviously he is not sure if he wants to chance it with either of us but is reluctant to retreat to the whimpering child posture again.) *I'm not used to talking that way to people.*

Therapist: *Then you'd better get used to it. You're going to have to shape up this family into a group that's worth living with, instead of a menagerie where your job is to come in periodically and crack the whip on the little wild animals.*

Husband: *You sure paint a bad picture.*

Therapist: *If I'm wrong, be man enough to disagree with me and don't wait to get outside of here to whimper to your wife about how you didn't know what to say here.*

Husband: (visibly bristling and speaking more forcefully) *I don't know that you're wrong about what you're saying.*

*(continued)*

*(CASE EXAMPLE continued)*

Therapist:  *But how do you like what I'm saying?*
Husband:  *I don't. Nor do I like the way you're going about it.*
Therapist:  *I don't like the way you're going about things either.*
Husband:  *There must be a more friendly way than this.*
Therapist:  *Sure, you know, whimper.*
Husband:  (with deliberate softness) *You're really a pusher, aren't you?*
Therapist:  *How do you like me?*
Husband:  *I don't.*
Therapist:  *You keep forgetting to say that part of your message. I can see it all over you, but you never say it.*
Husband:  (finally in anger) *I'll say what I damn please. You're not going to tell me how to talk ... and how do you like that?* (he socks his hand)
Therapist:  *I like it a helluva lot better than your whimpering. What is your hand saying?*
Husband:  *I'd like to punch you in the nose, I suppose.*
Therapist:  *You suppose?*
Husband:  (firmly) *Enough. Get off my back and stay off.*
Therapist:  (delighted to see his assertion) *Great. Now, about the rest of them* (waving to the family). *I'd like to see if there's anything you'd like to say to them.*
Husband:  (looks at each one of them and then settles on his wife) *He's right. I take an awful lot of nonsense from you, and I hate it* (still socking his hand). *I don't intend to take anymore. I'll settle with the kids my way. If you don't like it, that's too bad.*

This excerpt shows how Gestalt-oriented family therapy might be used to help a client reown something that has been disowned or projected. Unlike the typical empty chair technique, the therapist acted out the polarity of the client's aggressive side until the client took over the part.

life in the here and now or to try to deny or run away from the inevitable and therefore be ruled by fear and guilt.

Like Sartre, Moreno believed that experiences determine a person's essence. People are what they do or experience. Those holding this view do not deny the possibility of preexisting human nature but do not believe it is possible to discover it and therefore ignore its role in human development. The only reality worth considering is a person's experience. According to this view, the source of value is self-awareness and the commitment of the person to take responsibility for him- or herself, as well as exercising his or her ability to respond (responsibility). Evil involves the failure to act according to one's ability.

## Theoretical Constructs

**Theory of Cause**   Moreno clearly delineated the role of social forces in causing disturbances. The forces of the family, society, occupational groups, and religious groups all shape the personality. Moreno theorized that one of the main results of this socialization process is that most people lack spontaneity and live a sort of "as if" existence, never fully entering into their experiences. Moreno observed that young children were able to enter into spontaneous role playing and fantasy situations and freely express their feelings, but adults had great difficulty in doing so. He saw that people develop limiting scripts for their lives and rigid, stereotyped responses to most situations.

Moreno stated that instead of meeting eye-to-eye and face-to-face, parents see in their children only what they want to see and are unable to truly mirror for the child. On the other hand, children look at their parents and see omnipotent, perfect gods instead of scared, limited human beings. This condition may cause identity confusion for the child.

With this confusion as a base, most children grow up with distorted views of how the social order works. These distortions are best diagnosed through the use of role playing or action drama. If these distortions are not uncovered and removed before children leave their families, then the children's perceptions of the larger cultural milieu are also distorted, which leads to distortion at the universal level. The result of all these distortions is that people live in a world they hardly even recognize. Most people adapt to their own distortions; they are cut off from their own life force and spontaneity, living life in a bubble, unable to break out, and unable to grow and develop very much without feeling crowded and restricted (Moreno, 1951).

**Theory of Change**   The cure, so to speak, lies in the client's willingness to risk breaking the bubble through action. In this approach, insight comes as the result of some action. Moreno saw the psychodramatic method as the way to break through the bubble and learn how to be spontaneous. The method uses five instruments: the stage, the client, the director, the auxiliary egos, and the audience.

The *stage* provides the client with a living space that is multidimensional and highly flexible. As the reality of the client is usually much too limited, the stage allows for a new freedom to emerge. The clients are asked to be themselves on the stage and to portray their own private worlds. Once they are warmed up to the task, clients are asked to give a spontaneous account of some problem in their daily lives. The *client* is encouraged to become involved with all the people and things present in this problem, which can mean encountering internal parts of him- or herself as well as other people—past, present, and future—who are involved in some way in the problem.

The *director* serves as the producer, therapist, and analyst. As the producer, he or she develops the production in line with the life script of the client, never letting the production bog down or move too fast. As the therapist, he or she confronts, reflects feelings and content, summarizes, and gives information. The analyst interprets and helps the client integrate the material into his or her life space. *Auxiliary egos* are extensions of the client and are used to portray the actual or imagined personas of their real life drama. They help model and teach the client new ways to act in this and other similar situations. The *audience* is used as a sounding board of public opinion, helping the client see aspects of the drama that he or she overlooked. The client also helps the audience, because people from the audience see aspects of their own life drama being played out on the stage.

Psychodrama has three phases: (1) the warm-up phase, (2) the action phase, and (3) the discussion or sharing phase. The therapeutic element in psychodrama is *catharsis*, or release. This catharsis is produced *only* if a climate fostering spontaneity can be created in the warm-up stage. Such a climate requires that (1) the client feels safe and trusts the direction, (2) the expression of emotions and intuition is permitted, (3) an attitude of playfulness is established, and (4) a willingness to explore novel behavior is encouraged.

During the action phase, the spontaneity of the drama produces a catharsis that enables the client to reexperience repressed feelings and distorted thoughts. This catharsis can then be utilized by a skillful director to enable a new drama to emerge. With the help of the auxiliary egos, the director produces the new drama with the client and allows for new roles and actions to occur within the safety of the therapeutic setting. These new dramas can be properly rehearsed and reinforced by the director, the auxiliary egos, and the audience before the client tries them out in his or her life space.

During the discussion stage, the director protects the client from interpretative or negative feedback because the client is in a very vulnerable position. This protection is necessary to help the client integrate what he or she just experienced. The director asks for personal sharing by the audience, asking them how the psychodrama helped them. The catharsis that occurs in members of the audience helps them and the client achieve some integration (Moreno, 1983).

## Main Therapeutic Interventions

A number of psychodramatic techniques that lend themselves quite well to family therapy are listed and briefly described next.

1. *Self-presentation.* The therapist lets all family members present how they see themselves in relationship to every other family member. This technique enables the therapist to discover who is enmeshed in the family system and who is an outsider.
2. *Presentation of the other.* The therapist who wishes to know how family members see each other may ask them to present other family members as they see them. The therapist may wish to interview the person who is presenting another family member to get a more complete picture of how he or she sees the other family member.
3. *Role playing.* This is an extension of the "presentation of the other," with a possible role reversal. Two or more family members reverse roles and act out some scene. The therapist encourages maximum expression of feelings in conflict situations. The technique helps to quickly reveal the distortions in the relationships and to correct them, and it can produce new options and much insight into conflict situations.
4. *Double technique.* Sometimes the therapist or another family member has to act as a double for the person to express feelings and content that are blocked or repressed. This technique is often used as a catalyst to get a family member to express

feelings or thoughts that have been inhibited. It is possible to use multiple doubles to help portray mixed or conflicting feelings as well.

5. *Family sculpture.* In this technique, the therapist asks all the family members to sculpt the family the way they see it in relationship to themselves and in relationship to each other. This means physically placing them in postures and having them hold the position as a freeze frame to examine (Duhl, Kantor, & Duhl, 1973). This technique can also be used to choreograph new patterns by experimenting with different sculpture formations and allowing them to change in ways that members would like. This powerful intervention can help realign family relationships (Papp, 1980).

## Limitations of Psychodrama-Oriented Family Therapy

Although it is possible to uncover feelings and repressed material very quickly using this technique, it requires a sensitive therapist to use the material effectively. Another problem with the technique is that, like other experiential approaches, this approach does not have a strong research base (Rudestam, 1982). This approach requires specialized training and supervised experience; yet many practitioners utilize psychodramatic techniques without additional training or supervision.

# Summary

The main purpose of this chapter was to show how three humanistic/existential theories have been applied to family treatment. These applications provide a way for practitioners to bridge the gap from individual therapy to family therapy. In the next chapter, three major family systems theories will be examined and described.

**Psychodrama**

**C A S E**
**E X A M P L E**

*Mr. and Mrs. Thomas, their 17-year-old son, John, and their 15-year-old daughter, Ann, came to family therapy because of unresolved conflicts that had beset the family. In the initial interview, the major problem discussed was that Mrs. Thomas criticized her daughter and compared her unfavorably with her older brother. Ann was asked to present or role play the way she experienced her mother. Ann was happy to show her unexpressed feelings in the safety of the family therapy session as she portrayed her mother's attacks. She said, as her mother, "Ann, you are so lazy. Look at you, you don't do anything but sit around watching TV. John is always busy with his job, school activities, and his friends, and all you do is sit there."*

*Mrs. Thomas had initiated the family therapy. It turned out that she was also very critical of Mr. Thomas, who she said was always too busy at work. Mr. Thomas defended himself, saying that he stayed away because she was always nagging him.*

*The therapist attempted to uncover their patterns and help them discover new ways of behaving with each other through role playing. Ann became John, Mrs. Thomas became Ann, and John and Mr. Thomas reversed roles. The therapist helped them all express their feelings toward the rest of the family members. Ann, as John, said, "I feel isolated and alone inside this family. Everyone just expects me to do well, but I don't feel they like me, and I'm always afraid I'll screw up." Mr. Thomas, as John, said, "I'm a lot like Dad. I run away from conflict and just keep busy." Later Mrs. Thomas reversed roles with Mr. Thomas. As Mr. Thomas, she said, "I wish I could bring some order to this family."*

*The therapist worked with Mr. Thomas to show him what he could say and do to help bring order to the family. Using the double technique, with the coaching of the therapist, he tried out several possibilities. To his surprise, the family members responded positively. The therapist suggested scheduling a regular meeting time during which they could clear their feelings and plan family activities. Mr. Thomas was assigned the role of leading these meetings. The family role played an actual meeting during one session to learn how it might use this type of meeting to resolve conflicts.*

## SUGGESTED READINGS

Kempler, W. (1982). *Experiential Therapy with Families.* New York: Brunner/Mazel.

Moreno, J. L. (1946). *Psychodrama.* Boston: Beacon House.

Rogers, C. R. (1951). *Client Centered Therapy.* Boston: Houghton Mifflin.

Rogers, C. R. (1972). *Becoming Partners: Marriage and Its Alternatives.* New York: Dell.

Thayer, L. (1991). "Toward a Person-Centered Approach to Family Therapy." In A. Horne & J. L. Passmore, eds., *Family Counseling and Therapy*, 2nd ed. Itasca, IL: Peacock.

# 10

# Humanistic/Existential Systems Theories

*In this chapter, we will present two theories of family therapy based in humanistic and existential thought, the theories of Virginia Satir (1967, 1972) and Carl Whitaker (1976, 1981). Both of these theories emphasize individual differences and the belief in human potential. In addition, we will present the narrative/conversational approach to therapy developed by Michael White and David Epston (1990a and b). This approach includes elements of constructivist theory (Watzlawick, 1984), the human potential movement (Rogers, 1961), and poststructuralism (Parry, 1991); all of which suggest the ability of individuals to recreate themselves and their families through the use of new and more effective language and metaphors.*

Self-concept

Family communication

Family rules

Placater

Blamer

Computer

Distracter

Congruence

Battle for structure

Battle for initiative

Co-therapy

Three-generation therapy

Externalization

Therapeutic letters

Reauthored narrative

## QUESTIONS

## FOR DISCUSSION

1. According to Satir's communications theory, what is the cause of emotional illness in individuals?

2. Why did Satir believe the personal qualities of the counselor are so important in family therapy?

3. What types of problems are families typically experiencing when they seek treatment from a therapist trained in Satir's communications theory?

4. What are the major techniques Satir used to help family members develop self-esteem?

5. What are the characteristics of a healthy family according to Whitaker?

6. What are the battles for structure and initiative? Why are these important in therapy?

7. Why is having a co-therapist important in Whitaker's family therapy?

8. What are the common errors made by family counselors? How can these errors be avoided?

9. How does narrative therapy employ elements of the historical approach to treatment with elements of brief therapy?

10. How would you use therapeutic letters in your treatment of families? Do you think the time involved in preparing the letters would be justified? Why, or why not?

11. Why is externalization of problems so important in narrative therapy?

12. Why are exceptions so important in narrative therapy?

*T*he three theories presented in this chapter, those of Virginia Satir, Carl Whitaker, and Michael White and David Epston, are based in a belief in individual differences and human potential. Humanistic/existential therapists believe that individuals and families have a drive toward wholeness and health. Therapy should encourage the family members to identify and come into full contact with their experiences. This process of experiencing is the vehicle for enhanced self-worth and concomitant family improvement. Humanistic/existential therapists are more interested in what is currently occurring in the family than in past memories. To the extent that past events are directly related to current struggles, however, they may be explored in treatment.

The overall goal of humanistic/existential family therapy is to encourage family members to have a corrective experience based on experiencing immediate family issues. Throughout that corrective experience, family members learn how to deal creatively with future issues that will emerge in the family. The discussion of Satir's communications theory is followed by a description of the symbolic-experiential therapy formulated by Whitaker and the narrative approach used by White, Epston, and others.

## ▇ Satir's Communications Theory

Born in 1916, Virginia Satir completed her graduate degree in psychiatric social work and began training family therapists at the Illinois State Psychiatric Institute in Chicago in 1955. In 1959 she became one of the founding members of the Mental Research Institute in Palo Alto, California, where she worked with Don Jackson, Jay Haley, Jules Riskin, and others who were completing research on communication in schizophrenic families. In *Conjoint Family Therapy*, first published in 1964, she put forth her family therapy model. In a revised edition (Satir, 1983), she began to define the humanistic, existential foundation of her communications theory. Satir also had served as director of the residential training program at Esalen Institute, Big Sur, California. Satir was one of the most widely respected and emulated family therapists. Her genuine warmth and caring for families seemed to be always present. Satir died in 1988 at the age of 76.

## Philosophical Tenets and Key Theoretical Constructs

Satir viewed her theory as a dynamic and evolving concept rather than a set of rigid principles. As such, she considered her model of therapy with families to constantly be in process. She was continually seeking to improve the model by refining her techniques. In her work with families, Satir attempted to identify the processes that occur in all relationships involving human beings. She wanted to help heal those relationships, which would then lead to the growth and development of the self-concepts of the members of the family. According to Satir, every relationship is an encounter between two people at a particular moment in time. In contrast to the cognitive/behavioral systems theorists, Satir attempted to create genuine encounters between family members, to identify and deal with concealed feelings, and to heal the pain in the family.

Satir (1988) believed that an effective family therapy theory integrated the four basic parts of the self, which are: (1) the mind, (2) the body, (3) the report of the senses, and (4) social relationships. The order of this list suggests Satir may have placed more emphasis on the functioning of individuals within the family than other systems theorists included in this book. Satir believed that relationships would be stronger and more functional if the persons in the relationships had strong self-concepts. Thus, she placed much emphasis in therapy on development of strong self-concepts in the family members to make more functional relationships possible.

In keeping with her fluid and open process approach to therapy, Satir employed principles and ideas obtained from the disciplines of dance, drama, religion, medicine, communications, education, and the behavioral sciences. She believed that effective family counselors do not omit any useful tool to help the family, whether it comes from a discipline typically associated with psychotherapy or not (Satir, 1988).

Satir made three key points concerning therapy and change.

1. The individual needs to observe the self in interaction with significant others, including the family system.

2. The individual needs to recognize how behavior and self-concept are products of the family system itself.
3. All family members need to understand the points above; this understanding may occur in therapy when the process of therapy allows family members to experience each other genuinely and practice new interactional behaviors.

Further, Satir believed that effective therapy must be flexible and variable to be most helpful. She may have counseled families for an hour, or she may have worked with them in a marathon session lasting over a weekend. Thus, the *time* of therapy is flexible and variable. Satir may have treated families in her office, their home, or at a park or workplace. Thus, the *place* of therapy is flexible. After meeting with the family as a unit and gaining a solid understanding of the situation, Satir would meet with individuals, couples, siblings, spouses, or any other important family subsystem. Thus, *who will be seen* is flexible and variable. She worked alone, with a co-therapist, or with more than one co-therapist. The co-therapist could have been of either gender. Thus the *use of therapists* is flexible and variable.

Furthermore, Satir used techniques she believed would be helpful for the family from virtually any discipline. Thus, *techniques and procedures* for therapy are flexible and variable. This ability to use a wide variety of approaches and therapeutic plans is characteristic of therapists who work from humanistic/existential theoretical orientations. Because of this flexibility and variability of approach, however, duplication of the treatment methods of humanistic/existential therapists like Satir by other therapists and researchers is very difficult (Gurman & Kniskern, 1981b).

Like most therapists, Satir (1983) was interested in effective outcome for family treatment. She believed that the therapist's answers to the following questions strongly influence the type of therapy provided.

1. What causes illness?
2. What makes illness go away?
3. What makes people grow?

Satir provided answers to these questions and developed a model of treatment based on her answers. She believed that illness is caused when individuals are unable to establish the types of relationships they desire with the people who are most important to them. Specifically, these relationships are dysfunctional because of an inability of the family members to communicate effectively with each other. Illness goes away when people are able to honestly and openly relate to those who are important to them without fear of rejection and threat to their self-concepts. This objective is accomplished through therapy that emphasizes encounters between individuals in the family and the open discussion and resolution of important issues.

As a growth-oriented therapist, Satir did not believe that resolution of a presenting problem is sufficient. She believed that her therapy was effective only if she was able to create an environment for the family that was supportive of the continued positive growth of the individuals and of the relationships in the family.

Finally, in growth-oriented family therapy, the therapist is particularly important. Satir was willing to risk herself in therapy, to be spontaneous, and to establish intimate contact with family members to support their growth and self-esteem. The use of self in this manner is unique to the humanistic/existential approach to family therapy. The techniques are not designed to achieve specific behavioral outcomes. Rather, therapy and the encounters that occur within the therapy are designed to help individuals become more congruent, genuine, caring, and more capable of taking risks in relationship with others.

## Main Therapeutic Interventions

Because Virginia Satir held the optimistic worldview that individuals have within them the potential for growth and wholeness, her techniques and therapeutic interventions were designed to allow people to fully express their potential in relationships with other family members. This approach stresses individual growth and development within the context of the family, and it encourages individuals to take risks, to openly express their feelings to those they care about, and to take responsibility for their own behavior. Specifically, Satir believed that growth can take place only when the family communicates effectively and is able to validate and enhance the self-worth of its members.

In her book *The New Peoplemaking*, Satir (1988) described the family as a factory that is in the business of producing people. More specifically, she focused on the adults in the family as the peoplemakers. Thus, as the *architects of the family*, Satir placed special responsibility on the parents for nurturing their children and maintaining of an effective and loving family environment.

Families that chose Satir for therapy tended to be experiencing problems in one or more of the following ways:

1. The self-worth of family members was too low.
2. The ability of the members to share thoughts and ideas was weak. Communication was vague, indirect, and not really honest.
3. Family rules were autocratically developed, rigidly enforced, and everlasting.
4. The family's link to the societal system was based on fear, acquiescence, and blaming.

Through her therapy, Satir helped the family members develop increased self-worth; clear, direct, and honest communication; flexible and appropriate rules; and open and hopeful links to society (Satir, 1983).

Virginia Satir was a very charismatic and deeply caring therapist. She very much exemplified to her clients the characteristics she hoped to help them develop. Because she was warm and caring, her ability to develop meaningful relationships with family members was excellent. Thus, she was able to ask important and possibly threatening questions of family members without jeopardizing the relationships she had developed and nurtured.

For instance, Satir might ask each family member how it felt to be a member of the family right now. With this type of question, Satir accomplished at least two goals. She introduced affect, or feeling, to the therapy ("How does it feel?"), and she introduced the importance of the here and now ("right now"). Such questions elicit varied responses from family members that provide the therapist with data about the self-worth of members, communication within the family, family rules, and the family's link with society.

In *Conjoint Family Therapy*, Satir (1983) described in detail the role and functions of the therapist. We will describe some of the most critical skills she delineated for successful therapy.

First, the therapist recognizes that the family members coming to therapy will be fearful. They will be unsure whether therapy will help or hurt their situation. They are afraid that they may learn things in therapy that they don't want to know, and they are afraid to ask questions. Because the family is afraid, the therapist must be unafraid. In other words, the therapist is quite confident of her ability to help the family.

Furthermore, the therapist creates a setting in which the family members may take the risk of looking clearly at themselves and their behaviors and perhaps make changes to these behaviors. The confident therapist will ask the questions that are necessary to allow the family to experience this openness. The therapist is sensitive to the risk that the family members are taking as they disclose their feelings. Because all families are idiosyncratic, the therapist checks out all assumptions, including those made by family members and those of the therapist. The therapist gains the family's trust by being unafraid to help the family explore itself and the thoughts, feelings, and behaviors of its members. The therapist gives the family confidence by showing that therapy has direction and purpose and by asking questions that elicit the information the therapist and family members need to bring about family growth and change.

Once the therapeutic relationship has been established, the therapist continues to help family members look at themselves more objectively and talk to one another about what they are learning. Thus, the therapist encourages feedback among the family members about how each member may look to others. This feedback must be given in a helpful and nonjudgmental way. In daily living, most people do not get this type of feedback. Clients appreciate feedback from the therapist and other family members when it is provided in a sensitive manner. In addition, the therapist provides specific information about communication to family members and models effective communication through nonjudgmental feedback.

Central to effective therapy is the ability to help family members *develop positive self-esteem.* For the family members to be able to relate effectively to others and present their own points of view, they must feel good about themselves and their thoughts and feelings. The therapist assists each client in the development of self-esteem using these techniques:

1. Making "I value you" comments to the client
2. Identifying client strengths and reporting these to the client
3. Asking the client questions that are in his or her area of expertise. Thus, the client feels competent
4. Emphasizing that the client may ask for clarification if the therapist's communication is not clear
5. Asking each family member what he or she can do to bring happiness to other members (Satir, 1983).

Building self-esteem is a critical aspect of the therapy. Satir's communications theory emphasizes the idea of the therapist and the family working together as a team to solve family problems. The therapist must be perceived as a knowledgeable expert who works at the same level as members of the family, cares for them, and helps them along rather than telling them how they should proceed.

The therapist also needs the ability to structure the therapy sessions. The therapist sets rules for therapy that will encourage clients to listen to each other and respect the opinions of other members. For instance, a therapy rule might be that each person must speak for herself or that the family members do not engage in disruptive activities in therapy. By providing this structure, family members will feel secure and will begin to explore their issues in therapy.

The core of Satir's theory is the development of effective communication skills for all family members. Once these skills are developed, they may be used to maintain and enhance self-esteem, negotiate family rules, and connect the family with the external social system. Satir (1988) developed a creative description of the types of dysfunctional communication patterns that may be adopted by family members. These styles are:

1. *Placater.* This type of communicator attempts to keep others from getting upset. The placater says, "Whatever you want is fine with me," but in reality feels that he or she is of no value and is helpless to change.

2. *Blamer.* This type communicates in a way that makes the other person believe he or she is at fault and that the communicator is strong. The blamer seems to always say, "You can't do anything right," and finds fault with others. In reality, the blamer feels unsuccessful and lonely.

3. *Computer.* This type communicates in a logical and super-reasonable way that takes the emotion out of any situation. He or she establishes self-worth by out-reasoning others. The super-reasonable computer appears calm and in control. However, the computer uses his or her style to cover the vulnerability he or she feels in life.

4. *Distracter.* The distracter attempts to move the focus of attention away from a potentially threatening issue to some irrelevant or tangential situation. These types use themselves to deflect attention away from family problems. Distracters of-

ten seem flighty and scatterbrained, but inside they feel they are not valued and cared about.

Family members are taught about these communication styles and encouraged to identify which styles they and others in their family use. The therapist then works with them on ways to eliminate these ineffective styles and replace them with open, congruent, and direct communication.

Satir (1983) believed treatment should terminate when:

1. Family members can complete transactions and seek clarification without threat.
2. Members can recognize hostility from others and reflect this interpretation to the sender.
3. Members become able to understand how others view them.
4. Members can provide nonblaming feedback to others about their behavior.
5. Members can openly share hopes, fears, and expectations.
6. Members can disagree.
7. Members can make choices.
8. Members can learn through practice.
9. Members are no longer bound by past models and inappropriate rules.
10. Members can be congruent in communication with a minimum of hidden messages.

Satir helped families develop these characteristics so the family environment became a haven where children were nurtured and developed as responsible persons with high levels of self-esteem. She believed that effective communication is critical in this process and that parents, as the architects of the family, need to take responsibility for ensuring that these conditions exist in the family. Her warm, humanistic approach to treatment is acclaimed by many as a breath of fresh air in a profession that is dominated by technique-oriented theories.

## Strengths and Limitations of Satir's Communications Theory

This approach to family therapy is one of the most widely accepted by therapists trained in individual psychotherapy because it has the stated goal of increasing the self-worth of the individual family members. Increased self-worth is often one of the chief goals of individually oriented counseling theories. Thus, a major strength of this approach is that it is readily accepted by therapists working with individuals and is an excellent first theory for counselors to employ in family therapy. Other strengths of the approach are:

- Satir's approach emphasizes the importance of the personhood of the therapist. Family therapists are more than well-trained technicians. They should be warm, caring, and empathic to the needs of the family.
- Satir's approach recognizes and deals with the feelings of individual members of the family in treatment. The identification and exploration of feelings is recognized as an important aspect of the therapy.
- Satir' approach recognizes the importance of excellent communication skills in dealing with family members' feelings. By openly recognizing and dealing with feelings using healthy communication patterns, family members experience more respect from others and a heightened sense of self-worth. This increased self-worth through effective communication leads to increased family health.

The major limitation of Satir's approach to family therapy is that, although her charismatic style of treatment has attracted thousands of students, the approach remains uniquely Satir's. Satir's ability to connect with each family member in her own special warm, loving, and nurturing way had a major influence on the family's ability to change in treatment. Because the success of treatment relies heavily on the personality of the therapist, it may be difficult to train therapists in this approach. Thus, the major limitation of Satir's growth-oriented approach to family therapy is that it is not a systematic method for family treatment that can be easily replicated by other therapists.

## Whitaker's Symbolic-Experiential Family Therapy

Carl Whitaker (1918–1995) was a psychiatrist who had been active in family therapy since before its formal recognition in the early 1950s. Whitaker developed and refined his model of family therapy, called symbolic-experiential family therapy (Whitaker & Keith, 1981), through collaboration with several colleagues, including David Keith, Augustus Napier, and John Warkentin. Whitaker, who had previously been trained

### Satir's Communication Theory

C A S E

E X A M P L E

*Mr. and Mrs. Smith sought family therapy because their daughter was experiencing feelings of hopelessness about her future. The therapist requested that the entire family come for the initial sessions. At the first session, all members were present. Mr. Smith was a successful systems analyst for a data processing firm. Mrs. Smith was a homemaker with numerous interests and talents in the arts. Debby, the identified patient, was 15 years old and had average grades as well as a tremendous drive to play basketball, which was not supported by her parents. John was 7 years old. He was viewed by the family members as being very cute and not part of the problem.*

*The therapist began by gathering information about the family and how it resolved issues. During the information-gathering period, the therapist worked to develop the self-concept of each family member by identifying the strengths of the members. The therapist introduced the concept of communication styles and asked the family members to evaluate their styles. It was found that Dad was a super-reasonable computer; Mom was a placater trying to make everyone else happy at her own expense; Debby was a blamer who was angry at Dad for not encouraging her in her sports activity; and John was a distracter who could be counted on to be cute whenever family tensions increased.*

*Once the therapist helped the members recognize their communication styles, work began on developing effective communication patterns. As communication improved, hidden feelings were expressed by Mom, Dad, Debby, and John. Debby's symptoms of depression lifted. Mom became less concerned with making the family run smoothly and began to develop her artistic interests. Dad became more playful and experienced less need to analyze the feelings of family members. Finally, John remained cute, but his cuteness was no longer needed to distract family members from emerging issues in the family.*

as an obstetrician/gynecologist, became board certified in psychiatry during World War II. His early experience was as a psychiatric administrator at a small hospital. He later received training in child guidance and play therapy. He treated family members separately, as was the practice in those days.

Whitaker said that he began to formulate ideas about mental illness and its treatment because of what he learned from these experiences. In his work with patients, Whitaker noticed that his most effective interventions were made when he acted spontaneously and genuinely to a situation presented by a patient rather than when attempting to intervene based on some theoretical construct. Thus, Whitaker began to hypothesize that change was the result of client experiences rather than therapeutic education.

A classic example of this is when Whitaker used a baby bottle left by a previous patient's child for nurturing subsequent adult patients. This "technique" was effective for patients with all sorts of problems as long as Whitaker was invested in the notion of providing mothering to the patient. As he began to move on to other ideas about treatment, the baby bottle intervention was no longer effective. In a second classic example, Whitaker dozed off during an interview with a client and then shared his dream with the client as a part of the therapeutic process. This technique proved valuable when it was a spontaneous and experiential part of treatment. However, when it became a therapeutic technique to be taught to others, it lost its effectiveness.

As with many of the family therapy pioneers, Whitaker began to formulate ideas about family interaction in psychopathology based on work with schizophrenic patients and their families. His most widely recognized work began at Emory University in Atlanta, Georgia, and was continued when he accepted a position at the School of Medicine at the University of Wisconsin in 1965. As one of the senior members of the family therapy profession, Whitaker was a sought-after speaker and conducted numerous workshops throughout the country and the world.

## *Philosophical Tenets and Key Theoretical Constructs*

Classifying symbolic-experiential family therapy as a humanistic/existential theory may be questioned by some. Whitaker believed that theory itself can be harmful to clients because it allows the therapist to remain removed from the intimate contact he believed is necessary for therapeutic change to occur (Whitaker, 1976). Thus, Whitaker's approach to family therapy may be viewed as a moment-to-moment encounter with the family based on the therapist's own experience as well as caring for the family members. This moment-to-moment nature of symbolic-experiential therapy, coupled with the importance Whitaker placed on the ability of the therapist to become genuinely involved with the family, leads us to classify this "nontheory" in the humanistic/existential grouping.

Key tenets of symbolic-experiential family therapy are developed with caution because therapists using this approach do not want to establish a set of rules for therapy. Rather, this theory is constantly open to change and depends ultimately on the therapist's intuition and understanding of family problems. Key tenets of the theory were identified by Whitaker and Keith (1981) in their description of the healthy family. Therapy is designed to help families develop the following characteristics.

- Family health is a process of perpetual becoming.
- The healthy family is able to use constructive negative input to improve functioning.
- A healthy family is composed of three generations that maintain healthy separation and autonomy.
- Family roles are flexible, and members should be encouraged to exchange roles and explore various family roles.
- The distribution of power in a family is flexible.
- Healthy families develop an "as if" structure that allows tremendous latitude in behaviors tolerated in the family.
- Family members are free to behave temporarily in "crazy" ways without being viewed as permanently deviant by the family.
- The healthy family continues to grow in spite of adversities.
- The healthy family develops a functional reality about itself that is evolutionary and changes as necessary.
- Healthy families are not symptom-free; rather, they are able to deal with symptoms as part of family growth and development.
- Problems with children are opportunities for parents to look at themselves and determine how they will grow from the challenge. Whitaker would say, "We get the children we need to help us develop as parents."
- Healthy families are aware of the stresses experienced by each member and do not focus the stress and concomitant problems

permanently in one member. In other words, the identified patient in a healthy family moves from person to person rather than remaining fixed on one member.

- Healthy families change through crisis.
- Healthy families encourage expression of both positive and negative feelings. Children and parents should know they are loved and hated.
- In a healthy family, intimacy and separateness go hand in hand. Members are free to be both intimate and distant as required to meet individual needs.
- The healthy family encourages and supports outside relationships for its members.

In summary, Whitaker's followers support maximum autonomy so individuals can experience a full range of behaviors in family life. They encourage individuals to be serious as well as crazy, to know that they can choose to be either, and to know that this ability to choose is healthy. They encourage families to experience both pain and joy in family living and to grow from the experiences they encounter. Families who do not grow and change based on their experiences are most likely to seek or need therapy at some point in their development.

## Main Therapeutic Interventions

The major goals of symbolic-experiential family therapy are to increase members' sense of belongingness to the family while at the same time creating the opportunity for the members to individuate from the family. This objective can be accomplished by developing and exercising the creativity of the family in dealing with problems. To achieve these goals with a family in distress, certain therapeutic techniques may be employed. Both mediating and ultimate goals are part of this theory. Mediating goals create a therapeutic environment, while ultimate goals are selected by the therapist and the family to be attained through treatment (Roberto, 1991).

**The Battle for Structure and Initiative**  Two battles are typically waged as family treatment begins (Napier & Whitaker, 1978). The first is the *battle for structure*. This battle begins when the family attempts to tell the therapist what is wrong in the family as well as what should be done about it and who should be treated. To be effective, the therapist must control the therapy structure. If the therapist gives up this role and loses this battle, the family will bring the same ineffective structure to therapy that is currently creating problems in the family. The battle for structure begins with the first telephone contact between the therapist and a family member.

The symbolic-experiential therapist should set the unit of treatment, which is almost always the entire family. If the client resists this requirement for therapy, the therapist must be prepared to stand firm and be willing to refer the client to another therapist if the client refuses to agree to the proposed structure. Until the battle for structure is resolved, further therapeutic work cannot be accomplished, as the therapist and family will be engaged in a struggle for control. Therapy cannot be effective until the family has decided to trust the therapist and give responsibility for structuring the therapy to the therapist. Winning the battle for control is paradoxical, however, because when the therapist has won the battle, he or she will frequently defer to the family members' wishes about what they want to do to help improve the family.

The second battle to be fought is the *battle for initiative.* This battle must be won by the family. Any initiative for change must come from and be supported and maintained by the family. The therapist cannot ultimately be responsible for the choices made by the family members. Initially, members will want to lean on the therapist and become dependent on the therapist's leadership. The therapist rejects this type of leadership and instead supports family members in their decisions to change the way they deal with problems in their family. These two critical battles are the keys to an effective outcome in therapy. The therapist must be in charge of therapy, but the clients must be in charge of the changes they will or will not make.

**Co-Therapy**   Because symbolic-experiential family therapists become so intensely involved in their relationships with family members, a co-therapist is critical for effective therapy. The therapist is often reacting at a gut level with the family, and this reaction is more often than not therapeutic. However, on occasion, the therapist may become inappropriately involved and may not be able to withdraw from the intensity of the interaction. At this time, the co-therapist intervenes and directs therapy while the other therapist regains perspective on what occurred. The co-therapist in this situation might ask the other therapist and family member involved in the exchange to describe what happened and use that interaction for growth for both the family and the therapist. This use of the "experience" of the moment in the therapy is a critical element of the change process. Families (and therapists) need to be able to learn and make changes based on their life and therapeutic experiences (Napier & Whitaker, 1978).

Another reason co-therapy is used is that Whitaker believed that healthy interactions between co-therapists are a model for family members. Co-therapists can support each other, disagree, be confused, teach each other, and engage in many functional behaviors. The experience of observing this behavior is almost always helpful for the family (Whitaker & Keith, 1981).

Six specific techniques for therapy, described by Whitaker and Keith (1981), are discussed next. Remember, techniques are only useful insofar as they function to create a learning experience in the therapy for the family members.

1. *Redefine symptoms as efforts for growth.* Family members will enter therapy with complaints about the other members. The therapists will redefine these behaviors in some way that points out that the family needs to grow and that these behaviors are attempts to tell the family that this growth is necessary. For instance, the father may report that his son is neglecting his chores and behaving rudely at home. The therapist might suggest that the son is merely trying to get the husband and wife to grow in their relationship and work together in their efforts to discipline him.

2. *Teach family members to use fantasy alternatives rather than real life behaviors.* For example, if a rebellious adolescent reported wanting to kill his perfect older sister, the therapist might ask the youth how he would do the deed and how it would help his situation. Thus, the thought would not be considered abnormal, and the son would not be criticized or perhaps hospitalized because of his thoughts. Instead, by accepting the thoughts and encouraging fantasy expression, the need to turn the thought into action is dissipated.

3. *Assign homework that directs family members to change roles and, most important, not to talk about the family interviews between sessions.* As family members change roles, they experience increased autonomy and flexibility in the family. Role changes break up rigid patterns in the family, allow the family to experience itself differently, and support changes based on

that experience. Talking about the session between meetings will drain some of the emotional intensity from the family members. This intensity has to be present in the therapy session for symbolic-experiential family therapy to be most effective. Along the same line, co-therapists are advised not to talk about the family during the week either, as doing so may drain the therapists' energy from the session that would be better used there.

4. *Augment despair of family members.* When the therapists heighten the despair felt by a family member, the others will rally to provide support that was not previously present. Despair is one aspect of family life and must be acknowledged and respected. Denial of negative feelings leads to intensified family problems. Support is often lacking in troubled families, and development of a supportive climate eliminates many family problems.

5. *Engage in affective confrontation.* At times, the therapist will feel genuine affect toward family members based on their behaviors. The symbolic-experiential therapist will confront the family with his or her affective reaction. For example, a child may begin dismantling the therapist's office, and the parents may be ineffective in stopping the child's behavior. The therapist may say angrily, "Stop destroying my property and sit in your chair, now!" This affective confrontation would be experienced and assimilated by the child and, perhaps more important, by the parents and could lead to the parents and child choosing to change their behavior patterns.

6. *Treat children like children and not like peers.* This important principle clarifies that generational differences and boundaries must, at certain times, be acknowledged and respected. By recognizing generational differences, the spouses may win a "battle for structure" in their own family and develop a sense of order based on appropriate and flexible parental authority.

These specific techniques have been employed in symbolic-experiential family therapy. However, the co-therapy team is by no means limited to these techniques. Frequently, spontaneous reactions and corresponding interventions create experiences that foster a new awareness in the session and may be what is needed to facilitate family change.

Whitaker and Keith (1981) listed principles designed to help the therapist avoid errors, including:

- Do not become so much a part of the family that your ability to help is affected.
- Do not become so aloof from the family that you operate only from a technical perspective.
- Do not pretend that you do not feel stress or feelings of inadequacy.
- Do not employ a technique for change if it will only create another serious problem in another family member.
- Do not expect insight to produce change.
- Do not expect the family to operate from your value system.
- Move at the appropriate pace for the family. Therapists often move too fast and expect insight to produce change.
- Do not revere your intuitive leaps. Intuition is only intuition, and it may not be appropriate for the family. If the family resists, back off quickly.
- Failure of the therapist to recognize when he or she has the family's trust may waste time in the relationship-building phase when the family is ready to work.
- Do not create a new scapegoat in the family. Help the family understand that each person has a part in the problems that occur in the family.
- A final error that can be made is not realizing the benefits of not treating someone. Not all families need therapy, and not all families will benefit from therapy.

**Three-Generation Therapy**   When therapy reaches an impasse, the symbolic-experiential therapist may attempt to break the impasse by inviting the older generation to participate in therapy to help unlock the process (Napier & Whitaker, 1978). The grandparents are not invited to therapy as clients but rather as consultants to help the co-therapists and family members break the impasse that has developed. The insights brought to therapy by the grandparents frequently uncover a whole new arena of experience for the parents and the children and lead to other areas of family growth and development.

## Strengths and Limitations of the Symbolic-Experiential Approach

Symbolic-experiential family therapy as practiced by Whitaker and his colleagues has several important strengths. Two of the most important are that it fully recognizes the power a family has in maintaining its dysfunctional behavior patterns and the necessity for using a co-therapy team for work with families. Furthermore, Whitaker recognized the importance of the therapist winning the battle for structure so that the therapist and not the family is in charge of how therapy shall proceed. Finally, this approach more than any other encourages

## Whitaker's Symbolic-Experiential Family Therapy

### CASE EXAMPLE

*Mrs. Green called to set up an appointment for her 12-year-old son, who was regularly truant from school. She wanted the therapist to work with her son for a while and then she wanted to join the process. The therapist stated that he would need to see the entire family for his initial evaluation. Mrs. Green protested, and the therapist offered to give her the names of some therapists who would see the boy alone. Mrs. Green said that she wanted to work with this therapist because he had been highly recommended by a trusted friend, so she would comply with his desire to see the whole family.*

*The first few sessions were devoted to learning about the family and the problems with the son, James, and winning the battle for structure. When the family trusted the co-therapy team to direct therapy, the next phase of treatment began.*

*In this second phase of treatment, the therapists began challenging the family's reality of James being the problem and suggested that the entire family seemed to be experiencing a problem. James' behavior was defined as his attempt to point out to the entire family that growth and changes were needed. The rest of this phase of therapy was devoted to helping family members discover what they needed to change about themselves to increase family intimacy while allowing and encouraging autonomy. As therapy progressed, James' truancy stopped and the family began redefining what members of the family should reasonably be expected to do. This process was handled with very little assistance from the therapists, who suggested that the family was doing well on its own and that termination was in order.*

the therapist to use spontaneity and creativity to introduce new experiences to bring about family change.

The major limitation of this approach is that it lacks a systematic theoretical base for replication of the interventions in treatment. Because treatment in symbolic-experiential therapy is based strongly on the experiences and immediate reactions of the co-therapy team to the family members, no specific treatment interventions are suggested to intervene in specific situations. Thus, the ability of other therapists to replicate this treatment approach is very questionable. At best, therapists may attempt to develop their own version of this approach. Another weakness of this approach is that it suggests that it is unlikely that ineffective treatment could do lasting harm to a family. Gurman and Kniskern (1978a and b) have stated that deterioration may indeed occur in family therapy and that therapists should be cognizant of this fact. A third criticism is that, although much has been written about symbolic-experiential family therapy, the claims of this approach have little empirical support in the literature.

# White and Epston's Narrative Therapy

Narrative therapy has been heralded by many family therapists as the answer to the question, "How can we do in-depth therapy with clients under the constraints of short-term managed care regulations?" Narrative therapy, developed primarily by Australians Michael White and David Epston, may hold the key to dealing with difficult family problems based on past experiences and injunctions using brief therapy.

## Philosophical Tenets and Key Theoretical Constructs

Narrative therapy is simple in its tenets, yet, like most therapies, it is difficult to implement without training and practice. The narrative therapist establishes a warm, caring relationship with the client family and facilitates the clients' telling of their story, which will contain the precipitating elements of the problem situation within it. Imbedded in the client's story will be explanations rooted in the past for the client's present symptoms and current difficulties with life. Through a series of steps that will be described in detail later, the narrative therapist assists the client in *externalizing the problem* so that the problem, not the client, is understood as the reason for treatment. Moreover, the narrative therapist helps the client reauthor his or her life by retelling the life story in new ways that identify positive characteristics and strengths of the client. As the client comes to accept the reauthored narrative, significant life changes become possible and often occur.

Narrative therapists have great respect for the client's past. By telling their history, clients begin to realize they have the power to reshape their lives and to begin to live them in new and more productive ways. Unlike psychodynamic theories that assume that problems are the result of internal personality difficulties or contemporary individual and family therapy theories developed to work with small interactional systems such as families, narrative therapy helps the client look at the larger system consisting of all forces, past and present, that have shaped the attitudes and behaviors of the individual. Narrative theory assumes that clients adopt identities and behaviors based on numerous life influences. These influences define the client's problem-focused identity because clients assume that societal norms, family members' rules and opinions, and influences from other important relationships have the power and authority to define what is good or bad and what is a psychological problem. Narrative therapy helps clients understand the forces that have affected them over the years and make conscious choices to reshape and redefine their responses to these influences.

The key to successful narrative therapy is the fundamental understanding that the "person is never the problem; the problem is the problem" (O'Hanlon, 1994, p. 23). Through the therapy process, clients come to recognize that they are not the problem but that some external forces are influencing them to behave, think, and feel in ways that are unproductive. Externalization (White, 1986) of the problem gives clients a sense of their own personal worth as well as an active force to fight against—the externalized problem.

For example, a client may enter therapy believing he is a depressed person. The narrative therapist works with the client to help him understand that he has been influenced by societal messages to believe he is a depressed person and that he is the problem. In reality, however, the "forces of depression" are working on the client, and these forces of depression are the problem, not the client himself. When clients realize that they are not the problem, they come to understand that they need to develop new responses to combat the problem. Once this important insight is gained, powerful and creative client responses are possible. Externalization puts clients in the position of being responsible and accountable for the choices made responding to the problem. In the example above, the client might be asked how depression has been controlling his life. Then the therapist might ask what the client could do to fight depression and keep it from ruling him. This type of narrative questioning empowers the client and shows respect for the client's ability to respond in effective ways to the problem (O'Hanlon, 1994). In summary, the key element of this theory is the ability to separate, through the use of language, the problem from the personal identity of the client.

O'Hanlon (1994) listed the following fundamental elements of the narrative approach.

1. A collaborative relationship is established with the family, and a name for the problem is mutually agreed upon by all members. For example, a depressed father might name the depression "Agony."

2. The problem is personified and externalized (given its own identity) and oppressive characteristics are attributed to it. For example, Agony is identified as a powerful entity that steals the client's pleasant memories and time with family members.

3. The therapy proceeds to investigate how the problem has been disruptive, dominating, and discouraging for the client and the family. For example, family members are asked to describe how Agony has disrupted their lives and been a demoralizing factor for the family. This description encourages the family to mobilize resources to combat Agony. The therapist should not suggest that the problem "causes" client behaviors. The force of the problem only influences, tricks, confuses, or tries to recruit the client into certain unproductive actions, thoughts, or feelings. The language used in narrative questioning must highlight the client's choices in response to the problem.

4. Discover through narrative questioning moments when the problem has not dominated or discouraged the family members. For example, the therapist may ask the client to describe the longest period he has experienced without being influenced by depression. By identifying times when he or she is symptom-free, which are *exceptions* to the rule of being depressed, the client begins to understand that he has power over the problem in certain situations. Next, the therapist seeks ways to help the client develop power over the problem in most situations.

5. Discover historical evidence to support and reinforce the view that the client is competent enough to have stood up to, defeated, or escaped from the dominance of the problem. In this stage of the therapy, the client begins to *rewrite his life story through narrative.* The therapist and the client discover a reality very different from the one that brought the client to therapy. In this newly discovered reality, the client is competent and powerful and able to respond effectively to the problem. The therapist might ask: "As you continue to overcome the forces of depression, tell me how your life will be different from the one depression had planned for you?"

6. Ask family members to speculate on their future in a family with a strong competent person who is able to overcome the forces of the problem. This speculating becomes a *reauthoring of the family reality* and reinforces the identified patient's reauthoring of his life.

7. Establish an audience for the client that will support and reinforce the new life story and new identity created by this story. Problems develop in social contexts. Ensure that the client will be in a context that supports the reauthored life script. Involving family members is one way of developing the new audience. Discussing with the family how they will continue to live according to their new life story is an important aspect of the termination phase of the narrative approach.

## *The Use of Therapeutic Letters*

Epston (1994) found that narrative conversations with clients may be extended by the use of therapeutic letters to the clients that may be reread days, weeks, months, or years after the therapy has terminated to reinforces new narrative. Epston (1994) suggested that therapists use a letter to the family after most sessions. In addition to reinforcing the new narrative explored in therapy, it provides clients and the therapist with a record to work from in future sessions and clarifies what took place in previous sessions. While letters are initially very time consuming, with practice and effective in-session note taking, Epston felt most therapists could write a meaningful letter in about 30 minutes.

Nylund and Thomas (1994) conducted research concerning the efficacy of such letters. They surveyed 40 clients on the usefulness of the letters; 37 found them to be very useful and 3 found them to be useful. The "average worth" of one letter was 3.2 sessions. The clients believed that over 50% of the gains made in therapy were due to the letters alone. The average length of therapy was 4.5 sessions. These results certainly suggest that therapeutic letters are very powerful tools and support the use of letters in narrative and other therapies.

Nylund and Thomas (1994) proposed a format for therapeutic letters to help the novice begin using this powerful tool. They suggested that four areas be covered in the letter.

1. Join with the clients and reconnect them to the therapy process in an introductory paragraph.
2. Record statements that define the influences of the problem on the client and reinforce the concept of *externalization* of the problem.
3. Ask questions that might have been asked in the session but were not. For example, "I wish I had asked which of your friends will be most likely to support the changes you have made in resisting the influence of depression."
4. Document and reinforce elements of the session that show the client as competent and able to resist the influences of the problem. This focus on client strengths shown in the session often helps the client maintain the change by rereading the letter between sessions.

Obviously letters to clients are not a panacea. However, they offer the therapist an additional avenue of intervention and support for client change.

## Strengths and Limitations of Narrative Therapy

Narrative therapy offers an answer to the therapist's dilemma of how to attend to the client's past and yet focus on present change. Through the use of narrative and reauthoring client life stories, significant changes may be made in relatively brief therapeutic encounters. The therapist is able to work with the client as a colleague in this process and does not need to take a more powerful and directive position in the therapy. The use of letters to clients is viewed as a powerful adjunct to therapy.

Criticisms of the narrative approach suggest that by externalizing problems therapists may minimize the feelings clients have about their

## Narrative Therapy

**CASE**
**EXAMPLE**

*The Albertson family entered therapy because their son was anxious and fearful in most situations and was unwilling to go to school or to other places where he would be with strangers. The therapist used standard techniques in joining with family members. In the joining process, he had the family members come up with a name for the anxiety. The family called the anxiety "Mr. Fear." This personalization of the anxiety began the process of externalizing the problem. In the next phase of treatment, the therapist asked family members questions that demonstrated that the problem, Mr. Fear, was oppressive and producing havoc for the identified patient and family members. Next, the therapist investigated with the family the many ways the problem was disruptive to the family. All members were able to list several ways the externalized problem had adversely affected the family, and all agreed that the forces of Mr. Fear were great and very disruptive.*

*In the next phase of the narrative, family members were asked to identify times when Mr. Fear had not been influencing the family and the client had been able to withstand the power of the problem. This created a situation in which the identified patient and family members began to focus on times when the client and the family had been able to function in the face of the problem. If combating the problem had been done successfully in the past, perhaps it could be done in the future. The family was asked to record specific instances in their history when Mr. Fear was not in control and to discuss how the family worked to make such times happen.*

*Continuing the narrative approach, the therapist asked family members to speculate on how the family's life would be different without the power and influence of Mr. Fear present. The family responded quickly to ways they would be more productive and able to focus their energies on projects that were up to now impossible to contemplate. Finally, the therapist and the family searched for ways to create a context that would support the newly developed narrative suggesting that the client and the family could make choices that would defeat the influence and tricks of Mr. Fear. This context or audience is crucial to reinforcing and maintaining the new narrative.*

*A few weeks after termination of therapy the therapist sent the family a letter outlining the process of the therapy and specifically reminding the identified patient and family members what they did to overcome the powers of the externalized problem, Mr. Fear.*

problem situations and about themselves. Fish (1993) suggested that White and Epston engage in therapy that "denies the existence or relevance of differences in power at an interpersonal level" (p. 228). Moreover, Fish suggested that this theory does not deal with the realities of interpersonal power and power politics. Moreover, the reauthoring of life stories cannot exist outside the sphere of political, social, and economic realities.

# Summary

In this chapter, we have presented three systems-based theories of family therapy that will be of particular interest to therapists who believe family treatment must consider and emphasize the uniqueness of the individual within the family context. The theories of Virginia Satir, Carl Whitaker, and Michael White and David Epston place a premium on the genuine encounter between the therapist and the family members and seek to bring about family change through these encounters.

In the next two chapters, we discuss transpersonal theory, a relatively new approach to family treatment that offers potential direction for the future development of family therapy.

# SUGGESTED READINGS

"The Legacy of Virginia Satir." (1989). *Family Therapy Networker, 13*(1), 26–56.

Napier, A. Y., & Whitaker, C. A. (1978). *The Family Crucible.* New York: Harper & Row.

"The Promise of Narrative." (1994). *The Family Therapy Networker, 18*(6), 18–49.

Satir, V. M. (1983). *Conjoint Family Therapy,* 3rd ed. Palo Alto, CA: Science and Behavior Books.

Satir, V. M. (1988). *The New Peoplemaking.* Palo Alto, CA: Science and Behavior Books.

Satir, V. M. (1982). "The Therapist and Family Therapy: Process Model." In A. M. Horne & M. M. Ohlsen, eds., *Family Counseling and Therapy.* Itasca, IL: Peacock.

Whitaker, C. A., & Keith, D. V. (1981). "Symbolic-Experiential Family Therapy." In A. S. Gurman & D. P. Kniskern, eds., *Handbook of Family Therapy.* New York: Brunner/Mazel.

White, M., & Epston, D. (1990). *Narrative Means to Therapeutic Ends.* New York: Norton.

# 11

## Transpersonal Theories in Family Treatment

This chapter provides a detailed introduction to transpersonal therapy, including the historical background, key concepts, goals, process, and the advantages and disadvantages of transpersonal family therapy.

## KEY CONCEPTS

Transpersonal psychology
Validity of the core self
Oneness
Subjective experience
Life force and death urge
Thought is creative
Interim over-belief

Transcendent experiences
Karma
Namaste
Forgiveness
Universal laws
Unity of mind, body, and spirit
The law of attraction

## QUESTIONS
## FOR DISCUSSION

1. What are the characteristics of someone who has reached self-transcendence on Maslow's hierarchy of needs?

2. What transpersonal experiences have you had? How did they affect you, and how did you attempt to understand them?

3. How would a transpersonal family therapist identify the developmental needs of a family system?

4. What techniques would a transpersonal family therapist use to work with an addictive family system?

5. How do the "universal laws" operate in family systems?

6. How would a transpersonal family therapist use the concept of "oneness" in working with a family system?

*N*ear the end of his life, Abraham Maslow, one of the founders of humanistic psychology, began to perceive limitations in the somewhat ego-centered humanistic approaches. He believed that there had to be a way to transcend this ego-centered existence and take into account the deeply spiritual, psychic, and paranormal experiences of human beings as legitimate areas of study in psychology. In 1968, shortly before his death, he wrote, "I consider Humanistic, Third Force Psychology, to be transitional, a preparation for a still higher Fourth Psychology, transpersonal, transhuman, centered in the cosmos rather than in human needs and interest, going beyond humanness, identity, self-actualization and the like" (Maslow, 1971, p. 33).

Maslow had come to realize that the search for transcendence is a higher human need than the search for self-actualization, which is still centered in the self, or ego. Maslow also believed that transcendence cannot be achieved by attempting to avoid development of the ego. Only through mastery of the other ego needs in his hierarchy of needs (physiological, safety/security, love/belonging, self-esteem, and self-actualization) can people recognize and fulfill the deeper need for self-transcendence. Thus, an effective transpersonal therapist needs to be able to utilize all the other approaches that work with ego mastery, including psychodynamic, behavioral, and humanistic approaches.

Because most of Western psychology focuses primarily on ego functioning, a transpersonal therapist must also become familiar with Eastern psychology and philosophy, which focuses much more on working with transcendent states of being and so-called altered states of consciousness. As a result, much of transpersonal psychology deals with the study of yoga, meditation, chanting, movement, martial arts, and various body therapies based on oriental and Eastern medical practices and philosophies. In addition, numerous Western approaches have been utilized to help bridge the contrasting philosophies and practices. These techniques include dream work, biofeedback, bioenergetics, guided imagery, visualization, dance and movement therapy, art therapy, and music therapy.

The term *transpersonal* is difficult to define. The term was deliberately left in an undefined state during the first ten years of the transpersonal movement. Many of the early leaders feared that giving the word a definition would lead to limitation. They believed that transpersonal psychology should not be limited by our present knowledge of human behavior. Nevertheless, some broad definitions have begun to emerge. The Latin prefix *trans* has a number of different meanings. It can mean *connecting,* as in a *transcontinental* flight. It can mean *through,* in the sense of a *transparent* pane of glass, and it can mean *beyond,* as in a *transcendent* experience. In Latin, the word *personal* has a root word *persona,* which means mask. When we add the prefix *trans* to the word *personal,* the new term means bridging and connecting the parts of the personality or mask, allowing us to see through the mask and to move beyond the mask. In other words, transpersonal theory allows us to look through the persona or ego to get beyond the individual ego and connect with all egos.

The main transpersonal theory in Western psychology is Carl Jung's analytic theory. Jungian concepts such as the collective unconscious, synchronicity, the anima, and the animus point to higher forces that direct or influence our lives and lie beyond the human ego. The center of the personality, according to Jung, was the higher self, as opposed to the lower or ego self.

Arnold Mindell (1987), a practitioner of Jungian analysis, developed his global process work theory to apply Jungian and transpersonal principles to work with families. Mindell looks for the organizing principle or secondary process that is trying to happen in families. By supporting the primary process, the family therapist can discover the secondary process and facilitate its unfolding in the family. Mindell utilizes many nontraditional techniques to uncover the missing pieces in the family process.

Other body-oriented therapists have also developed techniques such as breath work, guided imagery, centering, dance and movement therapy, bioenergetics, and meditation to work with families. Gay Hendricks (Weinhold & Hendricks, 1993), using a variety of body-oriented techniques, works with family members to help free them from body-armoring and other dysfunctional patterns that show up in their body and breathing patterns. Coming out of a transpersonal framework,

Hendricks tries to move family members into transcendent states where they can experience the connection with their own core love and be able to connect with family members at the same level.

## ■ Theoretical Constructs of Transpersonal Theory

**Theory of Cause**    Some of the key ideas in transpersonal theory that may be useful for a marriage and family therapist are:

- oneness
- unity of mind, body, and spirit
- expanded context for human behavior
- the validity of the spiritual dimensions of life:
  — namaste
  — essence precedes existence
  — karma
  — thought is creative
  — life force and death urge
- the validity of subjective experience and the unconscious
- the validity of the core self-ego as a subpart of core self
- therapist and client are interchangeable
- everything is possible, acceptance of possibilities
- therapy is living

Basic to determining whether a therapist is using a transpersonal approach is whether he or she holds the basic beliefs and attitudes reflected in these concepts. We will now provide brief descriptions of these concepts and show how they may be utilized by a transpersonal therapist.

*Oneness*    Transpersonal therapists should see themselves as connected to all other people in a common human experience. From this perspective, most psychological problems in families are seen as denial of or forgetting our basic unity. Parents often react to their children as if they were strange alien beings and not parts of themselves being acted out. *Projection,* in this context, is not a failure to see our own behavior in the behavior of others but a recognition that what we see in others is really part of us. In families, the unintegrated parts of various family members are projected. In addition, the oneness belief allows us to strive to reclaim the disowned parts of ourselves and develop an increasingly deeper and more complete sense of inner unity.

*Unity of Mind, Body, and Spirit*   The transpersonal therapist views human behavior from a holistic perspective that focuses on the connections between mind, body, and spirit. A growing body of medical research clearly points to the interrelationship between mental and physical symptoms. Only recently have researchers begun to examine spiritual connections as well. By viewing all behavior as being interconnected, the transpersonal therapist can often see connections that are not immediately obvious.

For example, a father described his son as "a pain in the neck," and in a later session the son related a dream in which he was running at "breakneck" speed to avoid a dark figure who was chasing him. By having the son act out his dream in the session with his father taking on the part of the dark figure, the son finally realized that he was running away from the unreasonable demands of his father. He turned and faced his father and saw how he was being asked to fulfill the unfulfilled parts of his father.

*Expanded Context for Human Behavior*   The transpersonal therapist adopts an expansionist rather than a reductionist view of human behavior. An expansionist view looks for the broadest possible context when trying to understand human behavior. For example, when dealing with aggressive behavior, a reductionist view would be to ignore the possibility of an opposite or passive part of that person's behavior and attempt only to extinguish the aggressive behavior as quickly as possible. A transpersonal therapist might look for the opposite, allow that part to be played out, and seek ways to unify the two parts into a larger, more complete whole.

*The Validity of the Spiritual Dimensions of Life*   The transpersonal therapist recognizes the validity of certain spiritual principles that can guide our lives. One of these principles is *namaste,* which is a willingness to see and greet the highest in people. Traditional therapists can easily get bogged down in seeing only the problems and imperfections of themselves and their clients.

*Essence precedes existence* is another spiritual principle. It refers to the ability of the transpersonal therapist to wake up and transcend his or her own conditioning and be able to see the spiritual essence of people beyond their social, personal conditioning.

A core belief of most transpersonal therapists is that a human essence is present at birth for most people. This essence has been called the self, peace, love, soul (core self), and cosmic consciousness—our true nature. This true self can be lost or forgotten during childhood if it is not accepted and nurtured by wise and understanding parents and adults. To a transpersonal therapist, *karma* means the unconscious patterns of behavior we have learned from the adults who taught us, mainly those people in our family of origin. Putting it another way we could say, "What has been sown, thus shall be reaped." When a person is able to bring to consciousness those unconscious patterns, the person can begin to live under the *law of grace* rather than the *law of karma.*

The concept that *thought is creative* allows the transpersonal therapist to help people see more clearly how their own thoughts can create their reality. If we don't like the reality we have created for ourselves, we have to change our thoughts before a new reality can emerge.

And, finally, the transpersonal therapist must recognize the interplay of two basic energy forces in humans: the *life force* and the *death urge.* The transpersonal therapist attempts to see how these two interrelated forces are manifested in him- or herself so he or she can see them in the behavior of others.

**The Validity of Subjective Experience and the Unconscious**   Many therapies teach their practitioners to distrust or disregard the subjective and unconscious experiences of their clients. Transpersonal therapists learn to trust these experiences as having the most validity for themselves and for their clients. A transpersonal therapist does not believe in a definable objective reality. All experiences of reality are projections of a subjective experience. The therapist is not an objective observer but a subjective participant in the therapy process.

**The Validity of the Core Self/Ego as a Subpart of Core Self** Transpersonal therapists believe that the ego is not the center of the human personality; it is only a visibly socialized part of us. The core of who we really are is our core self. The ego tends to block our awareness of this core self, and often therapy is a process of "shrinking an inflated ego" so we can make contact with our core self again.

**Therapist and Client are Interchangeable**   This concept is difficult to grasp and probably runs counter to what most of us were taught about therapy. Yet it is the cornerstone of a transpersonal approach. According to this approach, clients bring the therapist all the therapeutic issues the therapist needs to work on. In giving therapy to a client, the therapist is really receiving therapy from him- or herself and the client. As a client, a person finds out what he or she already knows, and as a therapist, he or she helps remind others of what they already know.

*Everything is Possible; Acceptance of Possibilities* This belief is extremely important for both the therapist and the client. Therapists must believe in themselves as well as the client's ability to transcend limited views of the world. Without a strong belief in change and transcendence, no change or transcendence is possible.

*Therapy is Living* Transpersonal therapists have to be willing to work on themselves all the time. No matter what is happening, there is some opportunity for self-improvement and growth in awareness. All experiences in life can be divided into lessons and bliss. Once a person has learned these lessons, more time becomes available to experience bliss.

**Theory of Change** Transpersonal approaches are usually based on a set of universal laws or principles that the client and the therapist can move toward. The assumption is that if clients can reorient their lives more in line with these laws, clients' lives will be more effective. The following laws were assembled by Barry Weinhold (1982) from various esoteric and spiritual traditions.

- *The law of correspondence:* Truth on one level is truth on all levels of reality, and a breakthrough at one level can lead to a breakthrough at all levels.
- *The law of transcendence:* A person cannot move to a higher level of consciousness until he or she fully accepts and integrates all of his or her disowned parts. A person cannot flee to higher consciousness to avoid a part of the ego-self that is unwanted or unclaimed.
- *The law of grace:* People are never separate from God or the divine. Humanity has a divine essence that may be forgotten but is never lost.
- *The law of cause and effect:* Nothing ever happens by accident or by chance. Chance is merely a cause-and-effect relationship that isn't recognized.
- *The law of rhythm:* Everything in the universe is balanced. All energy expands and contracts in a natural ebb and flow. Ancient people knew how to stay in harmony and balance with the natural rhythms of the earth. In modern times most people have lost this ability.
- *The law of polarity:* Everything in the universe manifests in dual form, and everything has its opposite. All truths are really half-truths, and all paradoxes can be reconciled.

- *The law of oneness:* Everything in the universe is unified and connected. A person who feels separated from the rocks and trees or other people cannot feel at home in the universe.
- *The law of gender:* Everything has masculine and feminine energy. This law helps the universe to evolve. Our job is to balance and harmonize these seemingly competing energies.
- *The law of vibration:* Everything is in a state of motion; everything has a vibrational level. Spirit vibrates so rapidly it cannot be seen. Matter vibrates so slowly that at its most dense level it seems motionless.
- *The law of attraction:* People attract those relationships and situations that they need to help them solve unresolved problems or conflicts. It is as if "central casting" keeps sending people to us to help us resolve these issues and learn the lessons we are trying to learn.
- *The law of completion:* Any issue, problem, or lesson in a person's life will continue to press for completion until it is completed. A person cannot successfully avoid, ignore, or run away from these issues without some cost to the well-being of the individual.

## Goals of Transpersonal Therapists

Although some transpersonal therapists might use other terms, the following are the most commonly expressed goals of transpersonal therapists (Walsh & Vaughan, 1980).

1. Teaching themselves and their clients to achieve a daily experience of certainty; liberation; enlightenment, or gnosis; and self-transcendence.
2. Teaching themselves and others to "enjoy the world but not be attached to it, to be of service but not make a pest of oneself" (p. 180).
3. Teaching themselves and their clients the skills they need to handle their own problems as they arise.
4. Teaching themselves and others to increase their tolerance for paradox and ambiguity, as well as not to be satisfied with "easy answers" to life's problems.
5. Teaching themselves and others how to increasingly blend inner and outer experience.

6. Teaching themselves and others to develop compassion, generosity, inner peace, and the capacity for love and relatedness in the world.

# ■ *The Process of Transpersonal Therapy*

The transpersonal process is very complex and difficult to define, but we will attempt a brief summary of the basic elements of this process. Identification with the ego is the first step of the process, which involves bringing the functioning of the ego in each family member into consciousness. This includes understanding and taking back the ineffective defenses of the ego.

Disidentification with the ego is the next step. After a person has experienced his or her ego as completely as possible, the limitations of the ego become painfully apparent. Frequently, attachment to the ego is so strong that this stage of the process is often experienced as a death of the ego or a fear of physical death itself.

The next stage, self-transcendence, often includes archetypal awareness; the problems that remained insoluble at the ego level are transcended. For example, the fear of death that often surfaces during the previous stage is now transcended, allowing life to become larger than itself. The ordinary reality of "chop wood and carry water" is now seen in a new, expanded way. Nothing new happens, but an individual's perceptions about everything are changed. The deeper archetypal identities are now actively present as new sources of knowledge and being. The transcendent experience is unique in human existence and deserves a fuller description. Some common characteristics of a transcendent experience are:

1. A heightened sense of clarity and understanding of self and others.
2. Unique enough to almost defy verbal description. Words cannot describe it fully.
3. An altered perception of time and space in which everything may seem to slow down or speed up.
4. An appreciation of the connected nature of all things and our connections to or with everything.
5. An intensely positive feeling or sense of the perfection of everything in the universe.

6. The presence of a white or golden light surrounding every-thing or filling a person's vision.
7. All of a person's senses acutely attuned and open to the experience.
8. An experience of energy flowing through the body.

In the final stage of the process, these deeper identities dissolve into a state of direct knowing, gnosis, or enlightenment. We have very few models of this type of existence. Buddhists speak of it as nonattachment or just being awake. Once Buddha was asked by some of his followers, "Who are you? Are you a God? An Avatar?" Buddha answered, "I am awake."

# ▪ Advantages and Disadvantages of Transpersonal Family Therapy

A number of advantages might be seen in this approach. It provides the tools for self-therapy and is less dependent on the therapist having all the answers. The approach focuses on attainment of the highest ideals and principles, and it is transformative rather than remedial. It allows for deep, spiritual connections within and without, provides an expanded context for family therapy where there is no blame and everyone is seen as innocent rather than guilty, and frees families from a sense of isolation.

Some disadvantages can also be seen in transpersonal family therapy. One disadvantage is that there is an inadequate research foundation for this approach. Transpersonal therapists tend to engage in "interim over-belief," which means they trust their subjective experience *before* any research is done to confirm their perceptions. They could be wrong, or their perceptions could be distorted. There is now a substantial body of research on meditation and biofeedback, but few of the other concepts and techniques have been examined closely.

Furthermore, the success of the therapy is overly dependent on the personal growth and awareness of the therapist. There are few established guidelines for how to train transpersonal therapists not to become a barrier to the client. None of the other approaches requires the therapist to be as "squeaky clean" as does this one. Moreover, working with subtle energies demands more refined and less intrusive techniques. When people open up to their core, therapists must respect their vulnerability and learn to gently, lovingly assist them in their process of growth. Again, the sensitivity of the therapist is key to this issue, and there are possibilities of severe psychic damage if the therapist does not handle these issues properly. This danger exists with other therapies as well, but not as clearly as in the transpersonal realm.

### Transpersonal Family Therapy

### CASE
### EXAMPLE

*Mindell (1987) reported on an interesting family therapy case that illustrates his ideas about primary and secondary processes in families. He believes that the primary process, which usually involves the identified patient and the problem that brought the family to therapy, masks the secondary process that is trying to break through in the family.*

*In this case, Alex, a teenage son, is the identified patient. Someone stole the cookies his mother baked, and Alex is being accused as the thief. Because he has denied it, his mother is still very angry at him for taking the cookies and for his unwillingness to admit it. The therapist asks Alex's mother who she thinks stole the cookies, and why she thinks that way. While she is answering the question, the therapist notices that Alex is turning red.*

*Then the therapist asks Alex who stole the cookies, and his father burps. The therapist then asks the father the same question, and while he answers, Alex's sister, Marie, begins to fidget. Finally, the therapist asks Marie to tell him what is going on in the family. Marie answers that she believes that everyone in the family is guilty of something they haven't admitted. This gets everyone in the family laughing loudly, so the therapist asks each person to talk about his or her guilt. The family members share a story of something each did wrong, and as a result they all feel closer to each other. They no longer are pointing their collective finger at Alex as the irresponsible thief in the family.*

*This case illustrates how a family operates as a single unit to keep a secret. If the therapist had only met with Alex, he probably would not have uncovered the secondary process that was trying to happen in this family. Once the secret was revealed and everyone could "come clean," they were all free to share more of themselves in the family. This was the secondary process that was trying to happen in this family, and it led to a deeper level of communication and relationship.*

# SUGGESTED READINGS

Dossey, L. (1989). *Recovering the Soul.* New York: Bantam.

Weinhold, B., & Hendricks, G. (1993). *Counseling and Psychotherapy: A Transpersonal Approach.* Denver, CO: Love.

Zukav, G. (1990). *The Seat of the Soul.* New York: Simon & Schuster.

# 12

# Developmental Systems Theory:

# A Transpersonal Systems Theory

*In this chapter, we present a new
integrative transpersonal approach to
family therapy that has its roots in
existing psychodynamic, behavioral,
humanistic, and family systems theories.
In addition, this theory extends the study
of family therapy to include concepts and
techniques from metaphysical, esoteric,
and spiritual traditions. This emerging
theory, developed jointly by Barry K.
Weinhold and Janae B. Weinhold, is called
developmental systems theory. The
application of the theory, developmental
process work, is also presented, showing
how it can be used in therapy with
couples and families.*

## KEY CONCEPTS

Systematic eclectic
Intrapsychic
Process-oriented
Global process work
Reparenting
Talionic response
Psychological birth

Surface process
Deep process
Channels
Edges
Proprioceptive channel
Amplifying the signal
Double signal

## QUESTIONS
## FOR DISCUSSION

1. How do you know when you are following a person's process versus taking over a person's process?

2. What do you do if you identify a "double signal" in a family member's report of a problem he or she is having?

3. Which "channel" do you use most to access information?

4. What are your "edges" as a family therapist? What issues, problems, or clients can't you deal with in therapy?

5. What are your unresolved family-of-origin conflicts, and how have you dealt with them?

6. In what ways was your family-of-origin dysfunctional?

7. How does the talionic response operate in families?

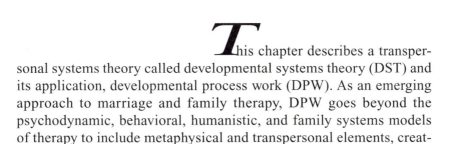

*T*his chapter describes a transpersonal systems theory called developmental systems theory (DST) and its application, developmental process work (DPW). As an emerging approach to marriage and family therapy, DPW goes beyond the psychodynamic, behavioral, humanistic, and family systems models of therapy to include metaphysical and transpersonal elements, creating an integrative approach that bridges individual and family systems theories.

Developmental systems theory is a *systematic eclectic* theory; key elements of various theories and various intervention strategies have been integrated in a systematic way to create a new theory. Much of the theory building in psychology has followed this model—previously existing theoretical material is reshaped and combined in a unique way to create a new theory. This is how most practitioners operate as well. They may have learned or been exposed to a variety of theories during their training as therapists, but when they attempt to apply the theories they have to adapt them to fit their own personality and the population with whom they work.

When engaged in transpersonal family therapy, it is necessary to use both objective and subjective information and to stay very personally involved in the therapeutic process. For this reason, this chapter is written from the viewpoint of Barry Weinhold, who created this therapeutic approach jointly with Janae Weinhold.

Utilizing developmental process work techniques with our clients, we found many transpersonal processes present in family and relationship problems. Once we learned to follow these processes as they emerged out of presenting problems, we often encountered relationship and family problems involving spiritual abandonment, demonic forces, intrapsychic structures, transcendent experiences, and other transpersonal phenomena. We have learned through these experiences to trust the "rightness" of whatever process is emerging. We believe openness to and acceptance of a wide range of psychological and spiritual experiences are necessary to do this kind of work. To work with people at these deep levels does require spiritual courage on the part of both the client and the therapist.

This kind of work can also produce a spiritual emergency in therapists if they have not done their own deep work. We have been challenged by our clients to do our own deep work. Sometimes we emerge from doing a piece of our own work only to find clients waiting for us to help them with a similar issue. We trust that our clients will bring us exactly what we need to work on and that only those clients we are ready to help will appear for therapy. Also, it is necessary for us to know our limitations and be ready to refer a client we don't feel ready to deal with. However, if this happens, we regard it as a "sign" that the client's issue is touching an important area of personal work for us.

# Our Personal Contributions to Developmental Process Work

Doing your personal work is very important in preparing to become a transpersonal marriage and family therapist. We discovered many of the elements of developmental process work while doing our own therapeutic work.

## Barry's Story

This theory has been developed in part out of several sets of transpersonal experiences I have had. My first awakening experience came in 1969 when I attended a workshop that was led by Dr. Herbert Otto. Dr. Otto had mentioned his interest in facilitating a process that helped people uncover their repressed death urges. He offered to do the process for those who were interested, and I volunteered. He told me to imagine my own death, including how I thought I would die, and also to attend my own funeral.

My only previous personal experience with death and dying was the death of my grandfather, who died of cancer in a hospital. I happened to be a patient in that hospital at the same time and visited him quite often. I imagined myself dying of cancer in a hospital, and almost immediately I began to experience a change in my breathing. My body began to shake and vibrate much like convulsions. At first I thought I must be creating these reactions through my breathing, but

I soon realized I had no control over what was happening to me. I thought, "My God, I must be dying." The more afraid I became, the more the shaking and vibrating continued. However, when I would let go of the fear and relax, I noticed that the shaking would subside and I would experience a deep sense of peacefulness. I remember deciding that I liked the peaceful feeling so much that I was willing to just relax and let go of trying to control the outcome.

Gradually the peaceful periods became longer and the shaking subsided until I sank into the most peaceful feeling I had ever experienced. I thought, "this must be what death is like." Then I felt myself rising out of my body. I rose up to about four feet above my body, and I remember looking down and seeing my body still lying on the floor. Finally, I floated up through the roof of the building and began to move very rapidly through dark space. I could see bright objects flashing past me. The colors were bright orange, blue, green, violet—all the basic colors, all vibrant and clear.

Slowly the blackness of deep space began to fade, and it got lighter and lighter until my whole consciousness was filled with a brilliant white light. I remember thinking, "This must be the beginning of the universe." Shortly after that everything faded, and I opened my eyes to see several people huddled around me with concerned expressions. Later I found out that Dr. Otto was quite concerned about me and had considered trying to bring me out of the experience. As he observed me closely, he reported seeing my lower jaw unhinge and my closed eyes roll back in my head. I was totally unaware of any of this and was surprised at his and other peoples' concern.

For weeks after this experience, I tried to understand its meaning, but none of my previous training in psychology helped me understand what had happened. One day I told a colleague about the experience, and he asked me if I had read the *Tibetan Book of the Dead*. I hadn't, so he told me that what I had described was recorded thousands of years ago in that book as the experience of people who had died and came back to relate their experience. After reading that book, I read lots of books with similar accounts of people who were declared clinically dead and then came back. There was a strong resemblance to what I had experienced.

About nine years later, in 1978, I went through a breathing process called *rebirthing*, and I experienced a very similar release of my body. This helped me formulate some hypotheses about the meaning of birth and death and the interplay between these experiences in our daily lives. I began to see that our notions of illness and death are somehow transmitted from generation to generation through our interaction with our birth family. I also began to see how thought patterns, behaviors, and beliefs are similarly transmitted (Weinhold & Hendricks, 1993).

This led me on an intensive study of my own family of origin and the thought and behavior patterns I had unconsciously taken on from growing up in my family. I saw that a process some would call forgiveness was necessary for me to break these patterns. I struggled to understand this process and eventually began to act on it. This led me to decide to "rebirth" my parents in 1979, which released many of the old relationship patterns that tied us together. Since that time, I have attempted to create new relationship patterns with members of my family of origin.

My individual search for a transpersonal relationship with myself, with a partner, and with the spiritual realms provided the laboratory where I synthesized, researched, and applied these theories. I believe that the theoretical foundations of this approach must work first on ourselves as individuals, then in our relationships with each other, and finally in our relationships with our families before we feel it is solid enough to use with our clients. As a transpersonal marriage and family therapist, I strive to "walk my talk" and teach by sharing my own journey to wholeness.

As I use this approach with my clients, I continue to discover more about myself. This interactive process helps me keep refining and expanding both myself and this model.

## Janae's Story

My contributions to developmental process work have come from my own experiences in healing deep psychological wounds from my early years in a highly dysfunctional family. My mother and father were locked in a deadly struggle that was never spoken out loud. Their struggle ended when I was 12 years old. At that time, my mother committed suicide by asphyxiation while she held my 5-year-old brother on her lap. My own place and role in this family system created experiences of abandonment, covert incest, caretaking, and confusion. Not until the age of 37 did I realize my need for therapy to help sort out all these family patterns.

When I finally opened myself up to comprehend the damage that had been done to me in my childhood, I began to understand the destructiveness of my family environment. It wasn't until I married Barry at the age of 41, however, that I began to feel at a deep level the degree of my childhood losses. The love and freeing environment of our relationship provided a safe place from which I began to plumb my own depths.

The transpersonal aspects of DPW also emerged from the discovery of how the unfinished business with my parents interfered with me being in a healthy relationship with my spiritual parents. As I surrendered more and more of myself to be guided by spirit, the obstacles to "spiritual intimacy" emerged. I began to see how I projected the faces of my human parents onto my spiritual parents. My inner child believed that Father/Mother God would respond to my prayers, ideas, dreams, and feelings just like my human parents had. I could see that I expected to be abandoned, judged, abused, and shamed as I had been as a child and that I would have to do everything myself by working very hard. The moment I saw how the developmental issues of my early childhood were creating a dysfunctional relationship with my spiritual parents was one I will long remember.

We both have personally experienced DPW as a highly effective treatment modality. It has helped us heal many of our narcissistic wounds and complete the developmental tasks necessary to recover our essence. We have used this approach with hundreds of clients and found it to be as effective with them as it has been with us.

We have also trained many therapists who have used this approach just as successfully with their clients. As we continue to work personally and professionally with this model, we see people experiencing the transpersonal part of themselves and of others. We regard DPW as a sacred technology to be used in "midwifing" people through their psychological birth, which we consider just as sacred and important as physical birth.

# Philosophical Tenets of Developmental Process Work

Developmental process work builds on the transpersonal paradigm outlined in the previous chapter and the various assumptions presented there. It adds numerous principles that apply directly to the therapeutic process and support the client in emerging from therapy through a more whole, individuated process. The main philosophical tenets are these:

1. The goal of developmental process work is to help people develop an intimate relationship both with their own soul and with their spiritual realms.

2. To develop spirit/soul intimacy, it is necessary for people to reclaim the parts of themselves that split off during childhood. At the core of each split-off part is some unmet developmental need that must be met before that part can be integrated.

3. The process of reclaiming split-off parts also includes doing core feeling work (for example, experiencing fear of abandonment/engulfment, shame, rage, grief, ecstasy, bliss, or unconditional love). Unexpressed core feelings help keep dysfunctional patterns recycling.

4. Developmental deficits occurred in our primary relationships from childhood. Healing these developmental deficits in adults requires safe, committed relationships. These may be committed love relationships or relationships between friends who are committed to helping each other get their unmet developmental needs met.

5. Every person has an innate desire to be whole and is always working in his or her best way (albeit unskilled) to become whole. Every behavior, whether it is effective or not, is an effort to reach the essential wholeness we were born with.

6. Each client enters therapy carrying a "healing process in progress." This healing is expressed in behaviors and body signals. It is the task of the therapist to discover this self-healing process and help the client become aware of it so he or she may do it more consciously. It is necessary to always see the client as evolving in this process, rather than as someone who is stuck in a particular psychological state. This requires "process-oriented" thinking rather than the "state-oriented" thinking associated with most medically oriented psychological models.

7. The client is always in charge of the therapy and dictates the speed at which his or her process moves. This puts the power back in the hands of the client and removes the therapist from a role that can be perpetrational or invasive.

8. It is possible to slow down a client's process, but it is not pos-

sible to speed it up. Clients truly move at their own pace. Hurrying them along often makes them skip important pieces of their learning process that then requires that they "cycle" the issue again.

9. Unmet developmental needs from childhood are carried along as "excess baggage" until they get met. They recycle again and again in different ways in our relationships with different people, always pressing to be met.

10. All current conflicts and problems are the result of unresolved conflicts from childhood. By following the client's process, it is possible to discover the sources of these conflicts.

11. Therapists will draw clients who have the same issues they have. The law of attraction can help both complete their unfinished business.

12. There is a "rightness" about all problems and body symptoms. Looking for the rightness of all problems and symptoms is a way of helping clients reframe their experiences. This removes judgment and avoids shaming.

13. It is never too late to get childhood developmental needs met. Human development is a life-long process that can get stunted or have gaps, but it never stops.

14. The therapist is seen as a protector. The first and foremost task of the therapist is to provide a safe and sacred space in which the client may open up his or her most vulnerable parts. Invasion, perpetration, and abuse of any kind in such a space might justify the label of "sin."

15. Developmental systems theory is a transpersonal theory that acknowledges the presence of both soul and spirit in the healing process. It acknowledges that the true power of healing comes from transpersonal realms. The role of the therapist is to access these realms and to facilitate the client in accessing them. This approach must be used with the utmost respect for the divine nature of both the client and the unseen forces that create the healing process.

# Theoretical Constructs of Developmental Systems Theory

The theoretical foundations of developmental systems theory are a synthesis of material from a broad psychological spectrum. The roots of developmental systems theory come from general systems theory, family systems theories, the Jungian-based global process work approach of Arnold Mindell, the psychoanalytic work of Alice Miller, transactional analysis reparenting theory, the developmental theories and research of Margaret Mahler, Eric Erikson, Robert Havighurst, and Jean Piaget, and various transpersonal and metaphysical theories, including rebirthing.

## Contributions from General Systems Theories

General systems theory originated in the early 1940s as mathematicians, physicists, and engineers searched for functional and structural rules that could describe all physical (nonhuman) systems. Norbert Weiner (1954) first applied these principles to develop the Norden bomb sight during World War II. He coined the term *cybernetics* to describe this emerging field of study. Books by Buckley (1967) and Bertalanffy (1968) attempted to apply systems concepts to human systems. Finally, in 1978 James Miller wrote a book that laid out a more complete application of the concepts of general systems theory to human systems.

## Contributions from Transactional Analysis

In 1970, Jacqui Lee Schiff published a book titled *All My Children* that described a revolutionary new therapy approach called "reparenting," which grew out of Eric Berne's work on transactional analysis. The book reported the work she and her husband did with schizophrenics no one else wanted to work with. Their treatment approach involved a residential treatment program that required 24-hour-a-day care. The results were that most of the people who went through their program went on to become successfully functioning adults, many becoming therapists themselves.

Their methods, which were highly controversial at the time, encouraged the client to regress to an infant stage and work there to heal the developmental deficits from that age. This included diapering clients, holding them and feeding them from bottles, as well as structured anger and rage reduction techniques. These methods were designed to reconnect clients with the sources of their original trauma, to allow them to express any unexpressed feelings related to the trauma, and then to provide them with support, nurturing, and new information to help them heal their early wounds.

As the practice of reparenting grew in the 1970s, many practitioners began to experiment with it on an out-patient format. From this early experimentation, practitioners were able to detail the kinds of interventions that produced lasting changes in their clients. Jacqui Schiff and her colleagues followed with a sequel book, *The Cathexis Reader* (Schiff, 1976), which described a set of passive or discounting behaviors that served to keep people stuck in symbiotic or co-dependent relationships.

Schiff also outlined effective methods for confronting these dysfunctional behaviors. For example, she found passive people often discount their own needs and focus on the needs of others, hoping to "win" some attention or approval from them. Passive people discount their ability to ask directly for what they want. Being forced to ask directly to get their needs met was an effective confrontation for dealing with this problem. As the Schiff and her colleagues studied passivity and discounting, they discovered that it wasn't just part of the pathology of schizophrenics but was also very much a part of everyday life for most people. They estimated that as many as two out of every five "transactions" or interactions between people involved some evidence of discounting or passivity.

TA practitioners Dorothy Babcock and Terry Keepers (1976) combined the passivity/discounting information with script analysis in a book for parents called *Raising Kids OK*. Others adapted this material in other types of TA therapy, such as redecision therapy (Goulding & Goulding, 1978).

During this period, Jacqui Schiff became embroiled in political battles within the International Association of Transactional Analysis over her approach and eventually was censured by the organization. This effectively stopped progress of this treatment modality except with a few of Jacqui's former students who continued to develop the theory. I (Barry) continued using some reparenting techniques with my clients in private practice as a psychologist but had gone on to explore other more transpersonal approaches by the time this had happened.

With the onset of the co-dependency movement, reparenting treatment modality again began to appear in the recovery literature. Jon and Laurie Weiss (1989), in their book *Recovery from Co-dependency*, described corrective parenting techniques they used in treating co-dependency. Jean Illsley Clarke and her colleagues (1978, 1989) wrote several books applying this evolving theory to parenting. Pam Levin also wrote several books that further developed reparenting theory, including *Becoming the Way We Are* (1988a) and *Cycles of Power*

(1988b). Our books, *Breaking Free of the Co-dependency Trap* (Weinhold & Weinhold, 1989) and *Counter-dependency: The Flight from Intimacy* (Weinhold & Weinhold, 1992), further developed aspects of this theory. *Breaking Free of Addictive Family Relationships* (Weinhold, 1991) describes the process of breaking dysfunctional transactions in present relationships using many concepts from reparenting.

Clarke and Levin added much to the understanding and use of developmental affirmations, which help people heal early developmental deficits. They also organized helpful lists of the developmental needs of early childhood.

## The Psychoanalytic Contributions of Alice Miller

Much of the revival of our own interest in the reparenting approach grew out of the work of Swiss analyst Alice Miller. Her pioneering books (1981, 1983, 1986, 1988, 1991) helped rekindle our interest in how early narcissistic wounds affect later development. Miller's work showed clearly some of the adverse effects of what might be called "standard parenting practices," as well as documenting the process of how the same dysfunctional patterns of behavior repeat from one generation to another.

## The Developmental Contributions of Eric Erikson, Robert Havighurst, and Jean Piaget

The work of Erikson (1950), Havighurst (1972), and Piaget (1951) were quite helpful to us in identifying the normal stages of physical development and the cognitive and emotional tasks that have to be mastered at each stage. We learned the most, however, by reading the research of Margaret Mahler (1968; Mahler et al., 1975). Mahler and her colleagues were able to chart the course of development from the early bonding stage of the infant (birth to nine months) through the separation stage (nine to twenty-four months). Kaplan's book, *Oneness and Separateness* (1978), which was based on Mahler's research, provided us with a clear narrative description of these two stages, including what might prevent the successful completion of each stage.

## The Global Process Work Approach of Arnold Mindell

These contributions were all coming together in 1985 and 1986 when we met Dr. Arnold Mindell, a Jungian analyst who was developing a new adaptation of Jungian theory called global process work, formerly known as process-oriented psychology (see Mindell, 1983, 1985a and b, & 1987). Earlier in this chapter we reported our first meeting with him.

While working as a Jungian analyst in Zurich, Switzerland, Mindell became ill with a life-threatening disease. After unsuccessfully attempting to cure himself using the standard analytic tools he had in his Jungian toolbox, he began to investigate the connections between body symptoms and dreams. He realized that he knew much less about his body than he did his dreams, so he began studying various body-oriented therapies in an attempt to heal himself. He studied yoga, bioenergetics, breath work, Rolfing, massage, movement therapy, psychodrama, neurolinguistic programming, Gestalt therapy, and meditation. In the process, he not only healed himself but began to find threads present in all these approaches that he could weave together into a totally new body/mind therapy he called the "dreambody approach" (Mindell, 1983).

Mindell also expanded on Jung's ideas about dreams and began to realize that most people are dreaming all the time. Their waking dreams, according to Mindell, are often ways to avoid unpleasant realities or unpleasant memories, while their sleeping dreams provide an outlet for unconscious material to emerge.

The real genius of Mindell's theory, however, was his expansion of information theories such as neurolinguistic programming (NLP) into six main channels for inputting and outputting information and the use of Taoist principles in his therapy. This information theory provided a mechanism the therapist could use to track information as it presented itself through the client's symptoms and problems. Mindell's uses of Taoist principles provided a context of "rightness" of all symptoms and problems, as well as the use of client-centered techniques for "following" the client.

In addition, he used the principles of unified field theory from quantum physics to show how problems move from one "field" or system to another. For example, according to his theory, an internal conflict that is not resolved at the individual level will move out into the relationship field and emerge there as a conflict. If not resolved at that level, he hypothesized that it will move out into the next level of system, the family. Using this theory to examine national and international conflicts, he began to hypothesize about how unresolved global conflicts can be the collective manifestation of many unresolved individual, relationship, family, and organizational conflicts.

In 1986 when we trained with Dr. Mindell, he was still evolving his theory. Since then, he has become interested in and involved with the resolution of global conflicts, so he has changed the name of his theory from process-oriented psychology to global process work. Many of the concepts from his theory have been adapted for use in developmental systems theory.

## Contributions from Family Systems Theories

As early as the late 1950s, the Palo Alto group led by Gregory Bateson began applying cybernetics to the study of family therapy. Their work eventually led to the major paradigm shift in the field of family therapy that now views the individual and each successively more complex social group as systems interacting with each other. This provided a new perspective in family therapy so that the family could be treated as a system containing various subsystems. Developmental systems theory utilizes both the systems language and the concept of a family as a dynamic system that is constantly changing and evolving.

Developmental systems theory also borrows from several of the established family systems theories. The work of Bowen and Framo forms a useful model for helping individuals and families sort out family-of-origin issues that are recycling in the current family dynamic. Bowen also was the first to emphasize the importance of family therapists doing their own family-of-origin work as part of training to become family therapists.

Structural family therapy has contributed useful definitions of the boundaries and rules present in each subsystem in a family. This helped us create the three interrelated subsystems used in DST: the individual, the couple, and the family.

The work of Don Jackson (1965) and Sager and his associates (Sager et al., 1971) helped us better understand how to bring together intrapsychic and family systems concepts. The basic assumption of their model is that unconscious and conscious aspects of family members' inner lives form an important part of the systemic feedback loop that can be observed in their interaction, communication, and behavior patterns. Taub-Bynum (1984) extended the family communication system developed by Jackson and others to include transpersonal aspects such as telepathy and extra sensory perception as ways the family's unconscious is communicated.

Like the strategic approaches, DST focuses on resolution of the presenting family problem. The belief is that following the family's process is going to be the most useful route for the therapist. Also, in the application of DST, paradox is utilized much the same way it is used by the strategic family therapist.

### Transpersonal and Metaphysical Contributions

As we synthesized the various theories, we realized the need for a solid spiritual foundation. We saw that a spiritual component was necessary both for helping clients move directly into their core issues and for moving through them in a permanent manner. Here we found the work of Ken Wilber (1980) very helpful in describing the transcendent and spiritual aspects of developmental psychology. His concepts of the transegoic stages of human development as well as the superconscious levels of awareness, helped us integrate the spiritual and transformative elements of human development into our own emerging model. His work led us to study other transpersonal and spiritual approaches that included Gnosticism and the teachings of spiritual masters from Eastern philosophies such as Integral Yoga, Taoism, Hinduism, Agni Yoga, and other so-called ageless wisdom traditions.

Leonard Orr (Orr & Ray, 1977), the founder of rebirthing, helped us understand the power of the breath in helping people reconnect with and heal early childhood traumas, including the birth trauma. We trained as "rebirthers," which helped us experience and understand the importance of natural childbirth techniques that respect the sanctity of the birth process and the need of the child to be in charge of his or her own birth.

The work of Frederick LeBoyer (1975), a French obstetrician, Igor Charkovsky, a Soviet physician; and the American midwifery movement helped us develop therapeutic methods to assist people in recreating an ideal birth. Our study of pre- and perinatal psychology helped us develop a variety of ways to link many adult problems to prebirth traumas and the trauma of birth.

# ■ The Stages of Development: Key Constructs of Developmental Systems Theory

This theory divides childhood and adolescence into four main stages of development: the *co-dependent stage* (pre-birth to 9 months), the *counterdependent stage* (10–36 months), the *independent stage* (3–5 years), and the *interdependent stage* (6–18 years). In each stage, certain key developmental tasks need to be mastered. If they are not met at their proper time, they become excess baggage that gets dragged along and interferes with the overall flow of development. These key tasks can be completed later only if effective interventions are made. We created developmental process work to provide parents, teachers, and therapists with the skills to make effective interventions that help children and adults complete these tasks (Weinhold & Hendricks, 1993; Weinhold & Weinhold, 1992).

The main developmental task of the *co-dependent stage* is bonding. If a child grows up in a child-centered family where the needs of the child are attended to with respect and nurturing, he or she will develop a solid foundation. The child will feel secure and will be ready to begin exploring his or her world at around 6 to 9 months. This ensures that he or she will develop a "love affair with the world" and continue to grow and learn. In addition to having basic physical needs met, the fully bonded child needs to be touched, sung to, talked to in loving ways, and have his or her essence mirrored back by patient and loving parents and other significant adults. Children who experience democratic parenting practices like these will likely grow up to create a similar loving and nurturing family of their own.

Unfortunately, with the increasing number of single-parent families or families where both parents have to work outside the home, many children do not receive enough bonding. Magid and McKelvey (1987), in their book *High Risk: Children Without a Conscience*, pointed out that poorly bonded children often become the sociopaths and psychopaths of society. These are the kids who join gangs, become criminals, or are unable to hold steady jobs. Research has also confirmed the connection between poor bonding and child abuse. When maternal and paternal infant bonding is strong, there is almost no child abuse.

The *counterdependent stage* requires that the child complete two important developmental tasks. The first task is to successfully separate from the constraints of the symbiotic relationship with mother to form an individual, autonomous identity. The second task is to learn to manage feelings of frustration and anger in response to normal limits imposed by the world in general and parents in particular. Temper tantrums and other forms of emotional outbursts must be handled gently by parents with clear limits given without shame or physical punishment.

If parents punish the child severely for these emotional outbursts by using physical punishment, shame, or humiliation, the child will suffer narcissistic wounds and experience the punishment as an attempt to annihilate the self. Anger and rage then become protective mechanisms against this fear of annihilation. Alice Miller (1983) reminded us that, "contrary to popular opinion, the injustice, humiliation, mistreatment and coercion a person has experienced (while growing up) are not without consequences" (p. 247).

One of the consequences Miller alludes to is activation of the deepest and most primitive of human defenses, called the talionic response. It is the response behind the Biblical statement, "an eye for an eye and a tooth for a tooth." If during the counterdependent stage children are not trained by understanding and sensitive parents to manage this primitive impulse effectively, they will likely develop violent or aggressive means for handling frustrations and conflicts. This becomes the basis for intergenerational patterns of child and spousal abuse, sometimes called "the vicious cycle of cruelty" (Weinhold, 1991). This is why older kids pick on younger kids on the playground or attempt to bully or intimidate other children, and it is likely that it plays a big part in all the youth violence we see.

The developmental tasks of the *independent stage*, namely mastery and autonomy, are impossible to complete if the child did not successfully complete the developmental tasks of the previous stages. If the child doesn't receive enough bonding during the co-dependent stage or receives abusive or neglectful parenting during the counterdependent stage, it is almost impossible for that child to develop as a separate, autonomous individual. The "psychological birth" of the individual is the important outcome of the successful completion of these crucial tasks. The independent stage is the time when the child learns to play independently, dress, feed, and nurture him- or herself. The child also asks questions to find out how everything works and learns to ask directly for what he or she wants and needs from others. Finally, the child learns to trust his or her own intuition and inner wisdom.

Without the proper foundation from the previous stages, the child is trapped in an endless web of self-doubts and insecurities. He or she may decide that it is too frightening to become a separate person and, instead, will turn away from him- or herself and learn how to be dependent on others to direct his or her life. This tragic decision makes it impossible for the child to think freely, feel all of his or her feelings, dream, or function later as an effective parent charged with the responsibility of guiding and directing the lives of his or her children.

The *interdependent stage* relies on the foundation created during the previous stages. The main developmental tasks are to learn how to cooperate with others and to resolve conflicts in nonviolent win-win ways. Again, if the foundation is weak, the child has great difficulty developing cooperative behaviors and resolving conflicts in win-win ways. The task is made more difficult because the schools operate on a competitive model rather than a cooperative one. Children with a poor foundation by the time they enter school tend to fluctuate between giving themselves up to get along with others or aggressively or narcissistically demanding that others do what they want. This is why youth gangs have replaced families; gangs allow children to give themselves up to the code of behavior in the gang (a distorted form of bonding) and they can band together to bully others into giving them what they want (a distorted form of autonomy).

Developmental systems theory presents a systemic approach to recovery of the self through couples and family therapy. One of the main goals of the family therapist using this approach is to create a therapeutic milieu in the couple relationship and in the family so people can help each other complete these vital tasks that hold them back from being effective parents and adults.

The theory posits that the same developmental stages that the individual system goes through are present in couple relationship systems and in family relationship systems. Figure 12.1 shows each stage with the developmental tasks to be completed during that stage for individuals, couples, and families. With the aid of this information, the family therapist can begin to locate the developmental "holes" in the individual, the couple, and the family system. By skillfully following the processes and presenting the individual's problems, the couple, the family, or the therapist can design interventions to help fill those holes and move the system to a higher level of functioning.

The *Map for Breaking Free* outlines the steps an individual, a couple, or a family needs to follow to achieve second-order change or transformation. Although the steps are presented here in linear form, they do not necessarily occur in this order. We are currently building assessment instruments to measure changes in each of the areas covered in these steps.

| The Stages of Development | Ways to Meet the Developmental Tasks of an Individual | Ways to Meet the Developmental Tasks of a Couple | Ways to Meet the Developmental Tasks of a Family |
|---|---|---|---|
| **Co-Dependent Stage** <br><br> **Task: Bonding** | Nonviolent birth <br> Establish basic trust with others <br> Nurturing touch, eye contact and physical comfort provided <br> Basic safety and survival needs met <br> Talked and sung to lovingly <br> Have needs respected and taken seriously <br> Recognition of child's essence | Acknowledgment of spiritual essence of each person <br> Respect for and validation of feelings and needs <br> Physical/emotional intimacy <br> Loving touch and talk <br> Mutual trust and love <br> Common values, beliefs and interests emphasized | Survival and safety needs of members met to provide safe and secure home <br> Time taken to build intimate family relationships <br> Ideas and feelings of members taken seriously <br> Exchange of loving words and touch among members <br> Develop a common view of reality |
| **Counterdependent Stage** <br><br> **Tasks: Exploration and Separation** | Permission and support to explore the world safely <br> Positive support for achieving self-sufficiency <br> Respect for personal boundaries, feelings, thoughts <br> Positive responses to wants and needs <br> Develop trust of senses | Separate nurturing touch from sexual touch <br> Respect for individual differences of values and beliefs <br> Mutual support for exploration <br> Mutual respect for boundaries <br> Direct negotiation to meet needs and wants <br> Identify the sources of unresolved conflicts | Respect for the personal space and property of others <br> Independent thinking, truthfulness and honesty in asking for what you want encouraged <br> Diversity of interests, beliefs and values supported |

**FIGURE 12.1**

**Developmental Systems Theory: A Systemic Approach to Change**

| The Stages of Development | Ways to Meet the Developmental Tasks of an Individual | Ways to Meet the Developmental Tasks of a Couple | Ways to Meet the Developmental Tasks of a Family |
|---|---|---|---|
| **Independent Stage**<br><br>**Tasks: Self-Mastery and Autonomy** | Delay gratification of wants<br>Achieve emotional separation<br>Master self-sufficiency<br>Achieve object constancy<br>Learn to tolerate frustration<br>Develop trust of inner guidance and wisdom<br>Achieve effective problem-solving from an "I'm okay/you're okay" life position | Develop self-mastery<br>Develop autonomous behavior<br>Develop ways for fulfilling needs separate from partner<br>Maintain self-identity<br>Tolerate ambiguity/confusion<br>Transcend gender/cultural role stereotypes | Permission for members to be emotionally separate<br>Members supported in developing individual mastery<br>Self-esteem of each family member a high priority<br>Individual initiative supported by family members<br>Uniqueness of members supported |
| **Interdependent Stage**<br><br>**Task: Cooperation** | Achieve appropriate gender identity<br>Cooperate with others without losing individuality<br>Make and keep agreements<br>Negotiate to get needs met<br>Achieve self-acceptance<br>Define and accept responsibility for psychological and physical territory | Use win/win conflict resolution methods<br>Shift from oneness to separateness when needed<br>Keep relationship agreements<br>Help each other resolve old conflicts from the past<br>Relationship a priority over career<br>Develop spiritual practices | Family meetings used to resolve conflicts, make consensus decisions and communicate wants and needs<br>Agreements honored and kept<br>Power used equitably<br>Members cooperate to achieve family goals and visions<br>Fullest development of all members a high priority |

**FIGURE 12.1** (continued)

1. Identify your conflicts, negative behaviors, and dysfunctional patterns.
   - Identify the betrayals, abandonments, rejections, abuses, and other traumatic events in the first five years of your life.
   - Identify your recurrent dysfunctional behavior patterns based on these traumatic events.
   - Identify the addictive and compulsive behaviors you learned in your family of origin that continue to recycle in your current relationships.
2. Identify the unfinished business from your childhood.
   - Learn about the healthy developmental needs and stages of relationships.
   - Identify the unmet developmental needs that are causing problems in your current relationships.
   - Identify appropriate activities necessary to meet these developmental needs.
   - Identify your unhealed narcissistic wounds.
3. Express core feelings related to your narcissistic wounds.
   - Find safe, supportive "family" relationships where you learn to express your feelings effectively.
   - Develop effective self-protective and self-nurturing skills.
   - Receive validation from your family members for your childhood experiences and feelings.
4. Contract with family members for help in completing your unfinished relationship issues.
   - Create corrective parenting contracts with family members to get your unmet developmental needs met.
   - Establish a therapeutic relationship, if necessary, to resolve old conflicts.
   - Do regular self-nurturing activities.
   - Learn to ask directly for what you want and need from others.
5. Develop autonomous behaviors.
   - Set limits and develop healthy boundaries for yourself without using violence or shame.
   - Confront and change any self-limiting beliefs or rules.
   - Develop mastery in the areas of self-care and self-nurturing.
   - Take personal responsibility for your own happiness and well being.

- Learn to resolve conflicts from a win-win place.
6. Begin a program of effective physical care.
   - Eat consciously to provide good nutritional support for your body.
   - Exercise regularly.
   - Get structural body work to break through any emotional patterns stored in your body.
7. Develop your spiritual life.
   - Use prayer, meditation, and other spiritual practices to help you reach deeper levels of spiritual mastery.
   - Find your life's purpose and your place in the world.
   - Develop forms of high service to others that help fulfill your purpose.
8. Create partnership relationships.
   - Create relationships with family members based on the principles of partnership, co-creation, flexibility, and intimacy.
   - Develop vocations and avocations that support the unfolding of your highest potential.
   - Create support systems that enable you to live in partnership with others and the earth.

## *Major Therapeutic Interventions of Developmental Process Work*

In DPW, the goal is to help family members gain access to material carried by some aspect of themselves that is split off or unconscious. Any therapeutic "doorway" can open a family member's unconscious to parts of the psyche that were closed off during childhood because of trauma or developmental disruptions. These split-off or unintegrated parts usually exist in opposition to other parts of the psyche that are owned or more integrated. Discovering these conflicting parts of the psyche that usually operate at an unconscious level is the first step in applying the principles of DPW. The second step is to help the family member or the family as a whole discover how the conflict between these two parts contains unmet needs or unresolved issues from childhood. The third goal is to help family members get these needs met and integrate this new learning in such a way that it helps the family become more whole, more interdependent, and more able to access transpersonal or spiritual realms.

## How to Follow the Multiple Processes of the Family and its Members

To discover the conflicting parts of the psyche, to identify the unmet developmental needs that are keeping them split off, and to help the client meet these needs, it is necessary to follow the client's signals. Each family member is seen as a system that constantly emits information through verbal and nonverbal signals. Following these signals can be a challenge for a therapist, for the signals may take the therapist through a confusing maze that can make him or her feel lost and out of control. For this reason, we always work as co-therapists when we do couples or family therapy. To follow the family member through this winding journey of signals, it is necessary to have a guiding structure. The following concepts help create a structure that allows therapists to follow the process more effectively.

1. *The surface process.* This is what the client is identified with at any given moment. It may be called the ego self; for example, "I am unemployed." Statements that begin with "I am" are indicators of the surface process of the client.

2. *The deep process.* This is what the client is not identified with in the given moment. It is usually described by the client as something that is happening to him or her. For the client who is unemployed, the deep process might be, "No one wants to hire me." The deep process is often associated with an unwanted or an unintegrated aspect of the personality that carries repressed feelings such as shame. Moving into the deep process with its unconscious material can be a very frightening experience for a client. It is important to move very slowly and respectfully into this material.

3. *The edge.* This is the point of conflict between the surface and the deep processes. It is also the edge of awareness between the known and unknown parts of the psyche. The edge can often be identified by statements that begin with, "I can't...." In the above example, the edge might be, "I can't get a job." Because it is often frightening to move into the deep process, it is important to work as long as necessary at the edge of it. At the edge, the client will learn many valuable things. He or she may learn about unmet developmental needs, about dysfunctional patterns of behavior, or about spiritual lessons. The

edge is the place where old feelings are stored that need to be released. The edge is also the place where people can build important intrapsychic structures that are needed to close the developmental gaps and ultimately repair the damage to the soul.

4. *Channels.* Channels are the ways in which information passes through a person's system. The channels we use are *auditory, visual, kinesthetic* (movement), *proprioceptive* (a combination of emotions and body sensations), *relationship* (between two people), and *family* (between three people or more). The therapist's task in DPW is to follow the flow of information as it winds its way through the client's information channels without interrupting, perpetrating, violating, or disturbing the client and his or her process until it is appropriate to make an intervention. When the information is flowing through a channel, the channel is "occupied." When a channel has no information or has unconscious information in it, the channel is "unoccupied." Terms such as these are simply tracking mechanisms for the therapist to use while watching the information flow.

   When information flows simultaneously through two channels and the information is not congruent, this is a "double signal." An example of this would be a woman saying, "I am in love with my husband" while she is also shaking her head side to side, which may be saying, "I don't think my husband loves me." Double signals are a quick way of helping the therapist identify the surface process ("I am in love with my husband") and the deep process ("I don't think my husband loves me") so that the work at the edge of the deep process can begin ("I can't face finding out that he may not love me").

5. *Amplification of signals.* This involves deliberately increasing or decreasing the strength of a signal to help the therapist and the client determine the actual meaning of the signal. For example, a therapist might ask a client who is shaking a foot while talking to shake it more or to stop shaking it altogether. Either approach may open up some new information that could be hidden in the movement.

6. *Mirroring.* Mirroring involves the therapist showing the client how his or her behavior looks from the outside. This technique can be useful for clients who cannot see their own behavior.

To do this, the therapist must be good at observing and acting out the observation.

7. *Taking over a signal or part.* This requires that the therapist act out or role play an unwanted part that exists in an unoccupied channel so the client can learn more about it. It is important that the therapist give the part back to the client during the therapy so the client can integrate it and so the therapist does not continue to carry it after the session is over.

8. *Interpretation.* Very little interpretation is done in DPW. Again, it is up to the client to determine what is meaningful and useful. It is appropriate to intervene or interpret only when the client needs cognitive information, mirroring, or help in completing some developmental task.

9. *Resistance.* There is no such concept in DPW. If you as a therapist suggest an intervention and the family doesn't respond favorably, this is considered negative feedback. The family is indicating that this is not the correct approach, or it is not the right time for the intervention. The family should never be forced to follow the therapist's agenda or program.

## Doorways to Enter the Deep Process

A family entering a therapy situation will already be exhibiting verbal and nonverbal signals that present the therapist with a number of doorways through which unconscious material can be accessed. These doorways are grouped under each of the channels described above: visual, auditory, proprioceptive, kinesthetic, relationship, and family.

1. *Visual.* Dreams are a visual doorway to the unconscious. Dreams can be analyzed for their symbolic, feeling, and spiritual content, and ultimately can be acted out in the form of a psychodrama. Through this analysis and enactment, it becomes possible for the client to determine what opposing parts of the psyche are showing up in the dream and what in the dream needs to be completed.

2. *Auditory.* An internal conflict often offers an auditory doorway to the unconscious. The conflict is experienced as a conversation between two opposing parts of the psyche. In this case, the family member might be asked to use dialoguing techniques to help him or her discover what is not finished about some old pattern in the internal conflict. Once this is deter-

mined, it may be possible to utilize Gestalt or psychodynamic techniques to complete the old pattern, thus allowing the family to construct a new pattern.

3. *Proprioceptive.* Body symptoms, both acute and chronic, are also a useful doorway to the deep process using the proprioceptive channel. Amplifying the pain of the symptom, such as an ulcer, will often help the family member remember some incident from the past in which there is unfinished business. The incident, which is long forgotten and has now somatized, can be examined to determine what the opposing parts of the psyche are and what in the process still needs to be finished. Once the family member completes a process and integrates the two parts, the pain or symptom usually disappears. If the pain reappears at some later date, we may advise a family member to consider it as an ally that can help her or him uncover even more unconscious patterning. Emotions also provide a doorway to the deep process. Expressing emotions often opens memories that may emerge as physical pain, pictures, conversations, or movements.

4. *Kinesthetic.* Unconscious movements offer a doorway to the deep process from the kinesthetic channel. Incomplete or abrupt movements in particular offer an opportunity to let the body reveal the opposing parts. Asking the client to consciously repeat a movement in slow motion can shift his or her awareness into some memory of a forgotten childhood event that reveals the opposing parts. At this point, the family member is encouraged to look for what in the event is not complete and to begin creating a plan for bringing the opposing parts together in an attempt to complete it. Family sculpting is an excellent tool to uncover the deep process in the family.

5. *Relationship.* Relationship conflicts provide a doorway to the deep process from the relationship channel. Relationship conflicts, which are usually a reflection of some unresolved relationship conflict from the past, can reveal the split-off parts each partner is projecting onto the other. When each family member identifies his or her projected parts and reclaims them, it becomes possible for them to locate some event or problem from the past that is trying to complete itself. By reclaiming the projected parts and completing the old event or problem, the two people are often able to resolve their conflicts.

6. *Family.* Family conflicts are a route to the unmet needs of the deep process using the family channel. In this case, we would assume that each family member involved is individually projecting some split-off part or unresolved family-of-origin issue onto other family members. The first part of resolving such a conflict would be to help each member identify both the personal aspect of the psyche being projected and the old issue (probably family-of-origin based) from which it originates. The second task would be for each individual to create ways in which his or her issue could be completed within the family setting.

Channels are essential in helping the family member gain access to a split-off part, for they help identify the place in the person where the splitting process may have occurred during a childhood trauma. For example, a sensitive man who was shamed by his mother when he was a child because she saw him as effeminate will often split off his feminine part. To reconnect with this part, the boy must go back into the proprioceptive channel to access the feeling of shame. Here he can remember the incident or incidents in which his receptive or innocent nature was ridiculed, feel the shame, and express his old feeling of shame. In hearing the shaming messages from his parents, he would also use the visual and auditory channels.

To reclaim his feminine part, this person would need to use all three channels. First, he would need to access the feeling channel where he would discover his old shame. Then he would need to have his shame identified as a feeling, have his experience of feeling shamed validated by the therapist, and have his feelings supported. In the visual and auditory channels he would need to see some nurturing person (perhaps the therapist) looking at him in a caring manner while speaking words that acknowledge the person's sensitivity, innocence, and receptivity. The client would also need to understand how he needs this part to function as a warm and compassionate person. He can then integrate his femininity into his psyche in such a way that he is more whole, more individuated, and more able to have functional relationships with both women and his spiritual mother.

Channels are also critical in helping people construct intrapsychic structures that are missing, particularly in those who have had severe trauma from neglect, abuse, or abandonment. These people often split off vital parts of themselves so severely that the parts may be almost impossible to find. If the parts are split off to an extreme, they may develop "personalities" that have names. Individuals with such severe intrapsychic gaps often lack inner structures that can help protect and nurture them. Without these intrapsychic structures, the person may have difficulty in problem solving during a crisis. The man mentioned above, for example, might regress into a childlike state if someone accused him of being a "sissy." Without an intrapsychic structure that serves as an inner protector, he may fall into an intrapsychic "hole" where he feels crazy.

The process of creating missing intrapsychic structures is a delicate one. It requires that the therapist follow the person's signals astutely, for somewhere in the flow of information through his or her channel system, the doorway to the part will appear. The task is to be very gentle and supportive, for most likely the person is in a regressive state, perhaps one that is preverbal.

For children to survive early traumas requires that they also receive some kind of nurturance and protection from some other human. Those without such care either die young or become psychotic very early. It is assumed, therefore, that adults who begin healing such trauma must have had some positive experiences to balance the negative ones. The therapeutic task is to recover these experiences in the channel where they occurred and use them to create the missing intrapsychic structures. To understand how this process works at a more technical level, we might use a computer-based analogy.

If, for example, the missing intrapsychic structure is a "nurturing parent," then we would insert into the computer a new disk that we name NP. Then, using channel theory, we would scan all the files (people from the client's past) looking for experiences. An older sister with whom the client slept as a small child might carry a proprioceptive memory of nurturing. A particular incident with a warm-hearted kindergarten teacher might carry a visual memory of nurturing. The voice of the grandfather reading a story to the person might carry an auditory memory, while the movement the person's mother made when she blew him or her a kiss goodnight might carry the kinesthetic memory. Once the person becomes aware that all the parts of a nurturing parent are already stored on the "hard drive," it becomes possible for him or her to imagine "copying" the nurturing memories onto the new disk. This allows the person to assemble the missing structure from his or her own experience.

Once copied and assembled, the new structure can be experienced piece by piece as the person remembers and reenacts these old memories with another person or persons. This grounds the structure physically, emotionally, and psychically within the client. It also allows the person to access the self-nurturing structure by remembering the nurturing component stored in each channel. If, however, there is a channel without a nurturing memory, the therapist can help the client fill that gap through the use of reparenting contracts.

Using such a precise psychological technology allows the therapist to exactly identify the developmental gaps. With such precision, the therapy can be much quicker, much easier, and much more effective. This technology also relieves the therapist of some of the intense transference from the client. The therapist will no longer feel the client demanding that the therapist become the ideal parent who can supply all that this person missed in childhood. This technology allows the therapist and the client to work more cooperatively without the intensity often involved in client-therapist transference. Clients find it highly empowering, and therapists find it highly freeing.

## How to Conduct a Therapy Session

The following steps show clearly how to conduct a therapy session using developmental process work.

*Begin therapy by asking for a contract with the family.* This may include both a general therapy contract regarding number of sessions, cost of sessions, and goals for therapy as well as specific desired outcomes for each session ("What do you want to accomplish in your session today?"). The initial contract is for a specific number of sessions, usually three to six. This is important for three reasons. First, it is important to put as much power as possible into the hands of the family. Reclaiming personal power and making clear and healthy agreements are important parts of the therapy process. Second, having a contract helps the therapist and the family have some measure of outcome both for the initial therapy contract and the session contract. Third, the initial series helps the therapist determine whether the therapist and the family can work together effectively.

*Support the family's surface process* by using reflective listening and clarifying statements, by supporting the feelings (expressed directly or indirectly), and by validating the experiences (often by naming; for example, "That sounds like abuse"). We also use warm, empathic verbal tones, attentive body language, and direct eye contact. These basic counseling skills help develop rapport and a sense of safety with each of the family members. This creates the safety and security needed for family members to reveal any hidden or deep material to the therapist. This step may take several sessions with a new family or only a few minutes with a family with whom there is already an established relationship.

During the first few minutes or hours of rapport building, the family members will reveal through the conversation a number of doorway opportunities. There may be movements in the hands or feet, a lowering of the head, the eyes may look up or to the side, or the client may describe a strong relationship or group conflict. Many such simultaneous signals can confuse the therapist. Patience is the best tool for the therapist to use, waiting until a signal appears that has a lot of energy in it or that reoccurs several times. At this point, it is safe to assume that this strong signal is a doorway through which to seek access to the unconscious material. Again, it is important to watch closely for the family member's feedback. If it is negative, then wait for another strong signal to appear that indicates another doorway to the unconscious.

The spiritual component of DPW must be kept in the forefront. When the unconscious material—the narcissistic wounds—of a family member appears, it is absolutely necessary for the therapist to assume a position of protector. When some aspect of these wounds appears after a long period of hiding, it can be assumed that some abuse or trauma was associated with its disappearance. When meeting this reemerging part, it is appropriate to assume an attitude of reverence, of sanctity such as that associated with the birth of an infant. The therapist may want to take the family member into the unconscious material too quickly in an attempt to get them through it rapidly. Guard against moving too fast for the family member. Find the person's rhythm and follow it.

Urges to move quickly can be ego-directed on the part of a therapist who sees him- or herself as the director of the therapy. In DPW, it is important to remember that the client is the director of therapy and that the therapist is following almost all the time. Interventions are appropriate only when the therapist sees a gap in the client's development that needs new information, options, or directions to help the client live more functionally. Even then it is necessary to have positive feedback from the client before continuing.

*Look for a signal that identifies the deep process.* When a strong signal appears in another channel, the therapist can offer feedback to the client such as, "I notice you keep rubbing your left ring finger when you talk about your ex-husband" (kinesthetic channel). Then notice how the client receives the feedback. If she responds with "I have an itch on this finger today, that's all," the therapist would not follow this signal because the client has given negative feedback. If she says "I was thinking about how sad I am not to be married to him anymore," the therapist can assume that the finger-rubbing is a safe signal to follow.

*Amplify the signal* by asking the person to do it more, amplifying the signal, or by forbidding the signal all together. For example, with the previous person, the therapist might say, "Just close your eyes and let yourself feel that sadness," or "What would happen right now if you stopped rubbing your finger?" Either statement could help her change channels (from kinesthetic into proprioceptive).

*Changing channels* generally happens spontaneously and brings a release of information from the unconscious to the client. If the change involves moving into the proprioceptive channel, it can also lead to a release of old feelings. A primary goal of the therapist is to facilitate the client in changing channels as many times as needed to help him or her access new information or release old feelings.

Information theory helps the therapist understand the different non-verbal body signals that indicate which channel is carrying the important information about the client's process at any given moment. When the eyes look up, it is usually a signal that a client is in the visual channel. When the eyes look sideways, it indicates that the client is accessing information in the auditory channel. Lowering the head or looking down is usually a sign that the client is in the proprioceptive channel, while movement of any kind indicates that information is flowing in the kinesthetic channel. Direct eye contact between client and therapist and congruent or mirroring body postures can be signs that the client is in the relationship channel with the therapist or with a partner who has also come to therapy. Multiple relationship or family issues indicate that the client is in the family channel.

*Work at the edge* is necessary if a family member or the family as a whole is not able to change channels. Here the client will learn valuable emotional, mental, physical, and spiritual lessons that indicate the real nature of the problem as well as the course of action needed to remedy it. Working at the edge is also a very sacred space and requires the most respectful and attentive attitude on the part of the therapist. It takes patience to let the client work at the edge without pushing him or her over. Most therapy time in DPW involves working at the edge. Some techniques for working at the edge are:

- Have the client explore options about going over the edge to make sure he or she has adequate intrapsychic structures for going over the edge without creating a psychotic break. This is particularly important when working with clients who have a personality disorder.
- Amplify or forbid the act of going over the edge.
- Role play or have another family member role play, going over the edge for the client.
- Have the client fantasize what going over the edge might be like.
- Help the client find a way around the edge.
- Have the client ask for the kind of support from other family members the client needs to go over the edge.

*Therapeutic interventions* in DPW are appropriate during a family therapy session when the therapist discovers evidence of incomplete developmental tasks emerging in a family member's process. These incomplete tasks may be related to incomplete bonding, separation, autonomy, or cooperation issues from the first five years of a family member's life. They also can be related to incomplete tasks of the parents in their couple relationship or incomplete tasks in the family system or all of the above. Figure 12.1 can be useful in determining the location of each person's developmental gaps.

The therapist must be able to recognize the nonverbal signals that indicate repressed feelings may be emerging in the therapeutic process. Rocking movements, a childlike tone of voice, curling up or lying down, and crossed feet are signals that often appear. Therapists should know the specific developmental needs and tasks of the four stages of development: co-dependent (bonding), counterdependent (separation), independent (autonomy), and interdependent (cooperation). Each stage will leave characteristic behaviors that indicate exactly what must be completed. For example, an adult with incomplete bonding will often have addictions to substances (food, drugs, alcohol), sex, and people. Adults with incomplete separation issues often have addictions to work or exhibit compulsive behaviors.

We have developed a series of skill-building exercises designed to help people complete these developmental stages. They are contained in our recent books (Weinhold, 1991; Weinhold & Hendricks, 1993; Weinhold & Weinhold, 1989, 1992, 1994). We give these handouts to family members to help them take charge of their own healing process. These exercises include:

- how to identify unmet developmental needs,
- how to get these needs met as an adult,
- how to express feelings appropriately,
- how to validate the client's childhood experiences and feelings,
- how to resolve old conflicts with members of the client's family of origin,
- how to resolve current conflicts in win-win ways,
- how to develop a vision of life beyond dysfunction, and
- how to conduct a family meeting.

We find that family therapy proceeds more rapidly and effectively if family members are also willing to work at several levels simultaneously. We recommend that they work alone with the handouts or by reading books, by attending workshops and seminars, and by using spiritual practices such as meditation and prayer. We also ask the family to hold regular family meetings where everyone can participate in the creation of a new family environment where trust and win-win conflict resolution can be practiced. If the family is having trouble creating effective family meetings, we will make a home visit and coach them until they are able to do so. This broad approach also supports family members in taking more and more charge of their own healing processes, which helps them reclaim personal power. This quickly shifts the therapist into the role of facilitator and consultant and helps prevent co-dependency between the family and therapist.

*Integration is the last step in a session of DPW.* The purpose of integration is to help the family system find ways to use the new information, insights, perceptions, and awarenesses gained during the session. The most effective way for family members to anchor new learning is to help them return to the channel that was first occupied at the beginning of the session. For example, if the person's presenting issue or problem emerged in the form of a dream or in a series of internal pictures, the occupied channel was visual. To integrate the session's learnings, the person needs to return to the visual channel. The therapist can help the client do this by asking, "How do you see yourself using what you learned in this session, especially with regard to the issue you began with?" The person would then have to create a new series of pictures related to the presenting issue and develop new behaviors congruent with the new learning.

This aspect of DPW is very important for several reasons. First, it provides a vision of the next steps in the family's process. Without a vision, we have found that it is almost impossible for people to develop new behaviors. Second, it asks the family to take information and experiences that may be of a transpersonal nature and translate them into practical, day-to-day behaviors or goals. Third, it returns the family and the therapist to the goal stated at the beginning of the session. This aspect of integration provides a sense of completion and also sets up closure for the session. It also provides an opportunity for the family members and the therapist to evaluate the therapy experience, and it can provide productive feedback to the therapist.

# ■ The Limitations of Developmental Process Work

The use of DPW in family therapy may be problematic in some cases because a long-term commitment may be required to break intergenerational family patterns. We usually recommend about one month of therapy for every year of life. But we have found that when a family works together to create a therapeutic milieu in the family, the time in family therapy is greatly reduced. Finally, this type of therapy requires the family to transcend the "conventional wisdom" and look at their problems and issues from an expanded perspective. Some families are just not ready or willing to do that and are not good candidates for this type of therapy.

# ■ Summary

The maps, charts, and tools needed to travel the mystical and mysterious world of the transpersonal have begun to reach over into the scientific world. With technologies such as those used in DPW, it becomes possible to identify, track, retrace, and recover the flow of transpersonal energy as it moves through individuals, couples, and families. The technologies, however, are there to explore the inner mystery of spirit and the deeper mystical nature of humans. In such an environment, where humans can begin to join with their own true transpersonal nature, co-creation becomes possible.

### Developmental Process Work

**CASE EXAMPLE**

*We recently had two people come to us for couples therapy in the midst of an intense crisis. The woman had just discovered that her husband was having an affair with another woman. She said she was angry enough to kill him. She claimed that a demon inside her was telling her to kill him and that she was afraid this demon would take over her behavior. After getting her to agree that she would use nonviolent means to resolve her conflict with her husband, we asked her to draw a picture of her demon and conduct a dialogue with him. With the picture of the demon she drew on a pillow in front of her, she carried on a Gestalt-like dialogue for about fifteen minutes.*

*Much to her surprise, she discovered through dialoguing with this demon that he served a useful purpose in her life. When she asked him what it was, he replied, "I have been waiting 900 years for you to work on this issue." When she asked what the issue was, he said, "You need to learn how to give up control. It was your need to control that led your husband to have an affair." He added, "I'm here to help you let go, and I am very patient." Eventually she asked the demon to help her work on her control issue. Later she began working on this issue in therapy. She also saw that her husband's affair provided her with another opportunity to learn to give up control over him and other people as well.*

*We wondered how more traditional therapists might have handled this client. We saw that she was, in effect, having a spiritual emergency precipitated by her husband's affair. Even though she looked and sounded psychotic, we knew it was important not to try to take her out of this state until we all better understood the purpose of this demon process. We trusted that there was something "right" about this process and decided to invite her to discover more about the demon. A more medically oriented therapist probably would have medicated and even hospitalized her to get her out of her "crazy" thinking process and through her emergency.*

# SUGGESTED
## READINGS

Miller, A. (1991). *Breaking Down the Wall of Silence.* New York: Dutton.

Weinhold, B. K. (1991). *Breaking Free of Addictive Family Relationships.* Walpole, NH: Stillpoint.

Weinhold, B. K., & Hendricks, G. (1993). *Counseling and Psychotherapy: A Transpersonal Approach.* Denver, CO: Love.

Weinhold, B. K., & Weinhold, J. B. (1989). *Breaking Free of the Co-Dependency Trap.* Walpole, NH: Stillpoint.

Weinhold, B. K., & Weinhold, J. B. (1994). *Soul Evolution: The Spiritual Uses of Conflict in Relationships.* Walpole, NH: Stillpoint.

Weinhold, J. B., & Weinhold, B. K. (1992). *Counter-Dependency: The Flight from Intimacy.* Colorado Springs, CO: CICRCL Press.

# III

## Special Issues in

## Marriage and Family

## Therapy

### CHAPTERS

# 13

# Treating Families with Special Needs

*Family therapy was originally developed as a method for working with schizophrenics and their families. Later, these theories and techniques were employed with families exhibiting a variety of problems. More recently, family systems theories have been employed to help with specific family problems, including blended families, ethnically diverse families, families with disabled children, alcoholic families, abusive families, families experiencing divorce, and families with a depressed or suicidal member. A brief discussion of family treatment for each of these specific problem situations will be presented in this chapter.*

## KEY CONCEPTS

Blended families
Families with disabled children
Alcoholic families
Abusive families

Depressed families
Ethnically diverse families
Divorcing families
Gender issues in family therapy

## QUESTIONS
## FOR DISCUSSION

1. *What important issues should a couple remarrying resolve prior to the marriage?*

2. *What is the best way for the family therapist to prepare to work with ethnically diverse families?*

3. *In what ways are the dynamics of families with disabled children similar to those of families without disabled children? In what ways do the dynamics of these family types differ?*

4. *What special problems should the family therapist be aware of when treating a family with an alcoholic member?*

5. *What are the critical issues to consider when treating a family with an abusive member?*

6. *What are the significant steps in the divorce process?*

7. *How can depression in one family member be maintained by the behaviors of other family members?*

8. *How might gender stereotyping affect the process of family therapy?*

*A*s family therapy has gained respect from the mental health community, new responsibilities have emerged for the profession. Clinical research has increased, and information has emerged that suggests strategies for treating families with specific problems. In this chapter, we will discuss treatment for several of these special situations.

## Blended Families

Blended families are created when one or both partners bring children from a previous marriage into a new marriage. Divorce and remarriage occur frequently; it has been estimated that in 1990, 69% of children in the United States lived with both parents and that for children born in the 1980s, 59% can expect to live with only one parent for a period of time and 35% can expect to live with a step-parent before the age of 18 (Glick, 1989). One of the most common problems in the remarried or blended family is that family members attempt to reconstitute as a traditional nuclear family (Visher & Visher, 1979). Frequently, the step-parent will attempt to assume the role of the "real" mother or father and quickly engage the step-child in an escalating battle to determine who will define the adult-child relationship. As this escalation takes place, the biological parent frequently enters the fray on the side of the child, which intensifies the problem because a division between the parents is now created.

When this type of family enters therapy, the therapist should quickly join with each member by understanding the frustrations inherent in each person's role. After establishing credibility as an expert on step-families, the therapist identifies the "myth of the nuclear family," which suggests that step-families will be similar in all respects to traditional families (Visher & Visher, 1979). Once the family recognizes the myth of the nuclear family, the myth will no longer drive the behavior of the family, and the family will stop attempting to duplicate the traditional family. At this point, members can discuss and negotiate how they would like their blended family to function. This intervention gives the step-parent the opportunity to hear directly from the step-children how they would like the relationship to develop. Therapy should also provide an opportunity for the parents to discuss how they wish their children to be treated by the step-parent. Therapy with a blended family can be an extremely positive experience after the family releases some of its idealistic notions concerning how blended families function. Structured premarital counseling (Fenell, Nelson, & Shertzer, 1981; Fenell & Wallace, 1986) can help couples prepare for certain problems associated with blended families and is advised whenever possible.

# ▉ *Ethnically Diverse Families*

Most family therapists will have the opportunity to work with client families of diverse ethnic backgrounds. This can be challenging as different ethnic groups value and respond to therapy in their own unique ways (McGoldrick, Pearce, & Giordano, 1982). When a therapist meets a client family from a different ethnic background, how should he or she respond? Each person and, indeed, each family is unique, and that uniqueness must be understood and valued by the therapist. If the therapist is open to learning about, understanding, and respecting the values and behaviors of one particular ethnically diverse group, this can lead to the possibility of successful therapy. Others contend that understanding a variety of ethnic groups and the characteristics of these groups better prepares the therapist to work effectively with all groups. A criticism of this approach is that the therapist may form stereotypical ideas about members of particular ethnic groups that, while valid for the majority of members of the group, may not apply to the specific individuals who are present for family therapy.

McGoldrick, et al., (1991) contend that the best preparation for a family therapist who will work with ethnically diverse clients is for the therapist to thoroughly study his or her own ethnic identity. By so doing, the therapist will come to understand the unique characteristics of the group and recognize that the values of the group, while understandable and useful for its members, may not be useful for other groups. The therapist comes to understand that the values of one group are no more true or correct than the values of some other group. Moreover, the therapist will come to recognize when he or she is operating out of a personal, ethnically based value in therapy. If the therapist is able to transcend ethnic identity, a "multiethnic" perspective develops, and the therapist no longer feels the need to convince clients to adopt his or her values.

The effective therapist knows how to "think" about ethnic differences and how these differences may have an impact on therapy rather than possessing a wealth of specific knowledge about a variety of ethnic groups. Specifically, various ethnic groups may have different responses toward suffering; different attitudes about helping professionals; a more formal or informal interactional preference with strangers; or differing attitudes about the appropriateness of childrens' expressiveness. The therapist will need to be sensitive to each of these and numerous other possible conditions in therapy.

While well aware of the problems associated with stereotyping members of ethnic groups and with no intention of doing so, McGoldrick and Rohrbaugh (1987) conducted a study that characterized differences among groups to help clinicians become aware of the range of values brought to therapy experience. Some of the most striking characteristics of several groups identified in the study are:

- Jewish families
    marry within group
    value success and education
    encourage children
    talk out problems
    shared suffering
    guilt used to shape behavior of children
- WASP families
    be strong and make it alone
    independence
    self-control
    suffer in silence
    conflicts hidden
- Italian families
    nothing more important than family
    expressiveness and enjoy a good time
    traditional sex roles
    relating through eating

    accomplishing tasks through personal connection
    males tend to be dominant
- African-American families
    strength to survive
    religiousness
    able to make it alone
    women seen as strong
    parents want children to succeed
- Asian families
    always have time for family members
    elders respected for wisdom
    bad behavior reflects on the whole group
    parents worry about children doing well in school
    parents want children to succeed
- Hispanic families
    family members take responsibility for care of elderly
    always have time for family members
    defined roles: men protect and women nurture
    elders respected for wisdom
    "losing face" viewed as catastrophic

Again, it must be emphasized that these characteristics are based on a preliminary study and should not be used to stereotype any group. Understanding the uniqueness of each family remains one of the most important tasks of the family therapist in dealing with ethnic minority families, or any family for that matter.

## ▇ Families with a Disabled Child

Fenell, Martin, and Mithaug (1986) have described therapy with a family with a disabled child. They suggested that once the initial shock of dealing with the reality of a disabled child subsides and reality of the situation is accepted, the parents begin working to provide the best possible environment for the child. At this point, two problems may occur. First, the parents may focus so much of their energy on the disabled child that they neglect their own relationship and perhaps the needs of their other children. Second, the family may do so much for the disabled child that the child does not learn what he or she is able to accomplish without assistance. It is the first problem that precipitates the need for therapy, as the marriage partners begin to experience the void in their own relationship or a nondisabled child begins to act out.

The first task of the therapist is to communicate that the sacrifices each member has made for the disabled child are noted, understood, and appreciated. Then the therapist points out that the family has not been able to make time for other members because they have organized their lives around the disabled child (Berger, 1982). Helping the family find time to reestablish other relationships takes patience and understanding by the therapist.

When the disabled child is the identified patient, the situation differs from most family therapy in that the disabled child often will be physically or mentally unable to make the improvements of a nondisabled identified patient. The therapist must always take this factor into consideration when working with a family system with a disabled family member and should devote considerable effort toward helping the other family members create an environment for the disabled child that will allow the child to fully develop his potential.

This objective is accomplished while strengthening the key subsystems of the family, especially the spousal subsystem and the subsystems between parents and nondisabled children. Frequently, parents do not know what resources are available in the community to help them with their child. Furthermore, they may feel guilty placing the child in short-term care so the family can enjoy some time away from the problems presented by the child. The therapist should be ready to help the family in both of these areas by providing necessary information about available support systems and by normalizing the parents' concern about leaving the disabled child. It is important for both the parents and the child to spend time away from each other.

When the parents begin taking their focus off the child, they may experience deficits in their own relationship. They may need support and training in communication to begin to relate to each other as individuals in meaningful ways. As the family begins to balance its time and energy better, it is not unusual to discover that the disabled child is able to accomplish many things the parents and siblings had previously done for him or her. This change in the disabled child has a systemic effect on the parents and siblings, who then begin to encourage further appropriate autonomy for the child.

# ■ Families with an Alcoholic Member

Families with alcoholic members are often treated with family therapy (Edwards & Steinglass, 1995). Many professionals consider alcoholism a disease, but others believe it is a behavioral problem. Regardless of the therapist's definition of alcoholism, it is clear that the alcoholic member not only affects the family system and the individuals in the family but is also affected by the family (Kaufman & Kaufman, 1979; Pattison, 1982). Family therapists have criticized treatment of the individual alcoholic outside the family context, and alcoholism treatment therapists have criticized family therapists for assuming that alcoholism can be cured by eliminating dysfunctional family patterns. All but the most minor problems of alcoholism may be treated most effectively by a combination of interrupting the drinking cycle through therapy with the individual and employing family therapy. The purpose of family therapy is to modify the family environment so the family does not precipitate and reinforce old drinking patterns.

Pattison (1982) identified four themes in the interaction of the alcoholic and the family. First, the alcoholic produces significant stress on the family system. Members may have to adopt roles to cope with the alcoholic member that are not in their own best interests. For instance, a young son may have to assume parental roles and care for an infant sibling because his mother is frequently drunk. Second, therapists must understand the effect the family has on the alcoholic. Conflict in the marriage or with children may precipitate excessive drinking and maintain the drinking pattern. Thus, alcoholism may serve as (1) a symptom of family dysfunction; (2) a method for coping with family stress; (3) a consequence of dysfunctional family rules, roles, and structure; or (4) a combination of these functions. Third, alcoholism is a family disease. It may be transmitted from one generation to the next. If one generation has an alcoholic, the chances increase that the next generation will also have an alcoholic. Nonalcoholic sons or daughters of alcoholics frequently marry an alcoholic and keep the intergenerational cycle functioning. Fourth, family participation in the treatment of an alcoholic improves the prognosis. Pattison (1982) reported that family participation in aftercare greatly enhances the positive outcome of treatment. He believed it critical that family members be included in the treatment of alcoholism.

However helpful it may be, family therapy alone is rarely sufficient. The alcoholic suffers from major physical, emotional, social, and vocational impairments. These problems must often be treated with specific rehabilitation methods, which may include inpatient therapy to break the drinking cycle (Pattison, 1982).

When couples and families with alcoholics seek family therapy, they almost never present their problem as being alcoholism. Rather, some other symptom almost always precipitates the decision to enter therapy. Too often, family therapists do not explore the possibility of an alcohol problem in the family, and many alcoholic families remain untreated. Usher and Steinglass (1981) encouraged family therapists to explore the possibility of an alcohol problem in the family. If one is detected, these authors maintain that the problem with alcohol must be dealt with before any other symptoms may be effectively treated. Initial treatment of the family must involve diagnosing the alcoholism as a *family problem*. All family members must understand that each of them has a role to play in resolving the family problem. The therapist's diagnosis of alcoholism will not be helpful unless the family members accept the diagnosis. Thus, the therapist must carefully gather and present data to support the diagnosis sensitively and firmly.

The first requirement of treatment is to interrupt the drinking pattern. The therapist will prepare the family for "slips" so that their expectations are not too high. Participation in Alcoholics Anonymous, Alanon, and Alateen are often useful adjuncts for the family while the drinking cycle is being stopped. After the drinking has stopped, the therapy focuses on reestablishing intimacy in the family that is not built around alcohol but on the genuine caring and respect of family members for one another. When alcohol is removed from the family system, it is not unusual for an intense void to be created. Members no longer know how to act or what to do. Family therapy can help the members move through this confusing and frightening phase to more productive family functioning. While family therapy is no panacea in the treatment of alcoholism, recent research suggests it is often very useful (Edwards & Steinglass, 1995).

# Gender Issues in Marriage and Family Therapy

The feminist critique of family therapy was one of the most powerful trends in the field during the past decade. Feminist family therapists questioned the notion of circularity in assessing families and the resulting conclusion that all family members are equally involved in maintaining a pattern of behavior (Goodrich et al., 1988). The feminists insisted that many family systems are unequal, with males having significantly more power than the women. Moreover, these writers condemned those who conceptualized systematically at the expense of an individual within the family, often a woman (Sprenkle, 1990).

In response to this criticism, family therapists have looked closely at the role of gender in family treatment. In the past, it may have been safe to assume that a family held traditional gender roles. Not so anymore. Therapists now need to spend time with males and females within families, attempting to understand how each person would like the family to function and how each person expects to be treated. Therapists also need to examine client family patterns to determine if those patterns are maintained by family hierarchical structures supported by implicit or explicit threat to other members. If such structures are identified, clarifying the effects of this way of functioning with all family members present is essential. Helping families develop alternative and more equal structures would be a goal of treatment.

In a special section of the *Journal of Marital and Family Therapy,* several authors comment on the role of men in marriage (Doherty, 1991). The conclusion appears to be that men need to change, and the jury is still out on whether this will happen. Doherty (1991) warned that moving men from the pedestal to the mud and women from the mud to the pedestal will not solve the gender problems. Doherty's concern is that we have moved from a model that recognized women as "men with deficits" to an equally problematic deficit model of recognizing men as "women with deficits." Berg (1991) criticized the movement to make men more like women and women more like men. She challenged the assumption that obliterating the differences between men and women will solve gender problems. Rather, Berg suggested an intervention that asks the question: "How can this particular woman learn to get what she wants in life using her strengths and talents? How can this particular man learn to get what he wants from life using his unique assets? How are we the same and different? Let us make these commonalties and differences work for us separately and together" (pp. 311–312).

How do mental health professionals develop a more gender sensitive approach to our work? Storm (1991) suggested that therapist training is critical to this shift. She has developed a training module that places gender at the heart of the training program. This approach to family therapy training continues to emphasize the importance of systems theory in treatment. However, it challenges the axioms and assumptions of systems theory throughout the training program. Black and Piercy (1991) have developed a research scale for assessing the effects of such a gender-based training program on students' attitudes toward a feminist-informed perspective on therapy.

## Families with an Abusive Member

Violence in families has long been a difficult problem for mental health professionals to treat. It is especially difficult because physical abuse is frequently a violation of the law as well as a threat to the family structure of those involved (Margolin, 1987). When abuse or neglect involves a child, therapists should be aware that they have a legal obligation to report the abuse in most states (Huber, 1994). Because abusive adults were often abused as children, their self-concepts are frequently quite low. Their ability to control their impulses and consider alternatives in a potentially violent situation are limited.

From a family systems perspective, physical abuse to a spouse or a child is considered to be part of a pattern of behavior that involves several family members. However, unlike most other types of presenting problems, the family therapist should not attempt to take the focus off the abuser, as this approach serves only to lead family members and community service agencies to believe that the therapist is excusing the violent acts. Families often enter treatment right after an abusing incident has taken place. At this time, the abuser usually feels bad about the violent actions and is ready to work at improving the family situation and eliminating the abuse. Other family members are generally hopeful that therapy will eliminate the abusive situation.

When the family enters treatment, the therapist has two basic goals. First, the therapist helps the abusive member learn to delay acting on impulses. Second, the therapist helps the abused client and the abuser develop the ability to recognize and consider several alternatives to potentially violent situations. The abuser must learn to recognize and select alternatives other than violence (Hatcher, 1981).

The first session is often a crisis intervention session. The therapist may be the first person outside the law enforcement system with whom the family has been able to discuss the problem. Therefore, it is important for the therapist to talk with each family member and allow all unexpressed feelings to be presented *without* allowing those feelings to escalate. At this point in treatment, escalation of feelings could precipitate abusive motivations that the family is not yet ready to handle. As the therapist discusses feelings about the problem with the family members without allowing them to escalate, a sense of control develops for the family. They are, perhaps for the first time, able to discuss what has happened without escalation. The sense of control that develops is the first step toward impulse control. As they begin to share their feelings, the therapist reinforces the aspects of the discussion that demonstrate control of their behavior. This initial process sets the stage for the family to deal with anger within controlled limits, a characteristic that violent families need to develop.

Davidson (1978) proposed a domestic violence cycle that therapists need to understand to be helpful to families in treatment. The stages of the cycle are: (1) tension builds in the family, (2) a violent incident occurs, then (3) the violent member is remorseful and seeks sympathy and understanding. From a systems point of view, it is possible to understand the violent incident through the provocation-response cycle. When the victim senses the tension building and realizes that a violent incident is going to occur, he or she may precipitate the incident to speed movement through the violence stage to the remorseful stage. If this behavior is occurring, it should be identified in a way that does not remove the responsibility of committing violence from the abuser. Again, the therapist must ensure that all family members understand that the abusive behavior is not acceptable while helping each member recognize his or her role in maintenance of the behavior. Furthermore, the therapist must ensure that the family knows that if the abuser does not learn to manage the violent behavior, the police and courts will. The therapist and family members must all agree that the behavior is unacceptable (Hatcher, 1981).

Hatcher (1981) suggested that a contract should be developed with the family. In this contract, members agree that when tension is building and violence is likely, the victims will leave the home. The contract should specify that the family will be in the "safe house" for six to twenty-four hours and that a call will be made to the home before the family returns. The place where the family will go should be arranged in advance but should not be known to the violent member. If this is not possible, the person agreeing to help the victims must be prepared to contact the police if the violent member should precipitate a potentially dangerous situation.

After the situation deescalates, each family member involved is instructed to call the therapist to describe how he or she managed the situation. These calls to the therapist are important because they reinforce that the leaving behavior on the part of the victims is appropriate behavior and that the victims have helped the violent member by leaving. The abuser must understand that when the family leaves the home, this is *good behavior* designed to strengthen the family relationships and not abandonment. The therapist plays an important role in helping the abuser recognize and accept this fact.

Therapists should attempt to develop a basic contract with the family in the first session with refinements occurring in later sessions. If the family cannot agree on the contract or if a contract is not finalized, the therapist may suggest that a temporary separation is needed if there is concern for the welfare of the family members.

After the family has been in therapy for several sessions, it may be establishing a pattern for impulse control and considering options other than violence. At this point, it is often helpful for the family members to attend support groups. These support groups for victims and abusers help the family members know that they are not alone in their struggle and that they are understood and supported by those who have been through similar circumstances. Furthermore, these groups provide additional support for the changes the family is making in therapy.

One of the major factors in long-term success with violent families is to help the violent member develop enhanced self-esteem. To accomplish this objective, it may be helpful to work individually with key family members in counseling sessions designed to enhance self-esteem.

A final caveat for the therapist working with an abusive family is the potential threat to the therapist. If a threat is made or implied, the therapist should take the threat seriously and deal with it in a matter-of-fact manner. If the threatening client is not appropriately responsive, the therapist should not be reluctant to discontinue treatment and take other appropriate protective measures (Benedek, 1982).

While the need to provide treatment to families with an abusive member is critical, outcome studies on the effects of treatment have been discouraging (Hamberger & Hastings, 1993). We have no conclusive studies to suggest effective intervention except for the permanent separation of the conflictual parties.

# Families with a Depressed or Suicidal Member

This specific problem is one that all therapists encounter several times in their careers. Olin and Fenell (1989) completed a study suggesting that when one spouse in a marriage is depressed, the other may also be depressed as well. They suggested marital therapy as an effective treatment for such "depressed marriages." Oftentimes depression may become severe and life-threatening as the depressed family member contemplates suicide. As in other life-threatening situations, the systems therapist should focus treatment initially on the presenting problem, the potential suicide. Although a systemic conceptualization may be helpful in understanding the family dynamics that support the suicidal ideation, it is usually a mistake to attempt to defocus the presenting problem until it has been thoroughly explored and steps have been taken to remove the immediacy of the suicide threat.

Thus, in the first phase of therapy it will be important to learn from the family members what has occurred in the past to lead to the depressed and suicidal feelings in one member. Frequently, the therapist will discover that because of intense worry about the suicidal member, the family is "overloading" the identified patient with love and concern, which may paradoxically cause the person to feel more depressed and hopeless. The therapist can help family members learn to express "just the right level of concern" to the depressed member. This change in the family's behavior will generally take some of the pressure off the identified patient and alleviate some of the depression and hopeless feelings.

Because depression and suicidal thoughts frequently occur together, the therapist should assess the client's life situation and explore the history that has precipitated the depression. Individuals who perceive their family-of-origin experiences to be positive are less likely to experience depression or other health problems than those who perceive their family-of-origin experiences to be problematic (Canfield, Hovestadt, & Fenell, 1992).

When a long-standing history of depression is identified, the client may be referred for an examination by a psychiatrist to determine whether antidepressant medication may be helpful in stabilizing the hopeless and helpless feelings that accompany depression. If medication is indicated, it will often help stabilize the client's mood and enable more effective work to take place in family therapy (Conye, 1987). The therapist should caution the family that antidepressant medication is very dangerous if excessive amounts are taken. The family should be instructed to monitor the use of the medication by the patient, especially during the early weeks of treatment when the effects of the medication may not be evident and when the depression is severe (Conye, 1987).

The behavior of family members toward the suicidal member is very important. Members must be concerned and attentive, but in a way that communicates to the person that the helpless feelings are understandable and that with the help of therapy, as well as changes in the family system, the feelings can be managed. Their attitude should communicate their respect for the client's ability to work through the situation. In situations where the family cannot develop the appropriate level of concern, the therapist may begin sessions with only the depressed individual present and gradually integrate the family into the sessions as the suicidal thoughts become less intense. It is important to involve the family in treatment as soon as possible because, as is always the case when the therapist chooses to focus on the presenting problem, the identified patient may be labeled by the family as the sick one. This attitude may validate the family's perceptions that it does not need to change.

One of the most effective ways to begin treatment of a family with a depressed or suicidal member is to develop a nonsuicide contract with the family. In this contract, the suicidal member agrees not to attempt suicide while involved in treatment. Whenever possible, it is also helpful to have other family members specifically identify in the contract what they will and will not do to assist the suicidal member in getting back to normal. By including all family members in the contract development, a systemic base is established that begins to broaden the family's understanding of the problem as a family problem that may be maintained and supported by the behaviors of all its members. The contract is helpful for the suicidal member because it formally offers a way for the person not to take his or her own life. Agreeing to a contract not to commit suicide often removes a tremendous burden from the suicidal member. A caution is in order, however. A contract will not stop a person who is determined to take his own life. If the therapist suspects that the client will attempt suicide despite a contract, hospitalization or some other type of inpatient treatment should be arranged.

Once the immediate threat of suicide has subsided, more traditional family therapy should begin. Rather than keeping the focus on the suicidal member, the focus may shift to other members and their impact on the overall health of the family.

# ■ *Therapy with Divorcing Families*

Divorce is a widespread phenomenon in American society. Everett and Volgy (1991) suggested that most therapists will deal with divorce-related problems in their practices and that the effects of divorce will touch the majority of adults and children in this country in some way. Kitson and Morgan (1990) projected that as many as one-half to two-thirds of recently contracted marriages may end in divorce. Fenell (1993b) reviewed current literature suggesting the potential harmful impact of divorce on children, extended family members, and the divorcing couple themselves. Despite the potential pain associated with it, divorce remains a common occurrence. The process of divorce is developmental, and the therapist may be included at various points in the process. For example, a therapist may work with:

- a couple in marriage counseling who discover they do not want to stay together,
- a spouse who has been informed that the marriage is to end and is devastated by the news,
- an acting-out child who is responding to the recent divorce of her parents, or
- a couple who intends to divorce and wants the process to be as positive as possible for all concerned.

Everett and Volgy (1991) developed a framework for the divorce process to help therapists understand and treat the various aspects of divorce with specific interventions. They postulated a series of steps in the divorce process and suggested that therapists be prepared to intervene at any of the steps. The most important steps in the divorce process as identified by Everett and Volgy are described here.

*Heightened ambivalence* occurs when parents begin to have serious doubts about the marriage. It is during this stage that children usually become aware that a problem exists. The therapist may be involved here, or the couple may let the relationship deteriorate without seeking help The next step is *distancing;* the marriage relationship begins to be characterized by both physical and emotional distance. This distancing may also occur with extended family and some friends. During this phase of the process, the couple may become aware that outside help is essential if the relationship is to improve. The third step in the process is *preparation fantasies and actions.* Here the partners begin to imagine that they will have their needs met by a return to the family of origin or by living a less restricted life after the divorce. *Physical separation* is the next step in the process. It is at this point that the reality of the divorce begins to have an impact on the children and may be a time when the children enter therapy.

*Pseudoreconciliation* may follow the separation stage. Events such as problems with the children or financial settlements bring the couple back together. While it is possible that this coming together could signify a reconciliation, normally this will not be the case. Moreover, this phase fuels childrens' fantasies that the parents will get back together, which can be devastating when the reconciliation is short-lived. After the temporary reconciliation, old problems resurface and reconfirm for the spouses why they want a divorce. At this stage, they often become more open with others about their plans. As children recognize this parting of the parents, they may develop symptoms or problems that might serve to slow the divorce process. Therapy is often sought at this point to help the children as well as to smooth the divorce process.

The *decision to divorce* occurs after the couple moves through the previous stages. During this stage, the legal system becomes actively involved, and it is important for the therapist to have a network of family law specialists to consult with. *Recurring ambivalence* resembles the earlier attempt at reconciliation. This time the overwhelming forces of the legal process lead one or both spouses to reconsider the decision to divorce. During this stage, children's hopes for reconciliation are renewed, and in a few cases, these hopes are rewarded as the divorce process is discontinued. The next step is dealing with *potential disputes.* The divorcing couple may choose to deal with disputes through the use of mediation or through adversarial methods. If the adversarial method is used, the therapist must be aware of the possibility of being called into court to testify concerning the case.

Once the divorce is finalized, the couple with children begins to establish a method of *postdivorce coparenting.* Clearly defined rules and responsibilities are essential here for the sake of the children. When coparenting problems arise, therapy may be of great value. Most couples who divorce will eventually remarry. More than 65% of women and 70% of men are likely to remarry after divorce (Norton & Mooreman, 1987). Many of these *remarriages* will require the intervention of the family counselor to help the new family define roles, rules, and responsibilities. And finally, the family counselor may be needed to help with the final stage of the divorce sequence, *dual family functioning,* where both partners from the former marriage are remarried and sharing children as well as assuming a parenting role for the new spouse's children. This is indeed a complex task that requires skill and perseverance and, occasionally, the help of a counselor.

Glang and Betis (1993) developed a list of suggestions to help children through the divorce process. These suggestions are:

- Both parents tell the children of the divorce with care and concern.
- Give children advance warning before one parent moves out.
- Ensure that children do not feel they are being divorced from either parent. Spend individual time with each child.
- The parent with whom the child is with most of the time will usually be the "anchor" parent. This is the parent who will most likely experience the child's anger and sadness
- Explain the divorce to kids in words they will understand. Reassure them that the divorce is the result of the adults' shortcomings, not the child's.
- Children should see your emotions and know that you feel and are human. However, too much emotionalism may lead children to believe there is no adult to rely on, and they may feel overwhelmed and frightened.
- Do not criticize the former spouse in front of the children. The children will find faults with both parents. Let the kids brings these up, not the parent.
- Let the kids see the new home as soon as possible. Ensure they have some space of their own. They may have a room, a closet, or perhaps only a chest of drawers, but it must be their private space.

- Children often wish parents would reconcile, even years later. Be aware of this and accept their feelings even though their will be no reconciliation.
- Help kids look forward to the visit to the other parent's home. These transitions can be difficult and stressful. Parents should help smooth the process.

Family counselors will have ample opportunity to work with divorcing and remarried families. Being aware of the stages of divorce and of ways to intervene during these stages can be useful in helping families through these most difficult times.

## Summary

For the marriage and family counselor to be best able to serve the divergent needs of clients, it is necessary for the counselor to have specific knowledge about numerous family-related problems. In this chapter, we have introduced and briefly discussed several specific family problems the family counselor will frequently encounter in clinical practice. We suggest that the reader use this chapter as an introduction and springboard to a more comprehensive study of these important issues, as well as other specific problems not covered here.

# SUGGESTED
## READINGS

Ammerman, R. T., & Hersen, M., eds. (1992). *Assessment of Family Violence: A Clinical and Legal Sourcebook*. New York: John Wiley.

Barnard, C. P. (1981). *Families, Alcoholism and Therapy*. Springfield, IL: Charles C Thomas.

Beck, A. T. (1976). *Cognitive Therapy and the Emotional Disorders*. New York: International Universities Press.

Beck, A. T., Rush, A., Shaw, B., & Emery, G. (1979). *Cognitive Therapy of Depression*. New York: Guilford Press.

Fenell, D. L., Martin, J. E., & Mithaug, D. E. (1986). "The Mentally Retarded Child." In L. B. Golden & D. E. Capuzzi, eds., *Helping Families Help Children: Family Interventions with School-Related Problems* (pp. 87–96). Springfield, IL: Charles C Thomas.

Goodrich, T. J., Rampage, C., Ellman, B., & Halstead, K. (1988). *Feminist Family Therapy: A Casebook*. New York: Norton.

Margolin, G. (1987). "The Multiple Forms of Aggressiveness Between Marital Partners: How Do We Identify Them?" *Journal of Marital and Family Therapy, 13*(1), 77–85.

McGoldrick, M., Pearce, J. K., & Giordano, J. (1982). *Ethnicity and Family Therapy*. New York: Guilford Press.

Visher, E. B., & Visher, J. S. (1979). *Stepfamilies: A Guide to Working with Stepparents and Stepchildren*. New York: Brunner/Mazel.

Wallerstein, J. (1989). *Second Chances: Men, Women and Children after Divorce*. New York: Ticknor & Fields.

# 14

# Professional Issues, Ethics, and Research

*The discipline of marriage and family therapy has emerged from the clinical experience and research of several older disciplines, including psychology, psychiatry, social work, group therapy, and others. Thus, marriage and family therapy has developed as both a separate discipline and as a specialty area of other established mental health professions. In this chapter, we will discuss several key issues influencing and confronting marriage and family therapy and its continued development. We will also discuss the ethical standards of marriage and family therapists with a focus on some of the ethical issues that may occur when the client is a family rather than an individual. Finally, we will present important research findings that have supported the continued development of marriage and family therapy.*

## KEY CONCEPTS

Professional organizations in family therapy
Clinical member, AAMFT
Confidentiality
Privilege

Informed consent
Preparation of MFTs
Outcome studies for MFT

## QUESTIONS
## FOR DISCUSSION

1. Do you think marriage and family therapy is a profession in itself, or is it a subspecialty of several mental health professions? Support your answer.

2. Why should a counselor use a professional disclosure statement?

3. What type of professional training do you think a counselor should undergo before beginning work with couples and families?

4. What are some unique ethical problems a therapist might encounter when providing marriage and family therapy?

5. Several research findings are reported in this chapter. Which of them do you believe are most significant? Why?

$T$he professional practice of marriage and family therapy grew tremendously during the 1980s and early 1990s. To represent the interests of the increasing number of professionals practicing marriage and family therapy, several professional organizations with a focus on marriage and family therapy have emerged.

## Professional Organizations

Four professional organizations specifically represent the professional interests of therapists who work with couples and families:

- American Association for Marriage and Family Therapy (AAMFT)
- International Association of Marriage and Family Counselors (IAMFC), a division of the American Counseling Association (ACA)
- American Family Therapy Association (AFTA)
- Division of Family Psychology, American Psychological Association (APA)

### The American Association for Marriage and Family Therapy (AAMFT)

The oldest and most widely recognized of these organizations is the AAMFT, which was established in 1942. Originally, this organization was the American Association of Marriage Counselors because the focus of the membership was on treating marriage problems. The organization was renamed the American Association of Marriage and Family Counselors in 1970 because of the growing interest of its members in family therapy. It was renamed the AAMFT in 1978 because the term counselor was not believed to accurately represent the thrust of the practice of most members in the organization (Broderick & Schraeder, 1991).

The AAMFT has served as a professional association and as a credentialing agency for its membership. AAMFT has three levels of membership: (1) student member, (2) associate member, and (3) clinical member. Student members are still in training to become therapists and are generally interested in obtaining clinical membership in AAMFT. Associate members have completed their qualifying degree and are seeking to complete the required courses in marriage and family therapy or are completing the two calendar years of postdegree supervised clinical experience prior to applying for clinical membership.

Clinical membership in AAMFT or state licensure are the only means of formal recognition that exist for marriage and family therapists. To obtain clinical membership, applicants must have completed a graduate program of study in marriage and family therapy containing appropriate courses as identified by AAMFT. In addition, a two-year, 1000-contact-hour supervised postdegree clinical experience is required. Clinical membership may also be obtained by licensure as a marriage and family therapist in one of the 50 states or by documentation of ten years of experience in marriage and family therapy with appropriate continuing education qualifications. Clinical membership identifies professionals with extensive and specific training in marriage and family therapy for consumers and mental health insurance providers. At the present time, several insurance carriers, including CHAMPUS, recognize clinical members in AAMFT as authorized providers of mental health services.

In addition to the membership categories described above, in 1983 the AAMFT designated approved supervisors, who have advanced training and experience in the supervision of the clinical work of prospective marriage and family therapists seeking clinical membership. Approved supervisors have submitted their credentials for careful review and have met the highest standards of clinical education and experience (Huber, 1994). The Commission on Supervision (now the supervision committee) was created by AAMFT in 1983 to administer the approved supervisor designation.

Furthermore, AAMFT has developed rigorous standards for accreditation of graduate and postdegree marriage and family training programs. In 1978, the Commission on Accreditation for Marriage and Family Therapy Education was recognized by the U.S. Office of Education, Department of Health, Education, and Welfare to establish standards for training programs in marriage and family therapy education. This recognition was continued under the U.S. Department of Education.

Until 1978, AAMFT was the only professional organization specifically designed to recognize and support mental health service providers specializing in marriage and family therapy. Other organizations have emerged on the professional scene offering alternatives for professional affiliation for marriage and family therapists.

## International Association of Marriage and Family Counselors (IAMFC)

The inaugural meeting of the IAMFC was held at the 1987 Annual Convention of the American Association for Counseling and Development (now the American Counseling Association). The purpose of the meeting was to approve bylaws and identify potential members so the IAMFC might petition the American Counseling Association for inclusion as a division of that larger organization. The IAMFC membership consists primarily of ACA members with a primary identity as professional counselors but who also identify themselves as marriage and family counselors.

The IAMFC was created to meet the needs of individuals with professional training in mental health disciplines other than marriage and family therapy. Professionals trained in other disciplines are often unable to meet the stringent academic requirements to obtain clinical membership in AAMFT. Thus, a need for professional affiliation has been met through creation of other marriage and family therapy professional organizations. Whether this diversity of professional organizations will have a beneficial effect on the training, practice, and regulation of marriage and family therapy remains to be seen.

## American Family Therapy Association (AFTA)

In 1977, a second professional organization was formed for family therapists. AFTA was created to offer a forum for relatively senior members of the family therapy profession who would convene annually to discuss a variety of clinical, research, and teaching topics (Huber, 1994).

## Division of Family Psychology

Because of rapidly growing interest by psychologists in marriage and family therapy, the Division of Family Psychology of the American Psychological Association was created in 1984. This division is composed mainly of professionals whose primary identity is that of psychologist but who have special interests in marriage and family issues and therapy. In 1989, Family Psychology was recognized as the seventh "diploma" specialty area by the American Board of Professional Psychology. A stringent application process must be completed to gain this recognition (Huber, 1994).

# Licensure of Marriage and Family Therapists

While it is true that marriage and family therapy is practiced by a wide array of licensed professionals, such as professional counselors, psychologists, psychiatrists, and social workers, marriage and family therapy is also licensed as a distinct professional practice in these 35 states, as of March 1996:

| | |
|---|---|
| Alaska | Nevada |
| Arizona | New Hampshire |
| California | New Jersey |
| Colorado | New Mexico |
| Connecticut | North Carolina |
| Florida | Oklahoma |
| Georgia | Oregon |
| Illinois | Rhode Island |
| Indiana | South Carolina |
| Iowa | Tennessee |
| Kansas | Texas |
| Kentucky | Utah |
| Maine | Vermont |
| Maryland | Virginia |
| Massachusetts | Washington |
| Michigan | Wisconsin |
| Minnesota | Wyoming |
| Nebraska | |

Because the content of these state laws differed in substantial ways and did not define the practice of marriage and family therapy consistently, the AAMFT developed a model for states who are pursuing marriage and family therapy licensure to use in defining the profession. Individuals interested in licensure should contact the regulatory board of the state for which licensure is sought to determine specific requirements for the license. Graduate students would be well advised to seek this information early in their programs to ensure that appropriate courses are completed. Clinical membership in AAMFT is available to professionals licensed by their state to practice marriage and family therapy.

# ▣ Professional Status of Marriage and Family Therapy

The issue of whether or not marriage and family therapy is a distinct profession is loaded with controversy (Gurman & Kniskern, 1981a). As can be seen by the descriptions of the four professional organizations above, the status of marriage and family therapy is not agreed on by various professional organizations. Fenell and Hovestadt (1986) gave four possible descriptions of the status of marriage and family therapy (see Figure 14.1):

- an independent profession
- a profession that partially overlaps with another mental health profession
- a professional specialty area within a specific mental health profession
- an area of elective study within a specific mental health profession.

Thus, family therapy is conceptualized on a continuum from an independent profession to an area of elective study within a specific mental health profession.

The AAMFT and IAMFC support the notion of marriage and family therapy as an independent profession or as a clearly definable professional area developed in conjunction with another mental health profession. Clinical membership in AAMFT is awarded to those who meet the rigorous academic and supervised experience requirements of that organization. Some members of other mental health professions, such as professional counseling, psychology, and social work, believe that their training programs, while possibly not meeting AAMFT requirements, adequately prepare graduates to work with persons experienc-

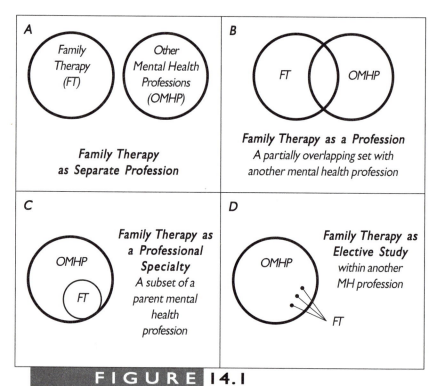

**FIGURE 14.1**

# Relationship of Family Therapy to Other Mental Health Professions

**Source:** "Family Therapy as a Profession or Professional Specialty: Implications for Training," by D. L. Fenell and A. J. Hovestadt, 1986, in *Journal of Psychotherapy and the Family, 1*(4). Used by permission.

ing marriage and family problems. Other therapists, however, would argue that marriage and family therapy graduate education should be conducted by institutions accredited by the Commission on Accreditation of Marriage and Family Therapy Education of the AAMFT or by the Commission on Accreditation of Counseling and Related Academic Programs (Marriage and Family Therapy specialty).

Nevertheless, many nonaccredited mental health graduate and postgraduate programs are training persons from a variety of mental health professions to work with marital and family problems. These therapists are providing marital and family services as licensed counselors, psychologists, social workers, psychiatric nurses, and pastoral counselors. Thus, the question of the status of the profession of marriage and family therapy remains unanswered. Will the field emerge as a distinct mental health profession? Or will it be recognized as a specialty area of other established professions, such as professional counseling, psychology, and social work (Fenell & Hovestadt, 1986)? Because many therapists from other professions do practice marriage and family therapy, it appears at this time that the field exists both as a profession in itself and as a professional specialty, depending on the background, training, professional affiliation, and perspective of the mental health professionals involved.

# Ethical and Legal Issues in Marriage and Family Therapy

The ethical guidelines developed by the American Counseling Association (ACA) and the American Psychological Association (APA) primarily address the therapeutic relationships that exist between one client and one therapist and the relationship between one therapist and a nonrelated group in group therapy. These ethical guidelines do not directly address many of the issues that face the marriage and family therapist. The marriage and family therapist may encounter specific legal issues surrounding confidentiality, child custody, and divorce problems. Marriage and family therapists must be familiar with the laws in their state to communicate effectively with clients who are dealing with legal issues in the family (Margolin, 1982).

## Ethical Considerations

Margolin (1982) identified six areas of specific ethical concern to the marriage and family therapist:

- therapist responsibility,
- confidentiality,
- client privilege,
- informed consent and right to refuse treatment,
- therapist values, and
- training and supervision.

These areas of concern will be briefly discussed next, with suggestions for how the marriage and family therapist may respond to each.

## Therapist Responsibility

The therapist working with individuals is responsible for the welfare of the client. In marriage and family therapy, this issue becomes more complex. Who is the client in marital therapy? Is it the two individuals involved in treatment, or is it the marital system? What may be in the best interests of the husband may not be in the best interests of the wife. Consider the following example. Mr. North has decided he wants to get out of his marriage. He is unwavering in this decision, yet has agreed to join his wife in marriage counseling to see if "something can change his mind." Mrs. North is a homemaker with no career and is terrified of going it alone. She pleads with the therapist to help restore the marriage. Over the course of several sessions, the scenario does not change. Mr. North still plans to leave the marriage. What is the ethical responsibility of the therapist, and to whom does the therapist owe allegiance? Should the therapist:

- support Mrs. North during the divorce process,
- support Mr. North as he extricates himself from the marriage he no longer wants, or
- continue to treat the couple and hope to save the marriage?

What is good for one family member is not always good for another. The therapist must be able to help the family system change in some manner that ultimately is reasonably satisfactory for all concerned. The therapist must attempt to balance the responsibility to help each individual while also working to help the marital and family system adjust to a more satisfactory condition, an oftentimes difficult position to reach.

## Confidentiality

The confidentiality of the relationship between client and counselor has long been an ethical hallmark of psychotherapy. Except in cases of child abuse, potential physical harm to the client, or potential physical harm to others by the client, the therapist is bound to maintain client confidentiality. Maintaining confidentiality may become a problem for the marriage and family therapist when individuals share secrets with the therapist. For example, suppose a couple is in therapy to attempt to rebuild the marriage because the wife has had an affair. The husband agrees to remain in the marriage if the wife agrees to stop her affair. In a private call to the therapist, the wife reveals that she is still involved in the affair but that she does not want her husband to know. How should the ethical marriage and family therapist respond to this situation?

Helping family members learn to communicate in an open manner is generally one of the goals of therapy. A serious problem may arise in therapy when a family member creates a situation that does not allow the therapist to communicate openly with all family members. The problem is especially complex when the other members may need the information to make responsible decisions.

Some marriage and family therapists respond to this problem by informing the family members before beginning therapy that secrets will not be kept. This stance, however, may keep a family member from sharing information that could be essential to the therapy. But therapists who agree too readily to maintain confidentiality often find themselves unable to intervene in a productive manner. A potentially productive middle ground is for the therapist to clearly articulate a position to the family at the beginning of therapy that states that any information provided may be used by the therapist in the interest of helping to resolve presenting issues. If information received in a private conversation would not be helpful to the therapy, the therapist would probably choose not to use it in a session. Whatever course of action is taken by the therapist regarding confidentiality, the policy must be clearly understood by the family members from the start. A *disclosure statement* signed by the clients that describes the therapist and the therapy process, including information on confidentiality in addition to being a legal requirement in many states, is an effective way to communicate this information to clients.

For some family therapists, the use of the one-way mirror is an important aspect of family treatment. Therapists who use the mirror as an adjunct to therapy often employ a team of one or more colleagues to observe the session and provide suggestions to the therapist during and after the session (Fenell, Hovestadt, & Harvey, 1986). In addition to the observation team, sessions can be videotaped for later review by the therapist, the team, and in some cases, the family. Involvement of these additional persons in the therapy process also creates issues of confidentiality. Family members should be fully informed about the mirror, videorecorder, and observation team. Again, a disclosure statement signed by the clients is an effective way to ensure that clients are informed and agree to the process. Family members must be told how the therapy process works in the amount of detail that they care to know. Furthermore, observation team members and family members alike should be reminded of the need for confidentiality regarding information revealed in the session.

## Client Privilege

Closely related to the issue of client confidentiality is the issue of *privileged communication.* Privileged communication protects the client from having confidences from therapy revealed on the witness stand in court. Privilege belongs to the client. However, when working with a family or couple, who is the client? When one family member seeks testimony from a therapist about another family member, courts have typically respected the client privilege and therapists have not been required to testify. However, this is not always the case. Herrington (1979) reported a case in Virginia in which the judge stated that when a husband and wife are in therapy together, there is no privilege because the statements were not made in private to a doctor but in the presence of a third party.

Marriage and family therapists may be able to avoid giving this type of testimony by claiming that the unit of treatment is the entire family rather than any single individual. Thus, as Gumper and Sprenkle (1981) suggested, testimony about any part of the family system would violate the privilege of the family. Nonetheless, courts may still order therapists to testify regarding information obtained in multiperson therapy sessions. Therapists are advised to determine what the laws of their own states require concerning client privilege in marriage and family therapy situations.

## Informed Consent and the Right to Refuse Treatment

It is becoming increasingly important that clients be clearly informed concerning their rights and responsibilities in therapy as well as the responsibilities of the therapist. Disclosure statements have been developed by many therapists to obtain informed consent from clients and advise them of their right to refuse treatment. Before families enter therapy, they should be adequately informed concerning the nature of therapy and important aspects of the process. Many states now have laws requiring therapists to use disclosure statements. Key information that may be of concern to clients and included in the disclosure statement was described by Gill (1982). These points of important consumer information are:

- Describe the purpose of psychotherapy.
- Describe what you believe helps people lead more satisfying lives.
- Describe what clients should expect as a result of therapy.
- Describe the responsibilities of clients in therapy.
- Describe your primary therapeutic approach and the techniques that emerge from this approach.
- Describe the problems you have been most effective in helping clients resolve.
- Describe the conditions that might precipitate a referral to another therapist or agency.
- Describe the limits of confidentiality in the therapeutic relationship.

The marriage and family therapist will want to ensure that all family members have agreed to participate in therapy and that all have signed the informed consent form. Clients engaging in marital and family therapy will also need to be informed of possible negative outcomes of therapy. When working with multiperson systems such as families, the outcome of therapy may be viewed as undesirable by one or more of the family members (Gurman & Kniskern, 1978b, 1981a; Wilcoxon & Fenell, 1983, 1986).

Finally, therapists who provide treatment only to whole families should not simply refuse treatment to a family that does not agree to have all members present. Rather, the therapist should be prepared to refer such families to other therapists who do not have this restriction on treatment (Margolin, 1982).

## Therapist Values

One of the most critical ethical issues confronting the marriage and family therapist concerns her values. With the tremendous plurality of family styles, the effective therapist carefully examines her values and ensures that these values do not adversely affect the client's goals for the treatment. When the therapist encounters family values in certain clients that are opposed to her own values, it is possible that the therapist may form biases against these clients and ally with the other family members who hold values similar to the therapist's own values. According to Margolin (1982), specific values that may cause problems for the therapist include:

- attitudes toward divorce,
- attitudes toward extramarital affairs, and
- attitudes toward sex roles in the family, especially as they pertain to women.

Concerning attitudes toward divorce, counselors should be very clear regarding their own values. Divorce is frequently a painful option, but at times it may be in the best interests of family members. Counselors must be certain that they are not pushing couples either to stay together or to divorce. The therapist's role is to help the couple identify issues in the marriage to be resolved and to help the partners make a joint decision about whether to stay in the marriage or to divorce. When couples ask a counselor about his or her biases regarding marriage and divorce, it is generally most helpful to be honest with the clients. If clients are not comfortable with the counselor's values, referral should be offered.

The counselor's attitude toward extramarital affairs can be a hindrance to therapy when it conflicts with the attitudes of one or both spouses. If the therapist believes affairs are acceptable and one or both of the marriage partners do not, the clients may perceive the counselor as advocating behaviors that may be destructive to a marriage that is in need of help. If the counselor believes affairs are harmful to the relationship, he or she must be careful not to side too heavily with the spouse who was faithful. This attitude may create the perception that the marriage problems are all the fault of the person who had the affair, a nonsystemic conceptualization. A counselor who employs systems theory will seek to discover how each partner engaged in behaviors that created marital problems and resulted in the affair. It is usually most beneficial to discover how the spouses share responsibility for the marital problems in any attempt to restore the marriage.

Concerning attitudes toward sex roles, some family systems therapists have stereotyped women and encouraged them to stay in unsatisfactory marriages. Therapists should be careful not to pay less attention to a woman's career, perpetuate the notion that children's problems are the result of poor mothering, exhibit a double standard that views extramarital affairs by the wife more severely than the affairs of the husband, or place more emphasis on the needs of the husband in a relationship. When values that may have a significant impact on the therapy exist, the therapist should inform the clients so they can make a responsible choice concerning the appropriateness of treatment with the therapist (Corey, Corey, & Callahan, 1993).

## Training and Supervision

Marital and family problems are quite widespread. Because of this fact, most mental health practitioners will have frequent opportunities to treat these problems. However, not all therapists are adequately trained to treat marital and family problems. Gurman and Kniskern (1981b) suggested that family therapists may need more forceful intervention methods than therapists for individuals are typically trained to employ if treatment is to be successful. Furthermore, Margolin (1982) reported that adequate preparation in marriage and family therapy is the exception rather than the rule among mental health service providers. Thus, therapists who work with couples and families must be careful not to exceed the bounds of their competence. Fenell and Hovestadt (1986) developed a three-level model of marriage and family therapist clinical training and suggested that therapists should evaluate their ability level and limit their practice to marital and family problems they are appropriately prepared to handle. It is important that therapists have access to clinical supervision by marriage and family therapists for assistance in evaluating couples and families who may need referral to a professional with more training and experience in family systems therapy.

# Ethical Standards for Marriage and Family Therapy

Most professional organizations have ethical standards for practitioners; the American Association for Marriage and Family Therapy (AAMFT, 1991) has developed standards specifically for marriage and family therapists. This set of standards is entitled the AAMFT Code of Ethics and addresses the following major points:

1. *Responsibility to clients.* Marriage and family therapists advance the welfare of families and individuals. They respect the rights of those persons seeking their assistance and make reasonable efforts to ensure that their services are used appropriately.
2. *Confidentiality.* Marriage and family therapists have unique confidentiality concerns because the client in a therapeutic re-

lationship may be more than one person. Therapists respect and guard confidences of each individual client.

3. *Professional competence and integrity.* Marriage and family therapists maintain high standards of professional competence and integrity.

4. *Responsibility to students, employees, and supervisees.*

5. *Responsibility to research participants.*

6. *Responsibility to the profession.* Marriage and family therapists must respect the rights and responsibilities of professional colleagues and participate in activities that advance the goals of the profession.

7. *Financial arrangements.* Marriage and family therapists make financial arrangements with clients, third party payors, and supervisees that are reasonably understandable and conform to accepted professional practices.

8. *Advertising.* Marriage and family therapists engage in appropriate informational activities, including those that enable laypersons to choose professional services on an informed basis.

The complete *AAMFT Code of Ethical Principles for Marriage and Family Therapists* is presented in Appendix A of this book for review by interested readers.

When a violation of the *AAMFT Code of Ethical Principles for Marriage and Family Therapists* is suspected, the AAMFT Ethics Committee is contacted and procedures are set in motion to determine if the complaint is against an AAMFT member, to determine if the complaint has validity, and to determine action by the Ethics Committee and the association. Complaints may proceed in three ways. First, the complaint may be dropped and no charges filed. Second, the charged member and the AAMFT may settle the complaint by mutual agreement. And third, the Ethics Committee may recommend that action be taken against the member. Actions taken may include:

- request to cease and desist,
- censure of member,
- probation of member,
- require supervision for member,
- require therapy or education for member,
- suspend or terminate Approved Supervisor designation, or
- suspend or terminate membership in AAMFT.

A thorough appeals process is provided for members who believe the process has been improperly managed. A booklet specifying the details for handling ethical complaints may be requested from the AAMFT.

Understanding and employing ethical principles for marriage and family therapists is critical in providing ethical services to clients and in maintaining a solid reputation for integrity in the profession.

The IAMFC (1993) has also developed ethical standards identified as the Ethical Code for the International Association of Marriage and Family Counselors. These standards cover the following key points:

- client well-being,
- confidentiality,
- competence,
- assessment,
- private practice,
- research and publications,
- supervision, and
- media and public statements.

The entire IAMFC ethical code is presented in Appendix B of this book. It is interesting to note the similarities that exist between the IAMFC code and the AAMFT code.

# Family Therapy Training

Family therapy claims to be more than another set of techniques for helping families change. Experienced practitioners believe that family therapy is a different way of thinking about problems that persons encounter. Because of the distinctions between the practice of individual and family therapy, training approaches have evolved for family therapists that differ from typical approaches used in training individual therapists (Fenell & Hovestadt, 1986; Fenell, Hovestadt, & Harvey, 1986; Liddle, 1991).

## Academic Preparation

Professionals who identify themselves as marriage and family therapists come from a wide range of academic training programs. Family therapy, for example, is taught in graduate departments of counselor education, family studies, psychiatry, psychology, social work, nursing, and pastoral counseling (Fenell & Hovestadt, 1986; Hovestadt,

Fenell, & Piercy, 1983). Many graduates of these programs seek clinical membership in the AAMFT. To be eligible for clinical membership, therapists must have completed an accredited graduate training program, be licensed as an MFT by their state, or complete a graduate degree meeting the following requirements or their equivalent:

- *Human development* (three courses). May include courses in human development, personality theory, human sexuality, psychopathology, and behavior pathology.
- *Marital and family studies* (three courses). Covers family development and family interaction patterns across the life cycle of the individual as well as the family. Courses may include the study of the family life cycle; theories of family development; marriage and the family; sociology of the family; families under stress; the contemporary family; family in a social context; the cross-cultural family; youth/adult/aging and the family; family subsystems; and individual, interpersonal relationships (marital, parental, sibling).
- *Marital and family therapy* (three courses). May include communications; family psychology; family therapy methodology; family assessment; treatment and intervention methods; and major clinical theories of marital and family therapy such as structural, strategic, transgenerational, experiential, object relations, contextual, and systemic theories.
- *Research* (one course). Includes research design, methods, statistics, and research in marital and family studies and therapy.
- *Professional studies* (one course). Professional socialization and the role of the professional organization, legal responsibilities and liabilities, independent practice and interprofessional cooperation, ethics, and family law.
- *Clinical practicum* (one year, 300 hours). Includes fifteen hours per week, with approximately eight to ten hours in face-to-face contact with individuals, couples, and families for the purpose of assessment and intervention.

Applicants for clinical membership who completed their qualifying degree prior to 1979 may establish coursework equivalency in the following manner:

- *Workshops/seminars.* Forty-five contact hours equals one three-credit semester course or four one-credit quarter courses.

- *Teaching courses.* One graduate-level course taught equals one three-credit semester or four one-credit quarter courses.
- *Extensive experience, publications, and educational qualifications* in the field may be considered on a case-by-case basis (AAMFT, 1986).

Clinical membership in the AAMFT is a highly regarded credential. In recent years, the AAMFT has developed policies to assist potential members interested in clinical membership. These new policies attempt to recognize the qualifications of professionals who are competent MFTs but may not have had the opportunity to attend an AAMFT prescribed graduate program.

In addition to these academic training requirements, the AAMFT requires prospective clinical members to complete two years of postdegree clinical experience under supervision of an approved supervisor recognized by the AAMFT or a supervisor acceptable to the AAMFT Membership Committee. At least 1000 hours of direct client contact must be completed during the two years of supervised experience, and at least 200 hours of supervision must be completed, of which at least 100 hours must be in supervision involving therapy with individuals.

## Clinical Training and Supervision

One of the features of marriage and family therapy that sets it apart from most treatment approaches for individuals is the focus on the family as a system. This emphasis is taught in the academic portion of the therapist's training program and is practiced in the supervised clinical experience. Many family therapy training programs have on-campus clinics where graduate students practice therapy under supervision. In most of these clinics, the therapist can be observed working with the couple or family from behind a one-way mirror. Often, a supervisor and a team of the trainee's colleagues will observe the therapist working in the session. This observation permits the supervisor to obtain an accurate impression of the work the therapist is doing and to offer immediate feedback to the student regarding the session.

Family therapy supervisors and trainees generally have an understanding that when the supervisor detects a way the therapist could be more effective, an in-session interruption may occur to inform the therapist of the possible intervention that could be used. Because family therapists can easily become emotionally engaged with the family system, having a supervisor and team of observers behind the glass offers a unique opportunity for feedback on what may be going on in a session that is outside the therapist's awareness. Initially, trainees may believe they are being judged and become defensive to in-session suggestions. However, over time and through their own participation in observing other trainees, they come to value the *metaperspective* of the supervisory team and learn to use the feedback effectively to improve their family therapy skills.

Much has been written about family therapy supervision (Fenell & Hovestadt, 1986; Liddle, 1991; Liddle & Halpin, 1978). However, little research has been attempted to demonstrate the effectiveness of family therapy supervision over traditional case presentation supervision (Kniskern & Gurman, 1979). One study using a small sample compared family therapy supervision with traditional supervision. The results showed no correlation between the acquisition of family therapy skills and the supervision method used (Fenell, Hovestadt, & Harvey, 1986). Liddle, Davidson, and Barrett (1988) discovered that live supervision could lead to excessive dependence on the supervisor, especially early in the training process. These authors suggested that assumptions regarding effective family therapy clinical training should be examined.

# Research in Marriage and Family Therapy

In 1952 Hans Eysenck shook the world of psychotherapy with the results of his research on psychotherapy effectiveness. Eysenck (1952) reported that, according to his analysis, about 67% of neurotic patients improved within two years whether they received therapy or not. Eysenck challenged psychotherapists to demonstrate the effectiveness of their approaches or to concede that these approaches were not useful.

Bergin (1967, 1971) was the first to respond to Eysenck's criticism. Bergin's reevaluation of Eysenck's data revealed that psychotherapy was at least moderately effective with neurotic patients, as 65% improved within two years with psychotherapy, while 43% of untreated neurotic patients improved within two years.

Despite Bergin's findings, the challenge to demonstrate the effectiveness of psychotherapy remains. As ethical practitioners, psychotherapists seek to provide the most beneficial treatment to clients.

How can we know what kinds of treatment are most beneficial unless effective research is conducted to demonstrate the results of various approaches? As ethical therapists, we want to know, within the limits available, whether the treatment works (Levant, 1984).

Paul (1967) phrased a question that described what psychotherapy research attempts to discover. His question clearly identified the complexities involved in conducting psychotherapy research. Paul asked, "What treatment, by whom, is most effective for this individual with that specific problem, and under what set of circumstances?" Attempting to respond to Paul's question has been and will continue to be a major challenge for psychotherapy researchers.

Following the publication of Bergin's findings (1967, 1971), investigators began to identify deterioration in clients as a result of psychotherapy (Lambert, Bergin, & Collins, 1977). Deterioration occurs when the client becomes worse as a result of therapy. It was discovered that deterioration occurred in less than 10% of the clients treated, with the rate higher for more disturbed clients.

Several research projects were conducted investigating the effects of the level of therapist empathy, warmth, and genuineness on the outcome of therapy (Mitchell, Bozarth, & Kraft, 1977; Rogers, 1957; Truax & Carkhuff, 1967; Truax & Mitchell, 1971). Although the results of these studies consistently suggested that these therapist qualities are important factors in client change, the mechanism for these results, as well as how widely the findings can be generalized, has been questioned (Mitchell, Bozarth, & Kraft, 1977). Nonetheless, when various theories of counseling are compared, results indicate that one approach is generally just as effective as another (Luborsky, Singer, & Luborsky, 1973; Smith & Glass, 1977; Strupp & Hadley, 1979). Thus, researchers have not been able to conclude precisely what it is about psychotherapy that brings about improvement. These studies lend indirect support to those researchers who have concluded that the therapist qualities of empathy, warmth, and genuineness are factors that facilitate change.

Later studies by Bergin and Lambert (1978) suggested that short-term therapy lasting six months or less was effective in providing symptom relief for the client. Smith and Glass (1977) completed a *meta-analysis* of 375 controlled-outcome studies that suggested that the typical client in therapy is better off than 75% of individuals with similar problems who are not treated. Thus, a fairly solid body of research has been compiled suggesting that psychotherapy is effective.

The preceding summary of some of the important findings in psychotherapy for individuals sets the stage for a review of the research in marriage and family therapy. The same problems that exist in research with individual clients exist in family therapy research, but with additional complications. In marriage and family therapy research, change is more difficult to assess. Are we looking for change in the identified patient? Other family members? Family subsystems? The family system itself? Without knowing what to look for or where to look, it is difficult to assess change (Gurman & Kniskern, 1981b). Olson, Russell, and Sprenkle (1980) stated that to evaluate family therapy, researchers need ways to identify and measure family system changes. A significant amount of work remains to be completed before researchers are able to reliably identify and accurately measure system change.

Four major reviews of the research concerning the outcome of marriage and family therapy have been conducted by DeWitt (1978); Gurman and Kniskern (1978a); Olson, Russell, and Sprenkle (1980); and Wells and Dezen (1978). Of these, the Gurman and Kniskern review is most often cited in the marriage and family therapy literature. Specific findings based on these comprehensive reviews indicate the following conclusions.

- Improvement rates in marriage and family therapy are similar to improvement rates in individual therapy.
- Deterioration rates in marriage and family therapy are similar to deterioration rates in individual therapy.
- Deterioration may occur because:
  — The therapist has poor interpersonal skills;
  — The therapist moves too quickly into sensitive topic areas and does not handle the situation well;
  — The therapist allows family conflict to become exacerbated without moderating therapeutic intervention;
  — The therapist does not provide adequate structure in the early stages of therapy; and
  — The therapist does not support family members (Gurman & Kniskern, 1981b).
- Conjoint marital therapy (with both partners present) is the treatment of choice over individual therapy for couples experiencing marital problems. Low improvement rates and high deterio-

ration rates are found when couples are treated separately for marital problems (Gurman & Kniskern, 1978b).

- Family therapy is as effective, if not more so, as individual therapy for problems involving marital and family conflict and even for treating an individual's problems.
- Brief therapy, limited to about twenty sessions, seems to be as effective as open-ended therapy.
- Participation of the father in family therapy increases the probability of a successful outcome.
- Co-therapy has not been shown to be more effective than one-therapist family therapy.
- Therapist relationship skills have an influence on the outcome of therapy. Good relationship skills produce positive outcomes, and poor relationship skills may produce deterioration.
- When the identified patient has severe diagnosable psychological problems, a successful outcome is less probable.
- Modified structural family therapy has been used to successfully treat psychosomatic problems (Minuchin, Rosman, & Baker, 1978) and drug and alcohol problems (Stanton, 1978; Stanton & Todd, 1979, 1981).
- Family type, family interaction style, and family demographic factors have not been demonstrated to be related to the outcome of family therapy.

A recent special issue of the *Journal of Marital and Family Therapy* (1995) has reviewed recent outcome studies concerning the effectiveness of marital and family therapy. These reviews suggest family therapy may be useful in the following specific problem situations:

- family psychoeducation with schizophrenic disorders (Goldstein & Miklowitz, 1995)
- family therapy with affective disorders (Prince & Jacobson, 1995)
- family therapy with selected behavioral disorders of childhood (Estrada & Pinsof, 1995)
- family therapy with adolescents with conduct disorders (Chamberlain & Rosicky, 1995)
- family therapy for the treatment of marital conflict and the prevention of divorce (Bray & Jouriles, 1995)
- family therapy for the treatment of alcoholism (Edwards & Steinglass, 1995)

- family therapy for the treatment of drug abuse (Liddle & Dakof, 1995)
- family therapy in the treatment of physical illness (Campbell & Patterson, 1995).

These findings reflect the synthesis of numerous studies conducted over the past twenty years. Psychotherapy research is still in a relatively primitive state, and these findings should be considered with this limitation in mind.

Several professional journals report the results of marital and family therapy research. These journals should be available for the interested reader at any university library:

- *Journal of Marital and Family Therapy*
- *The Family Journal: Counseling and Therapy for Couples and Families*
- *The Family Therapy Networker*
- *Journal of Family Psychology*
- *Family Process*
- *American Journal of Family Therapy*
- *Journal of Marriage and the Family*
- *Family Systems Medicine*
- *Family Therapy*
- *Journal of Sex and Marital Therapy*
- *Journal of Strategic and Systemic Therapies*

Future research should focus on evaluating specific aspects of treatment on specific targets in the family system. Because specific therapist behaviors to produce change may have little relation to the family therapy theory being practiced, identifying these specific, change-producing, theory-neutral factors will be important for all practitioners.

Future research designs should use a control group so findings can be generalized as much as possible. In addition, findings should be useful in practical ways to clinicians as well as statistically significant to researchers. Another need is for researchers to conduct follow-up evaluations of their subjects to determine the long-term effects of treatment (Gurman & Kniskern, 1981b).

In addition to providing practicing clinicians with information about the efficacy of certain treatment approaches, psychotherapy research provides a continuous flow of information to the increasingly critical

public concerning the effects of treatment for psychological difficulties.

## Summary

This chapter has introduced some of the critical issues in marriage
and family therapy that will be of interest to the psychotherapist beginning work with couples and families. It is important for family
therapists to know about professional associations because they provide information about the profession as well as opportunities for professional interactions with others interested in family therapy. Knowledge of the ethical and legal issues pertinent to the practice of family
therapy ensures that clients receive the quality of therapy to which
they are entitled. Finally, knowledge of the research in marriage and
family therapy is important so clinicians will be aware of the strengths
and limitations of family therapy.

# SUGGESTED
# READINGS

Gurman, A., & Kniskern, D. (1981). "Family Therapy Outcome Research: Knowns and Unknowns." In A. S. Gurman and D. P. Kniskern, eds., *Handbook of Family Therapy* (pp. 742–775). New York: Brunner/Mazel.

Huber, C. (1994). *Ethical, Legal and Professional Issues in the Practice of Marriage and Family Therapy*, 2nd ed. Columbus, OH: Merrill.

*Journal of Marital and Family Therapy* (1995). Special Issue: The Effectiveness of Marital and Family Therapy. Washington, DC, AAMFT.

Margolin, G. (1982). "Ethical and Legal Considerations in Family Therapy." *American Psychologist, 7,* 788–801.

Okun, B. F., & Gladding, S. T., eds. (1983). *Issues in Training Marriage and Family Therapists.* Ann Arbor, MI: ERIC/CAPS.

*Appendix*

# A

# AAMFT Code of Ethical Principles for

# Marriage and Family Therapists

*Reprinted by permission of the American Association for Marriage and Family Therapy. This revised code was approved in 1991. The AAMFT can make further revisions of the code at any time the association deems necessary.*

*T*he Board of Directors of the American Association for Marriage and Family Therapy (AAMFT) hereby promulgates, pursuant to Article 2, Section 2.013 of the Association's Bylaws, the Revised AAMFT Code of Ethics, effective August 1, 1991.

## *1. Responsibility to Clients*

Marriage and family therapists advance the welfare of families and individuals. They respect the rights of those persons seeking their assistance, and make reasonable efforts to ensure that their services are used appropriately.

**1.1** Marriage and family therapists do not discriminate against or refuse professional service to anyone on the basis of race, gender, religion, national origin, or sexual orientation.

**1.2** Marriage and family therapists are aware of their influential position with respect to clients, and they avoid exploiting the trust and dependence of such persons. Therapists, therefore, make every effort to avoid dual relationships with clients that could impair professional judgment or increase the risk of exploitation. When a dual relationship cannot be avoided, therapists take appropriate professional precautions to ensure judgment is not impaired and no exploitation occurs. Examples of such dual relationships include, but are not limited to, business or close personal relationships with clients. Sexual intimacy with clients is prohibited. Sexual intimacy with former clients for two years following the termination of therapy is prohibited.

**1.3** Marriage and family therapists do not use their professional relationships with clients to further their own interests.

**1.4** Marriage and family therapists respect the right of clients to make decisions and help them to understand the consequences of these decisions. Therapists clearly advise a client that a decision on marital status is the responsibility of the client.

**1.5** Marriage and family therapists continue therapeutic relationships only so long as it is reasonably clear that clients are benefiting from the relationship.

**1.6** Marriage and family therapists assist persons in obtaining other therapeutic services if the therapist is unable or unwilling, for appropriate reasons, to provide professional help.

**1.7** Marriage and family therapists do not abandon or neglect clients in treatment without making reasonable arrangements for the continuation of such treatment.

**1.8** Marriage and family therapists obtain written informed consent from clients before videotaping, audiorecording, or permitting third party observation.

## 2. Confidentiality

Marriage and family therapists have unique confidentiality concerns because the client in a therapeutic relationship may be more than one person. Therapists respect and guard confidences of each individual client.

**2.1** Marriage and family therapists may not disclose client confidences except: (a) as mandated by law; (b) to prevent a clear and immediate danger to a person or persons; (c) where the therapist is a defendant in a civil, criminal, or disciplinary action arising from the therapy (in which case client confidences may be disclosed only in the course of that action); or (d) if there is a waiver previously obtained in writing, and then such information may be revealed only in accordance with the terms of the waiver. In circumstances where more than one person in a family receives therapy, each such family member who is legally competent to execute a waiver must agree to the waiver required by subparagraph (d). Without such a waiver from each family member legally competent to execute a waiver, a therapist cannot disclose information received from any family member.

**2.2** Marriage and family therapists use client and/or clinical materials in teaching, writing, and public presentations only if a written waiver has been obtained in accordance with Subprinciple 2.1(d), or when appropriate steps have been taken to protect client identity and confidentiality.

**2.3** Marriage and family therapists store or dispose of client records in ways that maintain confidentiality.

## 3. Professional Competence and Integrity

Marriage and family therapists maintain high standards of professional competence and integrity.

**3.1** Marriage and family therapists are in violation of this Code and subject to termination of membership or other appropriate action if they: (a) are convicted of any felony; (b) are convicted of a misdemeanor related to their qualifications or functions; (c) engage in conduct which could lead to conviction of a felony, or a misdemeanor related to their qualifications or functions; (d) are expelled from or disciplined by other professional organizations; (e) have their licenses or certificates suspended or revoked or are otherwise disciplined by regulatory bodies; (f) are no longer competent to practice marriage and family therapy because they are impaired due to physical or mental causes or the abuse of alcohol or other substances; or (g) fail to cooperate with the Association at any point from the inception of an ethical complaint through the completion of all proceedings regarding that complaint.

**3.2** Marriage and family therapists seek appropriate professional assistance for their personal problems or conflicts that may impair work performance or clinical judgment.

**3.3** Marriage and family therapists, as teachers, supervisors, and researchers, are dedicated to high standards of scholarship and present accurate information.

**3.4** Marriage and family therapists remain abreast of new developments in family therapy knowledge and practice through educational activities.

**3.5** Marriage and family therapists do not engage in sexual or other harassment or exploitation of clients, students, trainees, supervisees, employees, colleagues, research subjects, or actual or potential witnesses or complainants in investigations and ethical proceedings.

**3.6** Marriage and family therapists do not diagnose, treat, or advise on problems outside the recognized boundaries of their competence.

**3.7** Marriage and family therapists make efforts to prevent the distortion or misuse of their clinical and research findings.

**3.8** Marriage and family therapists, because of their ability to influence and alter the lives of others, exercise special care when making public their professional recommendations and opinions through testimony or other public statements.

## 4. Responsibility to Students, Employees, and Supervisees

**4. 1** Marriage and family therapists are aware of their influential position with respect to students, employees, and supervisees, and they avoid exploiting the trust and dependency of such persons. Therapists, therefore, make every effort to avoid dual relationships that could impair professional judgment or increase the risk of exploitation. When a dual relationship cannot be avoided, therapists take appropriate professional precautions to ensure judgment is not impaired and no exploitation occurs. Examples of such dual relationships include, but are not limited to, business or close personal relationships with students, employees, or supervisees. Provision of therapy to students, employees, or supervisees is prohibited. Sexual intimacy with students or supervisees is prohibited.

**4.2** Marriage and family therapists do not permit students, employees, or supervisees to perform or to hold themselves out as competent to perform professional services beyond their training, level of experience, and competence.

**4.3** Marriage and family therapists do not disclose supervisee confidences except: (a) as mandated by law; (b) to prevent a clear and immediate danger to a person or persons; (c) where the therapist is a defendant in a civil, criminal, or disciplinary action arising from the supervision (in which case supervisee confidences may be disclosed only in the course of that action); (d) in educational or training settings where there are multiple supervisors, and then only to other professional colleagues who share responsibility for the training of the supervisee; or (e) if there is a waiver previously obtained in writing, and then such information may be revealed only in accordance with the terms of the waiver.

## *5. Responsibility to Research Participants*

**5.1** Investigators are responsible for making careful examinations of ethical acceptability in planning studies. To the extent that services to research participants may be compromised by participation in research, investigators seek the ethical advice of qualified professionals not directly involved in the investigation and observe safeguards to protect the rights of research participants.

**5.2** Investigators requesting participants' involvement in research inform them of all aspects of the research that might reasonably be expected to influence willingness to participate. Investigators are especially sensitive to the possibility of diminished consent when participants are also receiving clinical services, have impairments which limit understanding and/or communication, or when participants are children.

**5.3** Investigators respect participants' freedom to decline participation in or to withdraw from a research study at any time. This obligation requires special thought and consideration when investigators or other members of the research team are in positions of authority or influence over participants. Marriage and family therapists, therefore, make every effort to avoid dual relationships with research participants that could impair professional judgment or increase the risk of exploitation.

**5.4** Information obtained about a research participant during the course of an investigation is confidential unless there is a waiver previously obtained in writing. When the possibility exists that others, including family members, may obtain access to such information, this possibility, together with the plan for protecting confidentiality, is explained as part of the procedure for obtaining informed consent.

## *6. Responsibility to the Profession*

Marriage and family therapists respect the rights and responsibilities of professional colleagues and participate in activities which advance the goals of the profession.

**6.1** Marriage and family therapists remain accountable to the standards of the profession when acting as members or employees of organizations.

2 4 2003333222 22234444444444

**6.2** Marriage and family therapists assign publication credit to those who have contributed to a publication in proportion to their contributions and in accordance with customary professional publication practices.

**6.3** Marriage and family therapists who are the authors of books or other materials that are published or distributed cite persons to whom credit for original ideas is due.

**6.4** Marriage and family therapists who are the authors of books or other materials published or distributed by an organization take reasonable precautions to ensure that the organization promotes and advertises the materials accurately and factually.

**6.5** Marriage and family therapists participate in activities that contribute to a better community and society, including devoting a portion of their professional activity to services for which there is little or no financial return.

**6.6** Marriage and family therapists are concerned with developing laws and regulations pertaining to marriage and family therapy that serve the public interest, and with altering such laws and regulations that are not in the public interest.

**6.7** Marriage and family therapists encourage public participation in the design and delivery of professional services and in the regulation of practitioners.

## 7. Financial Arrangements

Marriage and family therapists make financial arrangements with clients, third party payors, and supervisees that are reasonably understandable and conform to accepted professional practices.

**7.1** Marriage and family therapists do not offer or accept payment for referrals.

**7.2** Marriage and family therapists do not charge excessive fees for services.

**7.3** Marriage and family therapists disclose their fees to clients and supervisees at the beginning of services.

**7.4** Marriage and family therapists represent facts truthfully to clients, third party payors, and supervisees regarding services rendered.

## 8. Advertising

Marriage and family therapists engage in appropriate informational activities, including those that enable laypersons to choose professional services on an informed basis.

### General Advertising

**8.1** Marriage and family therapists accurately represent their competence, education, training, and experience relevant to their practice of marriage and family therapy.

**8.2** Marriage and family therapists assure that advertisements and publications in any media (such as directories, announcements, business cards, newspapers, radio, television, and facsimiles) convey information that is necessary for the public to make an appropriate selection of professional services. Information could include: (a) office information, such as name, address, telephone number, credit card acceptability, fees, languages spoken, and office hours; (b) appropriate degrees, state licensure and/or certification, and AAMFT Clinical Member status; and (c) description of practice. (For requirements for advertising under the AAMFT name, logo, and/or the abbreviated initials AAMFT, see Subprinciple 8.15 below.)

**8.3** Marriage and family therapists do not use a name which could mislead the public concerning the identity, responsibility, source, and status of those practicing under that name and do not hold themselves out as being partners or associates of a firm if they are not.

**8.4** Marriage and family therapists do not use any professional identification (such as a business card, office sign, letterhead, or telephone or association directory listing) if it includes a statement or claim that is false, fraudulent, misleading, or deceptive. A statement is false, fraudulent, misleading, or deceptive if it (a) contains a material misrepresentation of fact; (b) fails to state any material fact necessary to make the statement, in light of all circumstances, not misleading; or (c) is intended to or is likely to create an unjustified expectation.

**8.5** Marriage and family therapists correct, wherever possible, false, misleading, or inaccurate information and representations made by others concerning the therapist's qualifications, services, or products.

**8.6** Marriage and family therapists make certain that the qualifications of persons in their employ are represented in a manner that is not false, misleading, or deceptive.

**8.7** Marriage and family therapists may represent themselves as specializing within a limited area of marriage and family therapy, but only if they have the education and supervised experience in settings which meet recognized professional standards to practice in that specialty area.

## Advertising Using AAMFT Designations

**8.8** The AAMFT designations of Clinical Member, Approved Supervisor, and Fellow may be used in public information or advertising materials only by persons holding such designations. Persons holding such designations may, for example, advertise in the following manner:

- *Jane Doe, Ph.D., a Clinical Member of the American Association for Marriage and Family Therapy.*
  Alternately, the advertisement could read:
  *Jane Doe, Ph.D., AAMFT Clinical Member.*

- *John Doe, Ph.D., an Approved Supervisor of the American Association for Marriage and Family Therapy.*
  Alternately, the advertisement could read:
  *John Doe, Ph.D., AAMFT Approved Supervisor.*

- *Jane Doe, Ph.D., a Fellow of the American Association for Marriage and Family Therapy.*
  Alternately, the advertisement could read:
  *Jane Doe, Ph.D., AAMFT Fellow.*

More than one designation may be used if held by the AAMFT Member.

**8.9** Marriage and family therapists who hold the AAMFT Approved Supervisor or the Fellow designation may not represent the designation as an advanced clinical status.

**8.10** Student, Associate, and Affiliate Members may not use their AAMFT membership status in public information or advertising materials. Such listings on professional resumes are not considered advertisements.

**8.11** Persons applying for AAMFT membership may not list their application status on any resume or advertisement.

**8.12** In conjunction with their AAMFT membership, marriage and family therapists claim as evidence of educational qualifications only those degrees (a) from regionally accredited institutions or (b) from institutions recognized by states which license or certify marriage and family therapists, but only if such state regulation is recognized by AAMFT.

**8.13** Marriage and family therapists may not use the initials AAMFT following their name in the manner of an academic degree.

**8.14** Marriage and family therapists may not use the AAMFT name, logo, and/or the abbreviated initials AAMFT or make any other such representation which would imply that they speak for or represent the Association. The Association is the sole owner of its name, logo, and the abbreviated initials AAMFT. Its committees and divisions, operating as such, may use the name, logo, and/or the abbreviated initials AAMFT in accordance with AAMFT policies.

**8.15** Authorized advertisements of Clinical Members under the AAMFT name, logo, and/or the abbreviated initials AAMFT may include the following: the Clinical Member's name, degree, license or certificate held when required by state law, name of business, address, and telephone number. If a business is listed, it must follow, not precede the Clinical Member's name. Such listings may not include AAMFT offices held by the Clinical Member, nor any specializations, since such a listing under the AAMFT name, logo, and/or the abbreviated initials, AAMFT, would imply that this specialization has been credentialed by AAMFT.

**8.16** Marriage and family therapists use their membership in AAMFT only in connection with their clinical and professional activities.

**8.17** Only AAMFT divisions and programs accredited by the AAMFT Commission on Accreditation for Marriage and Family Therapy Education, not businesses nor organizations, may use any AAMFT-related designation or affiliation in public information or advertising materials, and then only in accordance with AAMFT policies.

**8.18** Programs accredited by the AAMFT Commission on Accreditation for Marriage and Family Therapy Education may not use the AAMFT name, logo, and/or the abbreviated initials AAMFT. Instead, they may have printed on their stationery and other appropriate materials a statement such as:

*The* (name of program) *of the* (name of institution) *is accredited by the AAMFT Commission on Accreditation for Marriage and Family Therapy Education.*

**8.19** Programs not accredited by the AAMFT Commission on Accreditation for Marriage and Family Therapy Education may not use the AAMFT name, logo, and/or the abbreviated initials AAMFT. They may not state in printed program materials, program advertisements, and student advisement that their courses and training opportunities are accepted by AAMFT to meet AAMFT membership requirements.

Violations of this Code should be brought in writing to the attention of the AAMFT Ethics Committee, 1100 17th Street, NW, The Tenth Floor, Washington, DC 20036-4601, (telephone 202/452-0109).

# *Appendix*

# *B*

# Ethical Code for the
# International Association of
# Marriage and Family Counselors

*Reprinted with permission from the
International Association for Marriage
and Family Therapy. This code was
published in 1993. IAMFC can make
further revisions of the code at any time
the association deems necessary.*

## Preamble

The IAMFC (International Association of Marriage and Family Counselors) is an organization dedicated to advancing the practice, training, and research of marriage and family counselors. Members may specialize in areas such as: premarital counseling, intergenerational counseling, separation and divorce counseling, relocation counseling, custody assessment and implementation, single parenting, stepfamilies, nontraditional family and marriage lifestyles, healthy and dysfunctional family systems, multicultural marriage and family concerns, displaced and homeless families, interfaith and interracial families, and dual career couples. In conducting their professional activities, members commit themselves to protect and advocate for the healthy growth and development of the family as a whole, even as they conscientiously recognize the integrity and diversity of each family and family member's unique needs, situations, status, and condition. The IAMFC member recognizes that the relationship between the provider and consumer of services is characterized as an egalitarian process emphasizing co-participation, co-equality, co-authority, co-responsibility, and client empowerment.

This code of ethics promulgates a framework for ethical practice by IAMFC members and is divided into eight sections: client well-being, confidentiality, competence, assessment, private practice, research and publications, supervision, and media and public statements. The ideas presented within these eight areas are meant to supplement the ethical standards of the American Counseling Association (ACA), formerly the American Association for Counseling and Development (AACD), and all members should know and keep to the standards of our parent organization. Although an ethical code cannot anticipate every possible situation or dilemma, the IAMFC ethical guidelines can aid members in ensuring the welfare and dignity of the couples and families they have contact with, as well as assisting in the implementation of the Hippocratic mandate for healers: Do no harm.

## Section 1: Client Well-Being

A. Members demonstrate a caring, empathic, respectful, fair, and active concern for family well-being. They promote client safety, security, and place-of-belonging in family, community, and society. Due to the risk involved, members should not use intrusive interventions without a sound theoretical rationale and having thoroughly thought through the potential ramifications to the family and its members.

B. Members recognize that each family is unique. They respect the diversity of personal attributes and do not stereotype or force families into prescribed attitudes, roles, or behaviors.

C. Members respect the autonomy of the families they work with. They do not make decisions that rightfully belong to family members.

D. Members respect cultural diversity. They do not discriminate on the basis of race, sex, disability, religion, age, sexual orientation, cultural background, national origin, marital status, or political affiliation.

E. Members strive for an egalitarian relationship with clients by openly and conscientiously sharing information, opinions, perceptions, processes of decision making, strategies of problem solving, and understanding of human behavior.

F. Members pursue a just relationship that acknowledges, respects, and informs clients of their rights, obligations, and expectations as a consumer of services, as well as the rights, obligations, and expectations of the provider(s) of service. Members inform clients (in writing if feasible) about the goals and purpose of the counseling, the qualifications of the counselor(s), the scope and limits of confidentiality, potential risks and benefits associated with the counseling process and with specific counseling techniques, reasonable expectations for the outcomes and duration of counseling, costs of services, and appropriate alternatives to counseling.

G. Members strive for a humanistic relationship that assists clients to develop a philosophy of meaning, purpose, and direction of life and living that promotes a positive regard of self, of family, of different and diverse others, and of the importance of humane concern for the community, nation, and the world at large.

H. Members promote primary prevention. They pursue the development of clients' cognitive, moral, social, emotional, spiritual, physical, educational, and career needs, as well as parenting, marriage, and family living skills, in order to prevent future problems.

I. Members have an obligation to determine and inform all persons involved who their primary client is—i.e., is the counselor's primary obligation to the individual, the family, a third party, or an institution? When there is a conflict of interest between the needs of the client and counselor's employing institution, the member works to clarify his or her commitment to all parties. Members recognize that the acceptance of employment implies that they are in agreement with the agency's policies and practices, and so monitor their place of employment to make sure that the environment is conducive to the positive growth and development of clients. If, after utilizing appropriate institutional channels for change, the member finds that the agency is not working toward the well-being of clients, the member has an obligation to terminate his or her institutional affiliation.

J. Members do not harass, exploit, coerce, engage in dual relationships, or have sexual contact with any current or former client or family member to whom they have provided professional services.

K. Members have an obligation to withdraw from a counseling relationship if the continuation of services is not in the best interest of the client or would result in a violation of ethical standards. If a client feels that the counseling relationship is no longer productive, the member has an obligation to assist in finding alternative services.

L. Members maintain accurate and up-to-date records. They make all file information available to clients unless the sharing of such information would be damaging to the status, goals, growth, or development of the client.

M. Members have the responsibility to confront unethical behavior conducted by other counselors. The first step should be to discuss the violation directly with the counselor. If the problem continues, the member should first use procedures established by the employing institution and then those of the IAMFC. Members may wish to also contact any appropriate licensure or certification board. Members may contact the IAMFC executive director, president, executive board members, or chair of the ethics committee at any time for consultation on remedying ethical violations.

## Section II: Confidentiality

A. Clients have the right to expect that information shared with the counselor will not be disclosed to others and, in the absence of any law to the contrary, the communications between clients and marriage and family counselors should be viewed as privileged. The fact that a contact was made with a counselor is to be considered just as confidential as the information shared during that contact. Information obtained from a client can only be disclosed to a third party under the following conditions.
   1. The client consents to disclosure by a signed waiver. The client must fully understand the nature of the disclosure (i.e., give informed consent), and only information described in the waiver may be disclosed. If more than one person is receiving counseling, each individual who is legally competent to execute a waiver must sign.
   2. The client has placed him- or herself or someone else in clear and imminent danger.
   3. The law mandates disclosure.
   4. The counselor is a defendant in a civil, criminal, or disciplinary action arising from professional activity.
   5. The counselor needs to discuss a case for consultation or education purposes. These discussions should not reveal the identity of the client or any other unnecessary aspects of the case and should only be done with fellow counseling professionals who subscribe to the IAMFC ethical code. The consulting professional counselor has an obligation to keep all shared information confidential.
B. All clients must be informed of the nature and limitations of confidentiality. They must also be informed of who may have access to their counseling records, as well as any information that may be released to other agencies or professionals for insurance reimbursement. These disclosures should be made both orally and in writing, whenever feasible.
C. All client records should be stored in a way that ensures confidentiality. Written records should be kept in a locked drawer or cabinet and computerized record systems should use appropriate passwords and safeguards to prevent unauthorized entry.
D. Clients must be informed if sessions are to be recorded on audio- or videotape and sign a consent form for doing so. When more

than one person is receiving counseling, all persons who are legally competent must give informed consent in writing for the recording.

E. Unless alternate arrangements have been agreed upon by all participants, statements made by a family member to the counselor during an individual counseling or consultation contact are to be treated as confidential and are not disclosed to other family members without the individual's permission. If a client's refusal to share information from individual contacts interferes with the agreed upon goals of counseling, the counselor may have to terminate treatment and refer the clients to another counselor.

## Section III: Competence

A. Members have the responsibility to develop and maintain basic skills in marriage and family counseling through graduate work, supervision, and peer review. An outline of these skills is provided by the Council for Accreditation of Counseling and Related Educational Programs (CACREP) *Environmental and Specialty Standards for Marriage and Family Counseling/Therapy.* The minimal level of training shall be considered a master's degree in a helping profession.

B. Members recognize the need for keeping current with new developments in the field of marriage and family counseling. They pursue continuing education in forms such as books, journals, classes, workshops, conferences, and conventions.

C. Members accurately represent their education, areas of expertise, training, and experience.

D. Members do not attempt to diagnose or treat problems beyond the scope of their abilities and training.

E. Members do not undertake any professional activity in which their personal problems might adversely affect their performance. Instead, they focus their energies on obtaining appropriate professional assistance to help them resolve the problem.

F. Members do not engage in actions that violate the moral or legal standards of their community.

## Section IV: Assessment

A. Members utilize assessment procedures to promote the best interests and well-being of the client in clarifying concerns, establishing treatment goals, evaluating therapeutic progress, and promoting objective decision making.

B. Clients have the right to know the results, interpretation, and conclusions drawn from assessment interviews and instruments, as well as how this information will be used.

C. Members utilize assessment methods that are reliable, valid, and germane to the goals of the client. When using computer-assisted scoring, members obtain empirical evidence for the reliability and validity of the methods and procedures used.

D. Members do not use inventories and tests that have outdated test items or normative data.

E. Members do not use assessment methods that are outside the scope of their qualifications, training, or statutory limitations. Members using tests or inventories have a thorough understanding of measurement concepts.

F. Members read the manual before using a published instrument. They become knowledgeable about the purpose of the instrument and relevant psychometric and normative data.

G. Members conducting custody evaluations recognize the potential impact that their reports can have on family members. As such, they are committed to a thorough assessment of both parents. Therefore, custody recommendations should not be made on the basis of information from only one parent. Members only use instruments that have demonstrated validity in custody evaluations and do not make recommendations based solely on test and inventory scores.

H. Members strive to maintain the guidelines in the *Standards for Educational and Psychological Testing*, written in collaboration by the American Educational Research Association, American Psychological Association, and National Council on Measurement in Evaluation, as well as the *Code of Fair Testing Practices*, published by the Joint Committee on Testing Practices.

## *Section V: Private Practice*

A. Members assist the profession and community by facilitating, whenever feasible, the availability of counseling services in private settings.

B. Due to the independent nature of their work, members in private practice recognize that they have a special obligation to act ethically and responsibly, keep up to date through continuing education, arrange consultation and supervision, and practice within the scope of their training and applicable laws.

C. Members in private practice provide a portion of their services at little or no cost as a service to the community. They also provide referral services for clients who will not be seen pro bono and who are unable to afford private services.

D. Members only enter into partnerships in which each member adheres to the ethical standards of their profession.

E. Members should not charge a fee for offering or accepting referrals.

## Section VI: Research and Publications

A. Members shall be fully responsible for their choice of research topics and the methods used for investigation, analysis, and reporting. They must be particularly careful that findings do not appear misleading, that the research is planned to allow for the inclusion of alternative hypotheses, and that provision is made for discussion of the limitations of the study.

B. Members safeguard the privacy of their research participants. Data about an individual participant are not released unless the individual is informed about the exact nature of the information to be released and gives written permission for doing so.

C. Members safeguard the safety of their research participants. Members receive approval from, and follow guidelines of, any institutional research committee. Prospective participants are informed, in writing, about any potential danger associated with a study and are notified that they can withdraw at any time.

D. Members make their original data available to other researchers.

E. Members only take credit for research in which they made a substantial contribution, and give credit to all such contributors. Authors are listed from greatest to least amount of contribution.

F. Members do not plagiarize. Ideas or data that did not originate with the author(s) and are not common knowledge are clearly credited to the original source.

G. Members are aware of their obligation to be a role model for graduate students and other future researchers and so act in accordance with the highest standards possible while engaged in research.

## Section VII: Supervision

A. Members who provide supervision acquire and maintain skills pertaining to the supervision process. They are able to demonstrate for supervisees the application of counseling theory and process to client issues. Supervisors are knowledgeable about different methods and conceptual approaches to supervision.

B. Members who provide supervision respect the inherent imbalance of power in the supervisory relationship. They do not use their potentially influential positions to exploit students, supervisees, or employees. Supervisors do not ask supervisees to engage in behaviors not directly related to the supervision process, and they clearly separate supervision and evaluation. Supervisors also avoid dual relationships that might impair their professional judgment or increase the possibility of exploitation. Sexual intimacy with students or supervisees is prohibited.

C. Members who provide supervision are responsible for both the promotion of supervisee learning and development and the advancement of marriage and family counseling. Supervisors recruit students into professional organizations, educate students about professional ethics and standards, provide service to professional organizations, strive to educate new professionals, and work to improve professional practices.

D. Members who provide supervision have the responsibility to inform students of the specific expectations surrounding skill building, knowledge acquisition, and the development of competencies. Members also provide ongoing and timely feedback to their supervisees.

E. Members who provide supervision are responsible for protecting the rights and well-being of their supervisees' clients. They monitor their supervisees' counseling on an ongoing basis, and create procedures to protect the confidentiality of clients whose sessions have been electronically recorded.

F. Members who provide supervision strive to reach and maintain the guidelines provided in the *Standards for Counseling Supervisors* published by the ACA Governing Council (cf. *Journal of Counseling & Development,* 1990, Vol. 69, pp. 30–32).

G. Members who are counselor educators encourage their programs to reach and maintain the guidelines provided in the CACREP *En-*

*vironmental and Specialty Standards for Marriage and Family Counseling/Therapy.*

## Section VIII: Media and Public Statements

A. Members accurately and objectively represent their professional qualifications, skills, and functions to the public. Membership in a professional organization is not to be used to suggest competency.
B. Members have the responsibility to provide information to the public that enhances marriage and family life. Such statements should be based on sound, scientifically acceptable theories, techniques, and approaches. Due to the inability to complete a comprehensive assessment and provide follow-up, members should not give specific advice to an individual through the media.
C. The announcement or advertisement of professional services should focus on objective information that allows the client to make an informed decision. Providing information such as highest relevant academic degree earned, licenses or certifications, office hours, types of services offered, fee structure, and languages spoken can help clients decide whether the advertised services are appropriate for their needs. Members advertising a specialty within marriage and family counseling should provide evidence of training, education, and/or supervision in the area of specialization. Advertisements about workshops or seminars should contain a description of the audience for which the program is intended. Due to their subjective nature, statements either from clients or from the counselor about the uniqueness, effectiveness, or efficiency of services should be avoided. Announcements and advertisements should never contain false, misleading, or fraudulent statements.
D. Members promoting psychology tapes, books, or other products for commercial sale make every effort to ensure that announcements and advertisements are presented in a professional and factual manner.

*Reader's Note:* Mary Allison, R. P. Ascano, Edward Beck, Stuart Bonnington, Joseph Hannon, David Kaplan (chair), Patrick McGrath, Judith Palais, Martin Ritchie, and Judy Ritterman are members of the IAMFC ethics committee who formulated the IAMFC code of ethics.

# References

Ackerman, N. W. (1958). *The psychodynamics of family life.* New York: Basic Books.

Adler, A. (1927). *The practice and theory of individual psychology.* New York: Harcourt, Brace, Jovanovich.

Alexander, J. F. (1973). Defensive and supportive communications in normal and deviant families. *Journal of Consulting and Clinical Psychology 40*(2), 223–231.

Alexander, J. F., & Barton, C. (1976). Behavioral systems therapy with families. In D. H. Olson (Ed.), *Treating relationships.* Lake Mills, IA: Graphic Press.

Alexander, J. F., Barton, C., Schiavo, R. S., & Parsons, B. V. (1976). Behavior interventions with families of delinquents: Therapist characteristics and outcome. *Journal of Consulting and Clinical Psychology, 44,* 656–664.

Alexander, J. F., & Parsons, B. V. (1973). Short term behavioral intervention with delinquent families: Impact on family process and recidivism. *Journal of Abnormal Psychology, 81*(3), 219–225.

Alexander, J. F., & Parsons, B. V. (1982). *Functional family therapy.* Pacific Grove, CA: Brooks/Cole.

American Association for Marriage and Family Therapy. (1986). *AAMFT membership requirements.* Washington, DC: Author.

American Association for Marriage and Family Therapy. (1991). *AAMFT Code of Ethics.* Washington, DC: Author.

Anderson, W. J. (1989). Client/person-centered approaches to couple and family therapy: Expanding theory and practice. *Person-Centered Review, 4,* 245–247.

Anonymous. (1972). On the differentiation of self. In J. Framo (Ed.), *Family interaction: A dialogue between family researchers and family therapists.* New York: Springer.

Aponte, H. J., & Van Deusen, J. M. (1981). Structural family therapy. In A. S. Gurman & D. P. Kniskern (Eds.), *Handbook of family therapy.* New York: Brunner/Mazel.

Babcock, D., & Keepers, T. (1976). *Raising kids ok.* New York: Grove Press.

Bandura, A. (1969). *Principles of behavior modification.* New York: Holt, Rinehart, & Winston.

Bandura, A. (1977). *Social learning theory.* Englewood Cliffs, NJ: Prentice Hall.

Barker, P. (1992). *Basic family therapy.* New York: Oxford University Press.

Barton, C., & Alexander, J. F. (1977). Treatment of families with a delinquent member. In G. Harris (Ed.), *The group treatment of family problems: A source learning approach.* New York: Grune & Stratton.

Barton, C., & Alexander, J. F. (1981). Functional family therapy. In A. S. Gurman & D. P. Kniskern (Eds.), *Handbook of family therapy*. New York: Brunner/Mazel.

Bateson, G., Jackson, D. D., Haley, J., & Weakland, J. (1956). Towards a theory of schizophrenia. *Behavioral Sciences, 1,* 251–264.

Bateson, G., Jackson, D., Haley, J., & Weakland, J. (1971). Toward a theory of schizophrenia. In G. Bateson, *Steps to an ecology of the mind*. New York: Ballentine.

Baucom, D. H., & Epstein, N. (1990). *Cognitive-behavioral marital therapy*. New York: Brunner/Mazel.

Bauer, R. (1979). Gestalt approaches to family therapy. *American Journal of Family Therapy, 7*(3), 41–45.

Beck, A. (1976). *Cognitive therapy and the emotional disorders*. New York: International University Press.

Beck, A. (1991). Cognitive therapy: A 30 year retrospective. *American Psychologist, 46,* 368–375.

Beck, A., Rush, A., Shaw, B., & Emery, G. (1979). *Cognitive therapy of depression*. New York: Guilford *Press.*

Bell, J. E. (1961). *Family group therapy*. Public Health Monograph 64. Washington, DC: U.S. Government Printing Office.

Benedek, E. P. (1982). Conjoint marital therapy and spouse abuse. In A. S. Gurman (Ed.), *Questions and answers in family therapy* (vol. 2). New York: Brunner/Mazel.

Berg, I. K. (1991). Letter to the editor. *Journal of Marital and Family Therapy, 17,* 311–312.

Berger, M. (1982). Predictable tasks in therapy with families of handicapped persons. In A. S. Gurman (Ed.), *Questions and answers in family therapy* (vol. 2). New York: Brunner/Mazel.

Bergin, A. (1967). Some implications of psychotherapy research for therapeutic practice. *International Journal of Psychiatry, 3,* 136–150.

Bergin, A. (1971). The evaluation of therapeutic outcomes. In A. Bergin & S. Garfield (Eds.), *Handbook of psychotherapy and behavior change*. New York: Wiley.

Bergin, A., & Lambert, M. (1978). The evaluation of therapeutic outcomes. In A. Bergin & S. Lambert (Eds.), *Handbook of psychotherapy and behavior change: An empirical analysis* (2nd ed.). New York: Wiley.

Berne, E. (1961). *Transactional analysis in psychotherapy*. New York: Grove Press.

Berne, E. (1972). *What do you say after you say hello?* New York: Grove Press.

Black, L., & Piercy, F. P. (1991). A feminist family therapy scale. *Journal of Marital and Family Therapy, 17,* 111–120.

Bodin, A. M. (1981). The interactional view: Family therapy approaches of the Mental Research Institute. In A. S. Gurman & D. P. Kniskern (Eds.), *Handbook of family therapy*. New York: Brunner/Mazel.

Bowen, M. (1960). A family concept of schizophrenia. In D. Jackson (Ed.), *The etiology of schizophrenia*. New York: Basic Books.

Bowen, M. (1961). Family psychotherapy. *American Journal of Orthopsychiatry, 31,* 40–60.

Bowen, M. (1971). Family therapy and family group therapy. In H. Kaplan & B. Sadock (Eds.), *Comprehensive group psychotherapy*. Baltimore: Williams & Wilkins.

Bowen, M. (1976). Theory in the practice of psychotherapy. In P. J. Guerrin, Jr. (Ed.), *Family therapy: Theory and practice.* New York: Gardner Press.

Bowen, M. (1978). *Family therapy in clinical practice.* New York: Jason Aronson.

Bray, J. H., & Jouriles, E. N. (1995). Treatment of marital conflict and prevention of divorce. *Journal of Marital and Family Therapy, 21*(4), 461–474.

Broderick, C. B., & Schraeder, S. S. (1991). The history of professional marriage and family therapy. In A. S. Gurman & D. P. Kniskern (Eds.), *Handbook of family therapy* (Vol. 2). New York: Brunner/ Mazel.

Buckley, W. (1967). *Sociology and modern systems theory.* Englewood Cliffs, NJ: Prentice Hall.

Campbell, T. L., & Patterson, J. M. (1995). The effectiveness of family interventions in the treatment of physical illness. *Journal of Marital and Family Therapy, 21*(4), 545–584.

Canfield, B. S., Hovestadt, A. J., & Fenell, D. L. (1992). Family-of-origin influences upon perceptions of current family functioning. *Family Therapy, 19,* 55–60.

Carkhuff, R. (1969a). *Helping and human relations. Vol. 1: Selection and training.* New York: Holt, Rinehart, & Winston.

Carkhuff, R. (1969b). *Helping and human relations. Vol. 11: Practice and research.* New York: Holt, Rinehart, & Winston.

Carter, E. A., & McGoldrick, M., (Eds.) (1980). *The family life cycle: A framework for family therapy.* New York: Gardner Press.

Chamberlain, P., & Rosicky, J. G. (1995). The effectiveness of family therapy in the treatment of adolescents with conduct disorders and delinquency. *Journal of Marital and Family Therapy, 21*(4), 441–460.

Clarke, J. (1978). *Self-esteem: A family affair.* Minneapolis: Winston Press.

Clarke, J., & Dawson, C. (1989). *Growing up again: parenting ourselves, parenting our children.* Minneapolis: Hazelden.

Colapinto, J. (1991). Structural family therapy. In A. S. Gurman & D. P. Kniskern (Eds.) *Handbook of family therapy.* (vol. 2). New York: Brunner/Mazel.

Conye, J. (1987). Depression, biology, marriage and marital therapy. *Journal of Marriage and Family Therapy, 13*(4), 393–407.

Corey, G. (1991). *Theory and practice of counseling and psychotherapy* (4th ed.). Pacific Grove, CA: Brooks/Cole.

Corey, G. (1996). *Theory and practice of counseling and psychotherapy* (5th ed.). Pacific Grove, CA: Brooks/Cole.

Corey, G., Corey, M., & Callahan, P. (1993). *Issues and ethics in the helping professions* (4th ed.). Pacific Grove, CA: Brooks/Cole.

Davidson, T. (1978). *Conjugal crime.* New York: Hawthorne.

DeWitt, K. (1978). The effectiveness of family therapy: A review of the outcome research. *Archives of General Psychiatry, 35,* 549–561.

Dilts, R., & Green, J. D. (1982). Neuro-linguistic programming in family therapy. In A. M. Horne & M. M. Ohlsen (Eds.), *Family counseling and therapy.* Itasca, IL: Peacock.

Doherty, W. J. (1991). Beyond reactivity and the deficit model of manhood: A comment on articles by Napier, Pittman, and Gottman. *Journal of Marital and Family Therapy, 17,* 29–32.

Duhl, F. J., Kantor, D., & Duhl, B. S. (1973). Learning, space and action in family therapy: A primer of sculpture. In D. Bloch (Ed.), *Techniques of family psychotherapy.* New York: Grune & Stratton.

Edwards, M. E., & Steinglass, P. (1995). Family therapy treatment outcomes for alcoholism. *Journal of Marital and Family Therapy, 4,* 475–509.

Ellis, A. (1962). *Reason and emotion in psychotherapy.* Secaucus, NJ: Citadel Press.

Ellis, A. (1974). *Techniques of disrupting irrational beliefs.* New York: Institute for Rational Living.

Ellis, A. (1977). *Self-help report form.* New York: Institute for Rational Living.

Ellis, A. (1991). Rational-emotive family therapy. In A. Horne & A. Passmore (Eds.), *Family counseling and therapy* (2nd ed.). Itasca, IL: Peacock.

Ellis, A. (1992). First order and second order change in rational-emotive therapy: A reply to Lyddon. *Journal of Counseling and Development, 70,* 449–451.

Ellis, A. (1993). The rational-emotive therapy approach to marriage and family therapy. *The Family Journal, 1,* 292–307.

Ellis, A. (1995). Rational emotive behavior therapy. In R. J. Corsini & D. Wedding (Eds.), *Current psychotherapies* (5th ed.). Itasca, IL: Peacock.

Epston, D. (1994). Extending the conversation. *The Family Therapy Networker, 18*(6), 30–37.

Erikson, E. H. (1946). *The psychoanalytic study of the child.* New York: International Universities Press.

Erikson, E. H. (1950). *Childhood and society.* New York: Norton.

Erikson, E. H. (1959). *Psychological issues.* New York: International Universities Press.

Estrada, A. U., & Pinsof, W. M. (1995). The effectiveness of family therapies for selected behavioral disorders of childhood. *Journal of Marital and Family Therapy, 21*(4), 403–440.

Everett, C., & Volgy, S. (1991). Treating divorce in family therapy practice. In A. Gurman & D. Kniskern (Eds.), *Handbook of family therapy* (vol. 2). New York: Brunner/Mazel.

Eysenck, H. (1952). The effects of psychotherapy: An evaluation. *Journal of Consulting Psychology, 16,* 319–324.

Fairbairn, W. (1954). *Object-relations theory of the personality.* New York: Basic Books.

Falloon, I. (1991). Behavioral marital therapy. In A. S. Gurman & D. P. Kniskern (Eds.), *Handbook of family therapy* (vol. 2). New York: Brunner/Mazel.

Fenell, D. L. (1982). Counseling dual career couples. *Arizona Personnel and Guidance Journal, 7,* 8–10.

Fenell, D. L. (1993a). Characteristics of long-term first marriages. *Journal of Mental Health Counseling, 15,* 446–460.

Fenell, D. L. (1993b). Using Bowen's differentiation of self scale to help couples understand and resolve marital conflict. In T. S. Nelson & T. S. Trepper (Eds.), *101 interventions in family therapy.* New York: Haworth Press.

Fenell, D. L., & Hovestadt, A. J. (1986). Family therapy as a profession or professional specialty: Implications for training. *Journal of Psychotherapy and the Family, 1*(4), 25–40.

Fenell, D. L., Hovestadt, A. J., & Harvey, S. J. (1986). A comparison of delayed feedback and live supervision models of marriage and family therapy. *Journal of Marital and Family Therapy, 12*(2), 181–186.

Fenell, D. L., Martin. J., & Mithaug, D. E. (1986). The mentally retarded child. In L. B. Golden & D. Capuzzi (Eds.), *Helping families help children: Family interventions with school-related problems.* Springfield, IL: Charles C. Thomas.

Fenell, D. L., Nelson, R. C., & Shertzer, B. (1981). The effects of a marriage enrichment program on marital satisfaction and self-concept. *The Journal for Specialists in Group Work, 6*(2), 83–89.

Fenell, D. L., & Wallace, C. (1985). Remarriage: The triumph of hope over experience: A challenge for counseling professionals. *Arizona Counseling Journal, 10,* 12–18.

Fisch, R., Weakland, J. H., & Segal, L. (1982). *The tactics of change: Doing therapy briefly.* San Francisco: Jossey-Bass.

Fish, V. (1993). Poststructuralism in family therapy: Interrogating the narrative/conversational mode. *Journal of Marital and Family Therapy, 19,* 221–232.

Flugel, J. D. (1921). *The psychoanalytic study of the family.* London: Hogarth Press.

Foley, V. D. (1974). *An introduction to family therapy.* New York: Grune & Stratton.

Framo, J. L. (1981). The integration of marital therapy with family of origin sessions. In A. S. Gurman & D. P. Kniskern (Eds.), *Handbook of family therapy.* New York: Brunner/Mazel.

Framo, J. L. (1982). *Explorations in marital and family therapy.* New York: Springer.

Freud, S. (1909). Analysis of a phobia in a five-year-old boy. *Standard Edition, 10,* 3–152. (original work published 1909)

Freud, S. (1949). *An outline of psychoanalysis.* New York: Norton.

Freud, S. (1963). *Collected papers* (vol. 4). New York: Collier Books.

Friedman, E. H. (1991). Bowen theory and therapy. In A. S. Gurman & D. P. Kniskern (Eds.), *Handbook of family therapy* (vol. 2). New York: Brunner/Mazel.

Fromm, E. (1941). *Escape from freedom.* New York: Holt, Rinehart, & Winston.

Fromm, E. (1947). *Man for himself.* New York: Holt, Rinehart, & Winston.

Gaylin, N. L. (1989). The necessary and sufficient conditions for change: Individual versus family therapy. *Person-Centered Review, 4,* 263–279.

George, R. L. (1990). Counseling the chemically dependent: Role and function. Englewood Cliffs, NJ: Prentice Hall.

Gill, S. J. (1982). Professional disclosure and consumer protection in counseling. *Personnel and Guidance Journal, 60,* 443–446.

Gladding, S. T., Burggraf, M. Z., & Fenell, D. L. (1987). A survey of marriage and family therapy training within departments of counselor education. *Journal of Counseling and Development, 66*(2), (p. 90–92).

Glang, C., & Betis, A. (1993). Helping children through the divorce process. *PsychSpeak, 13* (4), 1–2.

Glick, P. (1989). Remarried families, stepfamilies and stepchildren: A brief demographic analysis. *Family Relations, 38,* 24–27.

Goldstein, M. J., & Miklowitz, D. J. (1995). The effectiveness of psychoeducational family therapy in the treatment of schizophrenic disorders. *Journal of Marital and Family Therapy, 21*(4), 361–376.

Goodrich, T. J., Rampage, C., & Ellman, B. (1989). The single mother. *The Family Therapy Networker,* Sept.–Oct., 52–56.

Goodrich, T. J., Rampage, C., Ellman, B., & Halstead, K. (1988). *Feminist family therapy: A casebook.* New York: Norton.

Gottman, J., Notarius, C., Markman, H., Bank, S., Yoppi, B., & Rubin, M. (1976). Behavior exchange theory and marital decision making. *Journal of Personality and Social Psychology, 34,* 14–23.

Goulding, M., & Goulding, R. (1978). *The power is in the patient: A Gestalt approach to psychotherapy.* San Francisco: TA Press.

Goulding, M., & Goulding, R. (1979). *Changing lives through redecision therapy.* New York: Brunner/Mazel.

Gumper, L. L., & Sprenkle, D. H. (1981). Privileged communication therapy: Special problems for the family and couples therapist. *Family Process, 20,* 11–23.

Gurman, A. S., & Kniskern, D. P. (1978a). Deterioration in marriage and family therapy: Empirical, clinical and conceptual issues. *Family Process, 17,* 3–20.

Gurman, A. S., & Kniskern, D. P. (1978b). Research on marital and family therapy: Progress, perspective and prospect. In S. L. Garfield & A. E. Lambert (Eds.), *Handbook of psychotherapy and behavior change: An empirical analysis* (2nd ed.). New York: Wiley.

Gurman, A. S., & Kniskern, D. P. (1981a). Family therapy outcome research: Knowns and unknowns. In A. S. Gurman & D. P. Kniskern (Eds.), *Handbook of family therapy.* New York: Brunner/Mazel.

Gurman, A. S., & Kniskern, D. P. (Eds.) (1981b). *Handbook of family therapy.* New York: Brunner/Mazel.

Gurman, A. S., & Kniskern, D. P. (Eds.) (1991). *Handbook of family therapy* (vol. 2). New York: Brunner/Mazel.

Haley, J. (1971). Family therapy: A radical change. In J. Haley (Ed.), *Changing families: A family therapy reader.* New York: Grune & Stratton.

Haley, J. (1983). *Problem solving therapy.* San Francisco: Jossey-Bass.

Hamberger, L. K., & Hastings, J. E. (1993). Court mandated treatment of men who batter their partners: Issues, controversies and outcomes. In Z. Hilton (Ed.), *Legal responses to wife assault.* Newbury Park, CA: Sage.

Harris, T. (1967). *I'm o.k., you're o.k.* New York: Harper & Row.

Hatcher, C. (1978). Intrapersonal and interpersonal models: Blending Gestalt and family therapies. *Journal of Marriage and Family Counseling, 4*(1), 63–68.

Hatcher, C. (1981). Managing the violent family. In A. S. Gurman (Ed.), *Questions and answers in family therapy.* New York: Brunner/Mazel.

Havighurst, R. (1972). *Developmental tasks and education.* New York: David McKay.

Herrington, B. S. (1979). Privilege denied in joint therapy. *Psychiatric News, 14,* 1.

Horne, A., & Ohlsen, M. (Eds.) (1982). *Family counseling and therapy.* Itasca, IL: Peacock.

Hovestadt, A. J., Fenell, D. L., & Piercy, F. P. (1983). Integrating marriage and family therapy within counselor education: A three-level model. In B. F. Okun & S. T. Gladding (Eds.), *Issues in training marriage and family therapists.* Ann Arbor, MI: ERIC/CAPS.

Huber, C. H. (1994). *Ethical, legal and professional issues in the practice of marriage and family therapy* (2nd ed.). New York: Merrill.

International Association of Marriage and Family Counselors. (1993). *Ethical Code for IAMFC*. Denver: Author.

Jackson, D. (1965). Family rules: The marital quid pro quo. *Archives of General Psychiatry, 12*, 589–594.

Jacobson, N. (1989). The maintenance of treatment gains following social learning based marital therapy. *Behavior Therapy, 20*, 325–336.

James, M., & Jongeward, D. (1971). *Born to win.* Reading, MA: Addison-Wesley.

Johnson, H. C. (1987). Biologically based deficit in the identified patient: Indications for psychoeducational strategies. *Journal of Marital and Family Therapy, 13*, 337–348.

Kaplan, L. (1978). *Oneness and separateness: From infant to individual.* New York: Simon & Schuster.

Kaplan, M., & Kaplan, N. (1978). Individual and family growth: A Gestalt approach. *Family Process, 17*, 195–206.

Kaufman, E., & Kaufman, P. (1979). *The family therapy of alcohol and drug abusers.* New York: Gardner Press.

Kempler, W. (1965). Experiential family therapy. *The International Journal of Group Psychotherapy, 15*, 57–71.

Kempler, W. (1968). Experiential therapy with families. *Family Process, 7*(1), 88–99.

Kempler, W. (1981). *Experiential therapy with families.* New York: Brunner/Mazel.

Kempler, W. (1991). Gestalt family therapy. In A. Horne & J. L. Passmore (Eds.), *Family counseling and therapy* (2nd ed.). Itasca, IL: Peacock.

Kerr, M. E. (1981). Family systems theory and therapy. In A. S. Gurman & D. P. Kniskern (Eds.), *Handbook of family therapy.* New York: Brunner/Mazel.

Kerr, M., & Bowen, M. (1988). *Family evaluation.* New York: Norton.

Kitson, G., & Morgan, L. (1990). Multiple consequences of divorce: A decade review. *Journal of Marriage and the Family, 52*, 913–924.

Klien, N. C., Alexander, J. F., & Parsons, B. V. (1977). Impact of family systems interventions on recidivism and sibling delinquency: A model for primary prevention and program development. *Journal of Consulting and Clinical Psychology, 45*, 469–474.

Kniskern, D. P., & Gurman, A. S. (1979). Research in training marriage and family therapists: Status, issues, and directions. *Journal of Marital and Family Therapy, 5*, 83–96.

Krumboltz, J., & Thoresen, C. (1969). *Behavioral counseling: Cases and techniques.* New York: Holt, Rinehart, & Winston.

Krumboltz, J., & Thoresen, C. (Eds.) (1976). *Counseling methods.* New York: Holt, Rinehart, & Winston.

Lambert, M. J., Bergin, A. E., & Collins, J. L. (1977). Therapist induced deterioration in psychotherapy. In A. S. Gurman & A. M. Razin (Eds.), *Effective psychotherapy: A handbook of research.* New York: Pergamon Press.

Lambie, R., & Daniels-Mohring, D. (1993). *Family systems within educational contexts: Understanding students with special needs.* Denver, CO: Love.

Lazarus, A. (1971). *Behavior therapy and beyond.* New York: McGraw-Hill.

Lazarus, A. (1981). *The practice of multimodal therapy.* New York: McGraw-Hill.

LeBoyer, F. (1975). *Birth without violence.* New York: Knopf.

Levant, R. (1978). Family therapy: A client-centered perspective. *Journal of Marriage and Family Counseling, 4*(2), 35–42.

Levant, R. (1984). *Family therapy: A comprehensive overview.* Englewood Cliffs, NJ: Prentice Hall.

Levin, P. (1988a). *Becoming the way we are.* Deerfield Beach, FL: Health Communications.

Levin, P. (1988b). *Cycles of power.* Deerfield Beach, FL: Health Communications.

Liberman, R. P. (1970). Behavioral approaches to couple and family therapy. *American Journal of Orthopsychiatry, 40,* 106–118.

Liddle, H. A. (1991). Training and supervision in family therapy: A comprehensive and critical analysis. In A. S. Gurman & D. P. Kniskern (Eds.), *Handbook of family therapy* (vol. 2). New York: Brunner/Mazel.

Liddle, H. A., & Dakof, G. A. (1995). Efficacy of family therapy for drug abuse: Promising but not definitive. *Journal of Marital and Family Therapy, 21*(4), 511–544.

Liddle, H., Davidson, G., & Barrett, M. (1988). Pragmatic implications of live supervision: Outcome research. In H. A. Liddle, D. C. Breunlin, & R. C. Schwartz, (Eds.), *Handbook of family therapy training and supervision.* New York: Guilford Press.

Liddle, H., & Halpin, R. (1978). Family therapy training and supervision: A comparative review. *Journal of Marriage and Family Counseling, 4,* 77–98.

Lowe, R. N. (1982). Adlerian/Dreikursian family counseling. In A. M. Horne & M. M. Ohlsen (Eds.), *Family counseling and therapy.* Itasca, IL: Peacock.

Luborsky, L., Singer, B., & Luborsky, L. (1973). Comparative studies of psychotherapies. *Archives of General Psychiatry, 29,* 719–729.

Lyddon, W. J. (1990). First and second order change: Implications for rationalist and constructivist cognitive therapies. *Journal of Counseling and Development, 69,* 122–127.

Lyddon, W. J. (1992). A rejoinder to Ellis: What is and is not RET? *Journal of Counseling and Development, 70,* 452–454.

Magid, K., & McKelvey, C. (1987). *High risk: Children without a conscience.* New York: Bantam Books.

Mahler, M. (1968). *On human symbiosis and the vicissitudes of individuation, Vol. 1, Infantile psychosis.* New York: International Universities Press.

Mahler, M. S., Pine, F., & Bergman, A. (1975). *The psychological birth of the human infant.* New York: Basic Books.

Margolin, G. (1982). Ethical and legal considerations in family therapy. *American Psychologist, 7,* 788–801.

Margolin, G. (1987). The multiple forms of aggressiveness between marital partners: How do we identify them? *Journal of Marital and Family Therapy, 13*(1), 77–85.

Maslow, A. (1968). *Toward a psychology of being* (2nd ed.). New York: Van Nostrand Reinhold.

Maslow, A. (1971). *The farther reaches of human nature.* New York: Viking Press.

McClendon, R. (1977). My mother drives a pick-up truck. In G. Barnes (Ed.), *Transactional analysis after Eric Berne.* New York: Harper & Row.

McFarlane, W. R. (1991). Family psychoeducational treatment. In A. S. Gurman & D. H. Kniskern (Eds.), *Handbook of family therapy* (vol. 2). New York: Brunner/Mazel.

McGoldrick, M., & Gerson, R. (1985). *Genograms in family assessment.* New York: Norton.

McGoldrick, M., Pearce, J. K., & Giordano, J. (1982). *Ethnicity and family therapy.* New York: Guilford Press.

McGoldrick, M., Preto, N. G., Hines, P. M., & Lee, E. (1991). Ethnicity and family therapy. In A. S. Gurman & D. P. Kniskern (Eds.). *Handbook of family therapy* (Vol. 2). New York: Brunner/Mazel.

McGoldrick, M., & Rohrbaugh, M. (1987). Researching ethnic family stereotypes. *Family Process, 1,* 89–100.

Meichenbaum, D. (1977). *Cognitive behavior modification.* New York: Plenum.

Miller, A. (1981). *The drama of the gifted child.* New York: Basic Books.

Miller, A. (1983). *For your own good.* New York: Farrar, Straus, Giroux.

Miller, A. (1986). *Thou shalt not be aware.* New York: New American Library.

Miller, A. (1988). *Banished knowledge.* New York: Doubleday.

Miller, A. (1991). *Breaking down the wall of silence.* New York: Dutton.

Mindell, A. (1983). *Dreambody.* Santa Monica. CA: SIGO Press.

Mindell, A. (1985a). *River's way.* Boston: Routledge, Kegan, Paul.

Mindell, A. (1985b). *Working with the dreaming body.* Boston: Routledge, Kegan, Paul.

Mindell, A. (1987). *The dreambody in relationship processes.* Boston: Routledge, Kegan, Paul.

Minuchin, S. (1974). *Families and family therapy.* Cambridge, MA: Harvard University Press.

Minuchin, S., & Fishman, C. (1981). *Family therapy techniques.* Cambridge, MA: Harvard University Press.

Minuchin, S., Montalvo, B., Guerney, B. G., Jr., Rosman, B. L., & Schumer, F. (1967). *Families of the slums: An exploration of their structure and treatment.* New York: Basic Books.

Minuchin, S., Rosman, B., & Baker, L. (1978). *Psychosomatic families: Anorexia nervosa in context.* Cambridge, MA: Harvard University Press.

Mitchell, K. M., Bozarth, J. D., & Kraft, C. C. (1977). A reappraisal of the therapeutic effectiveness of accurate empathy, nonpossessive warmth, and genuineness. In A. S. Gurman & A. M. Razin (Eds.), *Effective psychotherapy: A handbook of research.* New York: Pergamon Press.

Montalvo, B., & Thompson, R. F. (1988). Conflicts in the caregiving family. *The Family Therapy Networker,* July-Aug., 30–35.

Moreno, J. L. (1951). *Sociometry, experimental method and the science of society.* Boston: Beacon.

Moreno, J. L. (1983). Psychodrama. In H. Kaplan & B. Sadock (Eds.), *Comprehensive group* (2nd ed.). Baltimore: Williams & Wilkins.

Napier, A. Y., & Whitaker, C. A. (1978). *The family crucible.* New York: Harper & Row.

Norton, A. J., & Mooreman, J. E. (1987). Current trends in marriage and divorce among American women. *Journal of Marriage and the Family, 49,* 3–14.

Nylund, D., & Thomas, J. (1994). The economics of narrative. *The Family Therapy Networker, 18*(6), 38–39.

O'Hanlon, B. (1994). The third wave. *The Family Therapy Networker, 18*(6), 18–29.

O'Leary, C. J. (1989). The person-centered approach to family therapy: A dialogue between two traditions. *Person-Centered Review, 4,* 308–323.

Olin, G. V., & Fenell, D. L. (1989). The relationship between depression and marital adjustment in a general population. *Family Therapy, XVI,* 11–20.

Olson, D. H., Russell, C., & Sprenkle, D. H. (1980). Marriage and family therapy: A decade review. *Journal of Marriage and the Family, 42,* 973–993.

Olson, D. H., & Sprenkle, D. H. (1983). Circumplex model of marital and family systems VI: Theoretical update. *Family Process, 22,* 69–83.

Olson, D. H., Sprenkle, D. H., & Russell, C. (1983). Circumplex model of marital and family systems IV: Theoretical update. *Family Process, 22*(1), 69–83.

Orr, L., & Ray, S. (1977). *Rebirthing in the new age.* Millbrae, CA: Celestial Arts.

Paolino, T. J., Jr., & McCrady, B. S. (Eds.) (1978). *Marriage and marital therapy: Psychoanalytic, behavioral and systems theory perspectives.* New York: Brunner/Mazel.

Papp, P. (1980). The Greek chorus and other techniques of paradoxical therapy. *Family Process, 19,* 45–57.

Parry, A. (1991). A universe of stories. *Family Process, 30,* 37–54.

Parsons, B. V., & Alexander, J. F. (1973). Short-term family intervention: A therapy outcome study. *Journal of Consulting and Clinical Psychology, 41,* 195–201.

Patterson, G. (1971). *Families: Application of social learning in family life.* Champaign, IL: Research Press.

Patterson, G. (1976). *Families: Application of social learning in family life.* Champaign, IL: Research Press.

Patterson, G., Reid, J., Jones, R., & Conger, R. (1975). *A social learning approach to family intervention: Families with aggressive children.* Eugene, OR: Castalia Publishing.

Pattison, E. M. (1982). Family dynamics and interventions in alcoholism. In A. S. Gurman (Ed.), *Questions and answers in the practice of family therapy* (vol. 2). New York: Brunner/Mazel.

Paul, G. L. (1967). Strategy of outcome research in psychotherapy. *Journal of Consulting Psychology, 31,* 109–118.

Perls, F. (1969). *Gestalt therapy verbatim.* Moab, UT: Real People Press.

Piaget, J. (1951). *The child's conception of the world.* New York: Humanities Press.

Prince, S. E., & Jacobson, N. S. (1995). A review and evaluation of marital and family therapies for affective disorders. *Journal of Marital and Family Therapy, 21*(4), 377–402.

Rabin, M. (1980). *The field of family therapy: A paradigmatic classification and presentation of the major approaches.* Paper presented at the annual meeting of the American Personnel and Guidance Association, Atlanta, GA.

Raskin, N., & Van der Veen, F. (1970). Client-centered therapy: Some clinical and research perspectives. In J. Hart & T. Tomlinson (Eds.), *New directions in client-centered therapy.* Boston: Houghton Mifflin.

Reid, J., & Patterson, G. (1976). The modification of aggressive behavior in boys in the home setting. In A. Bandura & E. Ribes (Eds.), *Behavior modification: Experimental analysis of aggression and delinquency.* Hillsdale, NJ: Erlbaum.

Roberto, L. G. (1991). Symbolic-experiential family therapy. In A. S. Gurman & D. P. Kniskern (Eds.), *Handbook of family therapy* (vol. 2). New York: Brunner/Mazel.

Rogers, C. R. (1957). The necessary and sufficient conditions of therapeutic personality change. *Journal of Consulting Psychology, 21,* 95–103.

Rogers, C. R. (1961). *On becoming a person: A therapist's view of psychotherapy.* Boston: Houghton Mifflin.

Rogers, C. R. (1980). *A way of being.* Boston: Houghton Mifflin.

Rudestam, K. E. (1982). *Experiential groups in theory and practice.* Pacific Grove, CA: Brooks/Cole.

Sager, C. J., et al. (1971). The marriage contract. *Family Process, 10,* 311–326.

Satir, V. (1983). *Conjoint family therapy* (3rd ed.). Palo Alto, CA: Science and Behavior Books.

Satir, V. (1988). *The new peoplemaking.* Palo Alto, CA: Science and Behavior Books.

Schiff, J. (1970). *All my children.* New York: Pyramid Books.

Schiff, J. (1976) *The cathexis reader.* New York: Harper & Row.

Segal, L. (1991). Brief therapy: The MRI approach. In A. S. Gurman & D. P. Kniskern (Eds.), *Handbook of family therapy* (vol. 2). New York: Brunner/Mazel.

Smith, M. L., & Glass, G. V. (1977). Meta-analysis of psychotherapy outcome studies. *American Psychologist, 32,* 752–760.

Sperry, L., & Carlson, J. (1991). *Marital therapy: Integrating theory and technique.* Denver, CO: Love.

Spitz, R. (1965). *The first year of life.* New York: International Universities Press.

Sprenkle, D. H. (1990). Continuity and change. *Journal of Marital and Family Therapy, 16,* 337–340.

Stanton, M. D. (1978). Some outcome results and aspects of structural family therapy with drug addicts. In D. Smith, S. Anderson, M. Buxton, T. Chung, N. Gotlieb, & W. Harvey (Eds.), *A multicultural view of drug abuse.* Cambridge, MA: Schenkman.

Stanton, M. D., & Todd, T. (1979). Structural family therapy with drug addicts. In E. Kaufman & P. Kaufman (Eds.), *The family therapy of drug and alcohol abuse.* New York: Gardner Press.

Stanton, M. D., & Todd, T. (1981). Family treatment approaches to drug abuse problems. *Family Process, 18,* 251–280.

Storm, C. L. (1991). Placing gender at the heart of MFT masters programs: Teaching a gender sensitive systemic view. *Journal of Marital and Family Therapy, 17,* 45–52.

Strupp, H. H., & Hadley, S. W. (1979). Specific vs. nonspecific factors in psychotherapy: A controlled study of outcome. *Archives of General Psychiatry, 36,* 1125–1136.

Stuart, R. (1980). *Helping couples change: A social learning approach to marital therapy.* New York: Guilford Press.

Sullivan, H. S. (1947). *Conceptions of modern psychiatry.* Washington, DC: William Alanson White Psychiatric Foundation.

Sullivan, H. S. (1953). *The interpersonal theory of psychiatry.* New York: Norton.

Sullivan, H. S. (1954). *The psychiatric interview.* New York: Norton.

Taub-Bynum, E. (1984). *The family unconscious.* Wheaton, IL: Theosophical.

Thayer, L. (1991). Toward a person-centered approach to family therapy. In A. M. Horne & J. L. Passmore (Eds.). *Family Counseling and Therapy* (2nd ed.). Itasca, IL: Peacock.

Toman, W. (1961). *Family constellation.* New York: Springer.

Training of clinical psychologists. (1981). *Psychology Today, 16*(2), 85.

Truax, C. B., & Carkhuff, R. R. (1967). *Toward effective counseling and psychotherapy: Training and practice.* Chicago: Aldine.

Truax, C. B., & Mitchell, K. M. (1971). Research on certain therapist interpersonal skills in relation to process and outcome. In A. E. Bergin & S. L. Garfield (Eds.), *Handbook on psychotherapy and behavior change: An empirical analysis.* New York: Wiley.

Usher, M. L., & Steinglass, P. J. (1981). Responding to presenting complaints in an alcoholic family. In A. S. Gurman (Ed.), *Questions and answers in the practice of family therapy.* New York: Brunner/Mazel.

Van der Veen, F. (1977). Three client-centered alternatives: A therapy collective, therapeutic community and skills training for relationships. Paper presented at annual meeting of the American Psychological Association.

Visher, E. B., & Visher, J. S. (1979). *Stepfamilies: A guide to working with stepparents and stepchildren.* New York: Brunner/Mazel.

von Bertalanffy, L. (1968). *General systems theory: Foundation, development, applications.* New York: Brazillier.

Walsh, R., & Vaughan, B. (Eds.) (1980). *Beyond ego: Transpersonal dimensions in psychology.* Los Angeles: J. P. Tarcher.

Watson, R. (1977). An introduction to humanistic psychotherapy. In S. Moore & R. Watson (Eds.), *Psychotherapies: A comparative casebook.* New York: Holt, Rinehart, & Winston.

Watzlawick, P. (Ed.) (1984). *The invented reality.* New York: Norton.

Watzlawick, P., Weakland, J. H., & Fisch, R. (1974). *Change: Principles of problem formation and problem resolution.* New York: Norton.

Weiner, N. (1954). *Cybernetics, or control and communication in the animal and the machine* (2nd ed.). Cambridge, MA: MIT Press. (original work published 1948)

Weinhold, B. K. (1982). *A transpersonal approach to counselor education.* Colorado Springs: Author.

Weinhold, B. K. (1991). *Breaking free of addictive family relationships.* Walpole, NH: Stillpoint Publishers.

Weinhold, B. K., & Hendricks, G. (1993). *Counseling and psychotherapy: A transpersonal approach.* Denver: Love.

Weinhold, B. K., & Weinhold, J. B. (1989). *Breaking free of the co-dependency trap.* Walpole, NH: Stillpoint Publishers.

Weinhold, B. K., & Weinhold, J. B. (1994). *Soul evolution: The spiritual uses of conflict in relationships.* Walpole, NH: Stillpoint Publishers.

Weinhold, J. B., & Weinhold, B. K. (1992). *Counter-dependency: The flight from intimacy.* Colorado Springs, CO: CICRCL Press.

Weiss, L., & Weiss, J. (1989). *Recovery from co-dependency.* Deerfield Beach, FL: Health Communications.

Wells, R. A., & Dezen, A. E. (1978). The results of family therapy revisited: The non-behavioral methods. *Family Process, 17*, 251–274.

Whitaker, C. A. (1976). The hindrance of theory in clinical work. In P. J. Guerrin, Jr. (Ed.), *Family therapy: Theory and practice.* New York: Gardner Press.

Whitaker, C. A., & Keith, D. V. (1981). Symbolic-experiential family therapy. In A. S. Gurman & D. P. Kniskern (Eds.), *Handbook of family therapy.* New York: Brunner/Mazel.

White, M., & Epston, D. (1990). *Narrative means to therapeutic ends.* New York: Norton.

Wilber, K. (1980). *The Atman project: A transpersonal view of human development.* Wheaton, IL: Quest Books.

Wilcoxon, S. A., & Fenell, D. L. (1983). Engaging the nonattending spouse in marital therapy through the use of a therapist-initiated written communication. *Journal of Marital and Family Therapy, 9*, 199–203.

Wilcoxon, S. A., & Fenell, D. L. (1986). Linear and paradoxical letters to the nonattending spouse: A comparison of engagement rates. *Journal of Marital and Family Therapy, 12*(2), 191–193.

Wolpe, J. (1958). *Psychotherapy by reciprocal inhibition.* Stanford, CA: Stanford University Press.

Wolpe, J. (1969). *The practice of behavior therapy.* New York: Pergamon Press.

Wynne, L. C., (Ed.) (1988). *The state of the art in family therapy research: Controversies and recommendations.* New York: Family Prouss Press.

Wynne, L. C., McDaniel, S. H., & Weber, T. T. (1987). Professional politics and the concepts of family therapy, family consultation and systems consultation. *Family Process, 26*, 153–166.

Wynne, L. C., Ryckoff, I. M., Day, J., & Hirsch, S. I. (1958). Pseudomutuality in the family relationships of schizophrenics. *Psychiatry, 21*, 205–220.

# Author Index

# Subject Index

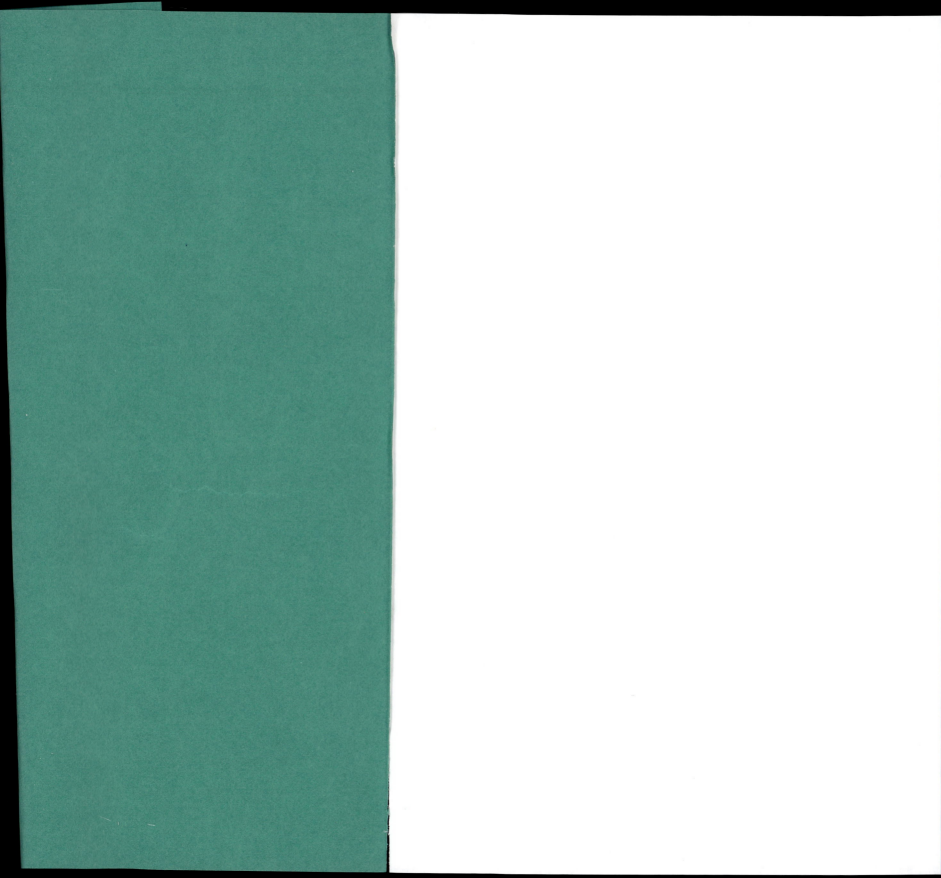

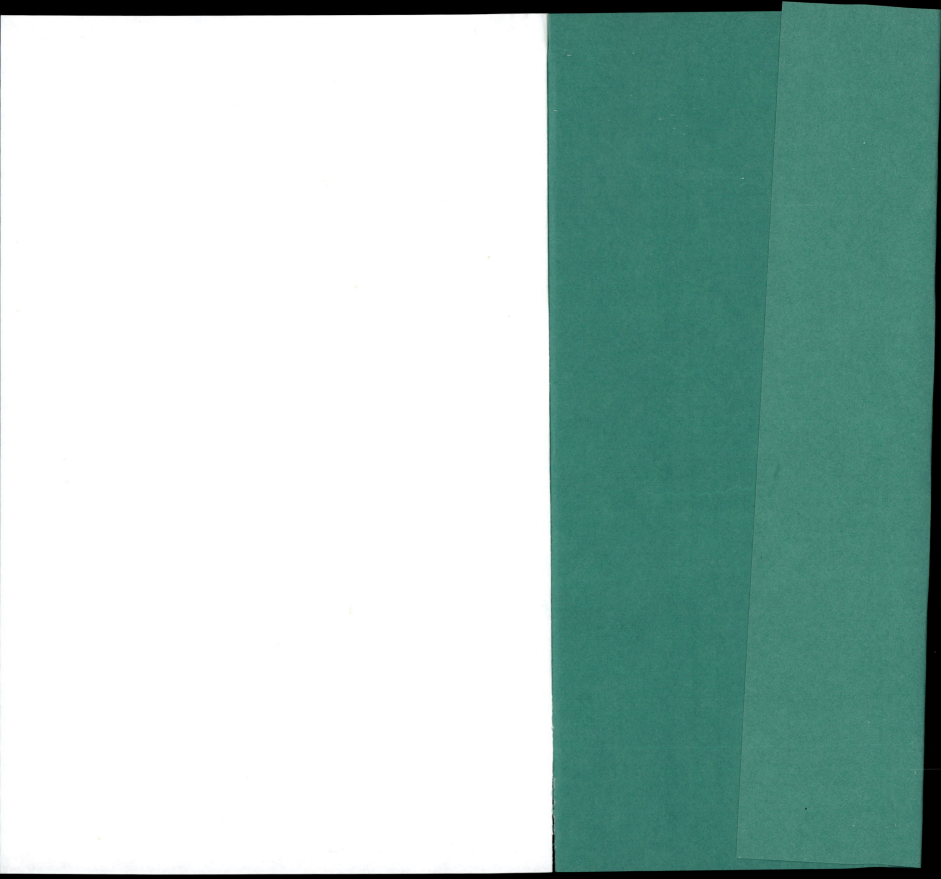